D1211920

ATANASOFF

Forgotten Father of the Computer

ATANASOFF

Forgotten Father of the Computer

CLARK R. MOLLENHOFF

Iowa State University Press, Ames

Unless otherwise attributed, all illustrations are courtesy of the Department of Special Collections, Iowa State University Library.

Composed by Iowa State University Press
Printed in the United States of America

First edition, 1988

Library of Congress Cataloging-in-Publication Data

Mollenhoff, Clark R.
    Atanasoff : forgotten father of the computer.

    Bibliography: p.
    Includes index.
    1. Atanasoff, John V. (John Vincent) 2. Electronic data processing—Biography. I. Title.
QA76.2.A75M65 1988   621.39′092′4 [B]   87-35261
ISBN 0-8138-0032-3

To Jane Cook Schurz Mollenhoff

An editor, a persistent critic, and a patient wife

CONTENTS

FOREWORD

THIS is a fast-moving account of a triumph of justice over
fraud and is centered on one of mankind's all-time great
inventions, the computer. Clark Mollenhoff's thorough research makes it plain that (1) Dr. John V. Atanasoff of
Iowa State College in Ames invented and built the world's first
electronic digital computer, and that (2) Dr. John Mauchly of Pennsylvania pirated the know-how and got the first computer patent.

Atanasoff emerges from the flow of facts as a too-trusting hero
while Mauchly emerges as a tarnished character. The narrative
leaves the reader with a sense of indignation over the unethical and
unfair treatment that is exposed in the record.

It took more than thirty years to right the wrong, and then only
as a by-product of a six-year legal battle between two industrial
giants.

It is a suspenseful story, intriguing as it unfolds, that has already sparked the curiosity and captured the attention of those who
have been involved in its production.

Mollenhoff spices his account with perceptive discussions of
several provocative questions: why did Iowa State College (now
Iowa State University) fail to get a patent on the Atanasoff Berry
Computer? Was Clifford Berry, Atanasoff's brilliant assistant, murdered or did he commit suicide? Why was the original computer
destroyed while Atanasoff was away and unconsulted? Why did it
take so long for the news of Atanasoff's legal vindication to get
through to the scientific community and to the public?

Mollenhoff was indeed well-suited to research and write about
just such a situation. It was clearly within the pattern of investigative reporting he had done so effectively as a newsman for over
three decades.

Clark became a legend in Washington where he won numerous

awards as correspondent for the *Des Moines Register* and for the Minneapolis dailies. Much of his success has come through hard work, long hours, and his courage in confronting formidable officials with unpleasant facts about illegal activities. He is big in size, big in energy, and big in use of the printed word to fight graft and corruption.

This book is a typical painstaking Mollenhoff operation. He used his legal skills as an attorney in sifting through more than 20,000 pages of federal court testimony in the computer case. He spent more than three months boning up on computer technology and terminology so that he might better understand the issues. Mollenhoff sticks closely to the record in this book. He is practically always "on the record." He rarely credits his reports to unnamed "reliable sources." You know where his material is coming from, and readers appreciate that.

Clark was awarded the Pulitzer Prize at the culmination of a five-year campaign that exposed major corruption in the teamsters union. Chairman John McClellan of the Senate select investigating committee wrote Mollenhoff saying: "Your ideas, advice, and guidance have been invaluable."

The Atanasoff book is a biography of the physicist-inventor as well as an analysis of the computer struggle. Atanasoff's father was a Bulgarian immigrant who came to the United States as a boy and became an electrical engineer of considerable merit. The son, now eighty-four-years old, is obviously a genius. His computer discoveries are only part of a long list of achievements in physics, national defense, and private industry.

This book may be the best of Mollenhoff's eleven books.

—GEORGE S. MILLS

PREFACE

THIS is the story of the invention of the Atanasoff Berry Computer at Iowa State College in the 1937 to 1941 period and the development of those basic concepts of the automatic electronic digital computer that are present in virtually all modern computers today. Although my book will necessarily deal with some of the history of computing beginning with the concept of an analytical engine as planned by George Babbage in the 1830–1842 period, it is not intended to be a history of the development of mechanical calculators and computers.

I am not unmindful of the work of Herman Hollerith and his tabulator that performed such miracles in connection with the United States census of 1880, or of the work done in England by William Thomson (Lord Kelvin) in developing a tidal harmonic analyzer to predict the rise and fall of tides and his early work on a differential analyzer, or of the work of Vannevar Bush in building a successful differential analyzer at the Massachusetts Institute of Technology at Cambridge.

I am aware that Konrad Zuse and George Stibitz were working independently on some important computer concepts during the late 1930s and early 1940s that involved some of the same concepts that Dr. John Vincent Atanasoff and his graduate assistant, Clifford E. Berry, were developing and constructing in the Physics building at Iowa State College.

The computing device that Konrad Zuse was developing in Germany in the late 1930s and 1940s was an electromechanical machine. The computer that George Stibitz was constructing at Bell Telephone Laboratories in New Jersey was an electromagnetic device. Neither the Zuse machine nor the Stibitz machine was an electronic device.

Dr. Atanasoff conceived his plans for an electronic digital computer in the winter of 1937–1938, and with the help of his graduate student, Clifford Berry, constructed a prototype in the fall of 1939 that proved the feasibility of his concepts. The Atanasoff Berry Computer was constructed and partially functioning before Christmas in 1940, but it had flaws in the card system converter used for changing the figures from base-two to base-ten – it permitted errors approximately once in 100,000 times.

However, it was the world's first electronic digital computer, and it was designed to find solutions for simultaneous algebraic equations with up to 30 unknowns. Atanasoff's achievement made it obvious that the electronic computer would be useful in hundreds of ways.

Litigation in the case of *Honeywell, Inc., v. Sperry Rand Corp., et al.* resulted in a massive record documenting the conception and construction of the Atanasoff Berry Computer at Iowa State College in the 1937–1941 period, and the planning and construction of ENIAC by Dr. John Mauchly and Presper Eckert at the Moore School of Electrical Engineering between 1942 and 1946.

One important aspect of the litigation was the question: Did Dr. Mauchly derive his basic concepts for an electronic digital computer from Dr. Atanasoff, Cliff Berry, and the Atanasoff Berry Computer which he examined in detail for several days in June 1941? John Mauchly contended that he learned nothing from his discussions with J. V. Atanasoff and Clifford Berry, from his examination of the machine, or from his reading of Atanasoff's thirty-five-page explanation of the construction and scientific theories involved in the Atanasoff Berry Computer. During the trial he produced no papers and no projects to demonstrate the state of his knowledge or interest in electronic digital computing before his meetings with J. V. Atanasoff.

My book does explore the controversy about what ideas John Mauchly may have derived from J. V. Atanasoff. I have tried to deal with the kind of detail that should make it possible for the reader to form his or her own judgment on that dispute without the necessity of reviewing the content of thousands of exhibits and reading the thousands of pages of testimony relevant to that issue.

I have read the full court record of the trial testimony of Atanasoff and Mauchly and the related documents. I have interviewed the late John Mauchly and Presper Eckert for purposes of determining if they had changed their position since the ruling by U.S. District Judge Earl R. Larson that John Mauchly had "derived" basic concepts of ENIAC from J. V. Atanasoff.

There can be no question that Mauchly and Eckert did a brilliant job of selling the ENIAC plan to the Army and in constructing what they now refer to as "the first general purpose electronic digital computer," to distinguish it from the Atanasoff Berry Computer which they refer to as "a special purpose" electronic digital computer.

However, the construction of ENIAC, remarkable as it may be, does not and should not excuse John Mauchly for his subsequent actions in trying to deny J. V. Atanasoff credit for his achievements.

The first electronic digital computer constructed by Atanasoff and Berry at Iowa State College in 1939 and 1940 was initially called "the Atanasoff Computer." It was referred to by Dr. R. K. Richards in his book on computer systems, published in 1966, as "the Atanasoff-Berry Computer." In 1967 during the early stages of the Honeywell and Control Data litigation, Atanasoff named the machine "the Atanasoff Berry Computer" to honor the great and invaluable assistance his graduate assistant, Clifford Berry, had given him in the development and construction of that machine.

To avoid confusing the reader, I have made reference to that original automatic electronic digital computer as "the Atanasoff Berry Computer" throughout the book, except in those instances when I am referring to the R. K. Richards book in which he used a hyphen.

I have used the title "Dr." in a few places with regard to Dr. Atanasoff and Dr. Mauchly, but otherwise have referred to them simply as Atanasoff or Mauchly. No disrespect is intended to either of these distinguished men of letters. The decision was made to avoid cluttering up the text with repetitious use of titles after their academic credentials were made clear to the reader.

I wish to express my appreciation to the following people for their assistance in researching, editing, or planning for the biography, *Atanasoff, Forgotten Father of the Computer:*

John Vincent Atanasoff, the co-inventor of the Atanasoff Berry Computer.
Mrs. Alice Atanasoff, the inventor's wife and research assistant.
Mrs. Richard (Elsie Atanasoff) Whistler, daughter of the inventor.
Mrs. Charles E. (Joanne Atanasoff) Gathers, daughter of the inventor.
John V. Atanasoff, Jr., son of the inventor.
Mrs. Grace Berry, mother of the late Dr. Clifford Berry, the co-inventor of the Atanasoff Berry Computer.
Mrs. Jean Reed Berry, wife of Dr. Clifford Berry who was also a secretary for Dr. Atanasoff.

Arthur and Alice Burks, authors of scientific computer articles.

David Beecher, former student of J. V. Atanasoff at Iowa State and his business partner at Rockville, Maryland.

Dr. R. K. Richards, author of a 1966 book on computer history, *Electronic Digital Systems,* who first noted the connections between the Atanasoff Berry Computer and Dr. John Mauchly, co-inventor of ENIAC.

Dr. Allan Mackintosh, Director of NORDICA, the Copenhagen-based Institute for Theoretic Physics and author of articles on the Atanasoff Berry Computer.

Dr. Theodore Sjoerdsma, head of the Department of Computer Science, Washington and Lee University.

Assistant Professor Kenneth A. Lambert, Department of Computer Science, Washington and Lee University.

Cecil A. Johnson, retired lawyer-businessman from Omaha, Nebraska, who first took the initiative to nominate J. V. Atanasoff for a Nobel Prize.

Bruce Bruemmer, archivist, the Charles Babbage Institute for the History of Information Processing at the University of Minnesota, Minneapolis.

Dr. Dwight Miller, archivist, the Herbert Hoover Presidential Library, West Branch, Iowa.

Jeff Coors, president of Adolph Coors Company, Golden, Colorado, who honored Dr. J. V. Atanasoff with the First American Ingenuity Award.

Al Pipkin, vice-president for financial management at the Adolph Coors Company.

Dr. Gordon Eaton, Iowa State University president.

Carl Hamilton, former Iowa State University vice-president and director of Information Services.

David L. Lendt, director of Information Services for Iowa State University.

O. S. (Steve) Knudsen, former director and writer on the Iowa State University film, "From One John Vincent Atanasoff."

Dr. Henry Black, emeritus professor of Mechanical Engineering at Iowa State University, and long-time friend of J. V. Atanasoff.

Dr. Bernice Black Durand, associate professor of Physics at the University of Wisconsin.

Dr. Blagovest Sendov, Director of the Bulgarian Academy of Sciences.

Dr. Boyan I. Penkov, member of the Bulgarian Academy of Sciences and director of a Bulgarian film on the life of Atanasoff.

Dr. Isaac M. Auerbach, senior associate in computer consulting firm known as Auerbach Associates.

Dr. Norman C. Fulmer, retired patent attorney for General Electric, who worked on the Atanasoff Berry Computer as an electrical engineering student at Iowa State.

Dr. Robert E. Mather, retired physicist, who worked on the Atanasoff Berry Computer as a physics student at Iowa State.

James E. Buck, retired industrial engineer, who was a boyhood friend of Clifford Berry when he was a student of industrial engineering at Iowa State.

Richard Kinney, director of Iowa State University Press.

Bill Silag, managing editor, Iowa State University Press.

Suzanne Lowitt, manuscript editor, Iowa State University Press.

U.S. District Judge Earl R. Larson of Minneapolis.

U.S. Clerk of Court Gerald Bergquist of Minneapolis.

D. Dennis Allegretti, Honeywell patent lawyer.

Charles G. Call, Honeywell patent lawyer-investigator.

Henry Hanson, general counsel for Honeywell.

Allen Kirkpatrick, Control Data patent lawyer.

Kevin Joyce, Control Data patent lawyer.

Jane Schurz Mollenhoff, editor, critic, and patient wife.

Florence Cook, secretary, Department of Journalism, Washington and Lee University.

Professor John K. Jennings, Department of Journalism, Washington and Lee University.

Professor Ronald H. MacDonald, Department of Journalism, Washington and Lee University.

Professor Hampden H. Smith, Department of Journalism, Washington and Lee University.

Professor Robert De Maria, Department of Journalism, Washington and Lee University.

Dean John Elrod, Dean of the College, Washington and Lee University.

Dr. Barbara Brown, Director of the Washington and Lee University Library.

George Mills, distinguished dean of Iowa political writers and commentators and widely recognized authority on the history of Iowa politics and institutions.

Frank Eyerly, distinguished former managing editor of the *Des Moines Register and Tribune* whose advice has been important in every reporting and writing assignment I have ever undertaken.

ATANASOFF

Forgotten Father of the Computer

CHAPTER 1

The Need to Set the Record Straight

O N 13 October 1967 Dr. John W. Mauchly testified under oath that he spent no more than "one and one-half hours" in the presence of the Atanasoff Berry Computer at Iowa State College, Ames, Iowa. Under questioning by Allen Kirkpatrick, a lawyer for Control Data, he swore under oath that he saw the computer machine only in the shadows and did not believe that the cover was off the Atanasoff Berry Computer at any time during his visit of "a couple of days."

"I do not remember getting any great detail or understanding as to what Dr. Atanasoff had in mind, because, again, he was communicating generalities rather than details with respect to any of his ideas," Mauchly testified. That testimony was in support of his claim that he was the true inventor of the first electronic computer and rightfully entitled to honors that he and J. Presper Eckert had received as the co-inventors of the first electronic digital computer.

While Mauchly persisted in his claim that he learned nothing from Dr. John Vincent Atanasoff, Clifford Edward Berry, or from his examination of the Atanasoff Berry Computer, his testimony did change substantially on important details.

As documents and testimony were produced that contradicted his 13 October 1967 deposition testimony, Mauchly changed his story slowly in three depositions when he was questioned by Honeywell Corporation lawyers and in the federal court trial.

Those highly relevant changes in Mauchly's testimony over a four-year period included:

1. Instead of spending only "a couple of days" with Atanasoff,

Mauchly acknowledged that he spent five days as Atanasoff's guest and examined the machine in some degree on four of those days.

2. Instead of not getting "any detail" about the Atanasoff Berry Computer, Mauchly acknowledged that Atanasoff and Clifford Berry had answered his questions freely and that he had access to the 35-page manuscript on the Atanasoff Berry Computer and probably read it. He testified that he probably asked Atanasoff if he could take a copy of the 35-page computer manuscript with him and that Atanasoff had on that one point refused his request.

3. Instead of merely seeing the Atanasoff Berry Computer in the shadows, Mauchly admitted that he had examined it closely in the company of Clifford Berry, saw it operate, and had the add-subtract mechanism explained to him. He acknowledged that it was "probably true" that he had his coat off and was helping Clifford Berry on some adjustment of the machine's position.

As these admissions were made under questioning by Honeywell lawyers, he blamed his initial inaccurate testimony on "a faulty memory."

In the face of a federal court opinion that his testimony was not credible when he claimed his electronic digital computer concepts were the product of his mind before he met Atanasoff, Mauchly did not give up his claim to being the co-inventor of the first electronic digital computer.

Mauchly, until his death in 1980, continued to speak with derision of the Atanasoff Berry Computer and of Atanasoff. Since then his widow, Kathleen Mauchly, and J. Presper Eckert have been highly critical of the decision by U.S. District Judge Earl R. Larson that Mauchly "derived" important digital concepts from Atanasoff.

Some computer historians have followed the line of Kathleen Mauchly and Eckert, and a good many computer textbooks and magazines have continued to refer to Mauchly and Eckert as "the co-inventors of the first electronic digital computer."

It is understandable why Kathleen Mauchly would loyally defend her husband's reputation against the finding that he stole Atanasoff's electronic digital computer ideas and falsely claimed to be the true inventor of those concepts. However, her arguments about what Mauchly knew or did not know in the period prior to 1940 must be analyzed against the fact that she did not meet him until 1944 or 1945 and did not marry him until 1948.

Eckert has testified as to his belief that he and Mauchly developed the electronic digital computer concepts at the Moore School of Engineering at the University of Pennsylvania in the 1943 and 1944 period. Significantly, he also has testified that he did not know Mauchly until the summer of 1941, some weeks after Mauchly's visit to Iowa State College.

It is also significant that Eckert testified he does not recall Mauchly mentioning the names of Atanasoff, Clifford Berry, or his trip to Iowa State College until some time in late 1943 or 1944.

Thus it is possible that Eckert, a particularly brilliant electronic expert, did not know what electronic digital computer concepts were the product of Mauchly's own thinking or what ideas might have been derived from Atanasoff.

At a party in Lexington, Virginia, in January 1986 I met Dr. Theodore Sjoerdsma who is head of the Computer Science Department at Washington and Lee University. Our conversation turned to the history of the electronic digital computer and its tremendous impact on education, on business, and on civilization generally.

While I had not met Sjoerdsma before, he said he had been in the Computer Science Department at the University of Iowa at Iowa City before joining Washington and Lee University and had been present at Iowa State University, Ames, Iowa, on 21 October 1983 when I had delivered a tribute to John Vincent Atanasoff and Clifford E. Berry, who had constructed the first electronic digital computer at Iowa State College. Sjoerdsma expressed his disappointment about the continuing reports in many computer textbooks stating that John W. Mauchly and J. Presper Eckert were the co-inventors of the first electronic digital computer at the University of Pennsylvania's Moore School of Electrical Engineering between 1943 and 1946. Sjoerdsma commented that hardly a month went by that he did not find some computer textbook or computer history stating that ENIAC (Electronic Numerical Integrator and Computer), the Mauchly-Eckert machine, was the first electronic digital computer.

Professor Sjoerdsma related that many books made no mention of the Atanasoff Berry Computer (ABC) that was constructed at Iowa State, and when the Atanasoff Berry Computer was mentioned, it was without the recognition of the decision in a U.S. District Court case stating firmly that Mauchly had derived important ideas for ENIAC from his examination of the Atanasoff Berry Computer and related papers on the visit he had made to the Iowa State campus in June 1941.

I told Sjoerdsma that I could understand how computer textbook authors and computer historians could have been confused on
the issue of inventor of the first electronic digital computer prior to
19 October 1973–the date of the decision by U.S. District Judge
Earl R. Larson of Minneapolis. However, I could not understand
how any computer historians or textbook authors could examine the
trial record and continue to have any doubts that Atanasoff and Cliff
Berry had constructed the first electronic computer at Iowa State.

The decision by Judge Larson had been preceded by six years
of litigation with thousands of pages of depositions by all of the
relevant witnesses, and many that were not relevant. The U.S. District Court trial had covered 135 days of testimony during which
time Atanasoff was on the stand for 9 days of direct testimony and
cross-examination about his relationship with Mauchly.

John W. Mauchly, who had been deposed at length several
times before the trial, was in the witness chair for several days on
direct examination by lawyers for Sperry Rand, who were trying to
establish the validity of patent rights the corporation had purchased
from Mauchly and Eckert, including rights for the ENIAC computer. Mauchly was cross-examined extensively for several days by
lawyers for Honeywell, who were trying to establish that he had
obtained important concepts in the ENIAC and the Electronic Discrete Variable Automatic Computer (EDVAC) from his examination
of the Atanasoff Berry Computer and related papers during his visit
to Ames, Iowa, in June 1941.

It was one of the longest trials in the history of the federal court
system. The defendant corporations–Sperry Rand and its subsidiary, Illinois Scientific Development, Incorporated–had almost un-
limited resources in pursuing any evidence they believed might establish proof that Mauchly had originated or invented any of the key
electronic digital concepts in ENIAC prior to his contacts with John
V. Atanasoff and Clifford E. Berry. In the opinion of Judge Larson
they failed to produce any credible evidence to corroborate Mauchly's claim that he had the ideas in his mind. Mauchly had never
reduced those ideas to a written form until several months after
visiting with Atanasoff and Berry at Iowa State.

It was estimated by Honeywell lawyers that more than $3 mil-
lion was spent by Honeywell in pursuing the litigation. They calcu-
lated that Sperry Rand and Illinois Scientific Development spent in
excess of $5 million in defending the patent rights they held through
Mauchly and Eckert.

The record shows that the trial commenced in the U.S. District

Court in Minneapolis on 1 June 1971 and continued with few interruptions until it closed on 13 March 1972. It consumed over 135 days or part days. Judge Larson heard testimony from seventy-seven witnesses and the deposition testimony of an additional eighty witnesses was introduced into the record. The Honeywell lawyers called the attention of the court to a total of 25,686 exhibits, and lawyers for Sperry Rand and Illinois Scientific Development directed Judge Larson's attention to 6,968 exhibits.

There could be no doubt that both sides took full advantage of the opportunity to explore every piece of evidence that might be relevant to their cause. It was the kind of record no author or group of historical researchers could afford to compile. It was a record that included direct testimony from the key figures taken under oath and under cross-examination designed to spotlight flaws that might relate to questions of credibility.

Honeywell lawyers had the opportunity to review the history with Atanasoff and to reach out to obtain documents and corroborative testimony. Sperry Rand lawyers had an equal opportunity to subpoena witnesses and documents that would be supportive of Mauchly.

Judge Larson, in his detailed summary of the case, commented: "The Court further had the benefit of numerous documentary aids in dealing with the special terminology and contents of complex electronic and financial evidence, as well as rules and customs of patent practice, involved in the reconstruction of over three decades of past history underlying the modern day computer industry."

Although the case involved a wide range of antitrust issues arising out of the procurement, licensing and enforcement of patent rights, and other business conduct of Sperry Rand in the electronic data processing industry, one of the central issues was the question of whether Mauchly had derived any of the concepts in ENIAC from the Atanasoff Berry Computer. On that central issue of who was the inventor of the first electronic digital computer, Judge Larson did not equivocate.

From a standpoint of chronology there could be no doubt that the Atanasoff Berry Computer was constructed at Iowa State College in the period between 1939 and 1941.

The chronology is equally clear that Mauchly did not draw up the proposal for his electronic digital computer until 1942. The ENIAC machine was constructed under plans that Mauchly did not complete until 1943. The construction of ENIAC under an army ordnance contract at the Moore School of Electrical Engineering at the University of Pennsylvania was not completed until early 1946.

Judge Larson's opinion stated emphatically: "Eckert and Mauchly did not themselves first invent the automatic electronic digital computer, but instead derived that subject matter from one Dr. John V. Atanasoff." In his opinion he explained that "although not necessary to the finding of derivation of 'the invention' of the ENIAC patent, Honeywell has proved that the claimed subject matter of the ENIAC patent relied on in support of the counterclaim herein is not patentable over the subject matter derived by Mauchly from Atanasoff. . . . As a representative example, Honeywell has shown that the subject matter of detailed claims 88 and 89 of the ENIAC patent corresponds to the work of Atanasoff which was known to Mauchly before any effort pertinent to the ENIAC machine or patent began."

He further declared that the testimony demonstrated clearly that between 1937 and 1942 Atanasoff "developed and built an automatic electronic digital computer for solving large systems of simultaneous linear algebraic equations."

The judge noted that in December 1939 Atanasoff and Berry "completed and reduced to practice his [Atanasoff's] basic conception in the form of an operating breadboard model of a computing machine."

"This breadboard model machine, constructed with the assistance of a graduate student, Clifford Berry, permitted the various components of the machine to be tested under actual operating conditions," Judge Larson stated. "This breadboard model machine established the soundness of the basic principles of the design, and Atanasoff and Berry began construction of a prototype or pilot model, capable of solving with a high degree of accuracy a system of as many as 29 simultaneous equations having 29 unknowns."

The unchallenged record, according to Judge Larson, demonstrated that "by August, 1940, in connection with efforts at further funding, Atanasoff prepared a comprehensive manuscript which fully described the principles of his machine, including detail design features." Judge Larson found that this manuscript also demonstrated that the Atanasoff Berry Computer was "already far advanced" and that "the description . . . was adequate to enable one of ordinary skill in electronics at that time to make and use an ABC computer."

Judge Larson pointed out that Atanasoff's manuscript at that time "was studied by experts in the art of aids to mathematical computation, who recommended its financial support, and these recommendations resulted in a grant of funds by Research Corporation for the ABC's continued construction."

These facts were set forth by Judge Larson to demonstrate the advanced stage of development and testing of the breadboard model and the prototype Atanasoff Berry Computer before Atanasoff's first meeting with Mauchly in December 1940 and Mauchly's later visit to Iowa State College in June 1941 to observe the functioning of the Atanasoff Berry machine.

"Mauchly went to Ames, Iowa, as a houseguest of Atanasoff for several days, where he discussed the ABC as well as other ideas of Atanasoff's relating to the computing art," Judge Larson said. "Mauchly was given an opportunity to read, and did read, but was not permitted to take with him, a copy of the comprehensive manuscript which Atanasoff had prepared in August, 1940."

Judge Larson noted that at the time of Mauchly's visit to Iowa State in June 1941 the Atanasoff Berry Computer "was not entirely complete" but that "its construction was sufficiently well advanced so that the principles of its operation, including detail design features, was explained and demonstrated to Mauchly."

It was important for Sperry Rand to establish evidence of the extent of any work that Mauchly had been doing on ideas related to the development of an automatic electronic digital computer before the time of his visit to Iowa State in June 1941. Judge Larson declared that "prior to his (Mauchly's) visit to Ames, Iowa, Mauchly had been broadly interested in electrical analog calculating devices, but had not conceived an automatic electronic digital computer."

"As a result of this visit (to Iowa State), the discussions of Mauchly with Atanasoff and Berry, the demonstrations, the review of the manuscript, Mauchly derived from the ABC 'the invention of the automatic electronic digital computer' claimed in the ENIAC patent."

Judge Larson, in an exercise of judicial restraint, stopped short of stating that Mauchly had lied under oath when he testified that he had learned nothing important from his talks with Atanasoff and Berry, his reading of Atanasoff's manuscript, and his observation of the operation of the Atanasoff Berry Computer. Judge Larson believed it was adequate to state that the corroborative evidence produced to support Atanasoff as well as Atanasoff's demeanor and testimony made him conclude that Atanasoff was a truthful witness. The implication was that Mauchly was not truthful. Thus the judge ruled that "the court has heard the testimony at trial of both Atanasoff and Mauchly, and finds the testimony of Atanasoff with respect to the knowledge and information derived by Mauchly is credible."

Despite Judge Larson's findings and the massive court record, there are some writers of computer textbooks and some magazines and newspapers who refuse to acknowledge that the first electronic digital computer was constructed at Iowa State by J. V. Atanasoff and Cliff Berry. Some of this misinformation remains in texts because of the practices of textbook writers to pick up the copy from earlier books without any effort to check the record or analyze the court record or judicial findings that are at odds with their own version of computer history.

The record has continued to be muddied by articles and speeches by Mauchly, and since his death by his widow, that are for the most part only repetitions of his uncorroborated depositions and court testimony that already have been discredited.

Since Mauchly was given the opportunity in court to provide any documents, devices, or witnesses to corroborate his contention that he had been giving some thought to an electronic digital computer before his first meeting with Atanasoff in December 1940, and his visit to Ames in June 1941, little credibility can be given to the embroidered repetition of those vague and uncorroborated tales by others.

Where it is in their own best interests to believe Mauchly's account, the friends, relatives, and business associates of Mauchly will probably continue to rely on his uncorroborated self-serving accounts even when Mauchly's claims are sharply contradicted by his own letters written to Atanasoff and others in the period immediately after his visit to Iowa State College. Those friends, relatives, and business associates of Mauchly will probably resist the suggestion they do an objective analysis of the evidence in the massive record that supports Judge Larson's opinion that Mauchly derived his ideas from Atanasoff.

The opinions and conclusions of friends, relatives, and business associates are irrelevant unless accompanied by hard documentary evidence that would support Mauchly's work on an electronic digital computer prior to his meetings with Atanasoff in 1940. That evidence will be difficult or impossible to produce since Sperry Rand lawyers spent millions of dollars already in the futile effort to obtain evidence for the depositions and the trial before Judge Larson.

Now it is time for those who claim to be computer historians to stop accepting the self-serving statements and unsupported new theories of what Mauchly might have thought in the 1937 to 1944 period. He had his chance in several depositions and in the trial, where Sperry Rand and Illinois Development Corporation lawyers had the motivation and the financial support to produce every scrap of evidence and every bit of testimony that might support his contention that ENIAC was the product of his intellect and was not derived from knowledge he gained from the Atanasoff Berry machine.

It is time for those who argue that a record made in a court of law may not be as valid as scientific historic research to come forward and point out where that court decision in the Honeywell case was in error. It is time for those who purport to challenge Judge Larson's decision to do so in a manner that gives some indication that they have read at least the relevant parts of the testimony of the key figures—John V. Atanasoff and John W. Mauchly.

That Judge Larson did not bluntly call Mauchly a liar and chose to say he "derived" rather than stole the ENIAC computer concepts from Atanasoff should not blind those who hold themselves out to be researchers and computer historians.

After my discussions with Theodore Sjoerdsma, I returned home and reviewed my 1974 newspaper stories on Judge Larson's decision. Those stories included a brief report of my conversations at that time with Mauchly. I decided it was time to write a book with in-depth documentation to set the record straight. The facts are stranger than fiction.

CHAPTER 2

Precocious Physicist: John V. Atanasoff's Early Years, 1903–1925

J OHN VINCENT ATANASOFF was born on 4 October 1903 at the home of his maternal grandfather, Preston Hill farm, a few miles west of Hamilton, New York. His maternal grandfather was Monmouth Purdy, a farmer who could trace his paternal lineage to Jeremiah Purdy who fought with General George Washington and wintered with him at Valley Forge.

John Vincent Atanasoff's father was a Bulgarian immigrant named Ivan Atanasov. His name was Americanized to John Atanasoff through the ignorance or arrogance of immigration officials at Ellis Island in 1889 when he arrived here with an uncle, Constantine Zhelescov. Ivan's father, a Bulgarian patriot, had been killed when Ivan was a baby. Ivan's widowed mother, wanting her son to have the opportunities that America offered far away from the turmoil of war and revolution that had cost her the life of her husband, sent him to America with his uncle.

Ivan Atanasov was thirteen years old when he arrived at Ellis Island. When he was fifteen years old his uncle returned to Bulgaria, leaving the youth to fend for himself with a small amount of money his mother had given him. The young Bulgarian immigrant washed dishes and did other chores to work his way through Peddie School for Boys, a private high school at Hightstown, New Jersey.

After completing his schooling at Peddie School, the young immigrant worked at a series of odd jobs in New Jersey and New York until he became acquainted with a Baptist minister who suggested that he attend Colgate College, at Hamilton, New York, which at that time maintained its Baptist affiliation.

While working his way through Colgate College, the young man, now known as John Atanasoff, became acquainted with two of Monmouth Purdy's sons. Through them he met Iva Purdy, a pretty younger sister. Iva, a high school graduate with a talent for mathematics, was teaching in a nearby rural school.

They were married before John received his Bachelor of Philosophy degree (a general degree) from Colgate in 1901, and John Vincent was the first born of this marriage. John's college courses at Colgate included mathematics, algebra, geometry, chemistry, and physics, for which he had a special liking and aptitude. Later, John became a self-taught electrical engineer with the help of some correspondence school courses, and this special aptitude was to be a significant force in John Vincent's early interest in electricity and electric gadgets.

John Atanasoff worked at a number of electrical jobs including employment at a plant operated by Thomas A. Edison near Orange, New Jersey, in the months just prior to John Vincent's birth. After the birth of John Vincent, his father worked at a series of electrical engineering positions in the Hamilton, New York, area and in northern New Jersey before moving to Osteen, Florida. The family lived in Osteen for about a year, and then moved to Brewster, Florida, where John Atanasoff obtained another job as an electrical engineer. It was at Brewster that John Vincent completed grade school and demonstrated his first fascination with, and understanding of, electricity. The two-bedroom frame house in Brewster was the first home the Atanasoff family lived in with electric lights, and John Vincent as a nine-year-old boy found and corrected faulty electric wiring in a back-porch light.

It was also in 1913 that John Vincent had his first adventures in the field of mathematics. He had been a good student from his first years in school but also had a normal youthful interest in sports. The young man viewed himself as having a special talent for baseball until his first introduction to the more fascinating world of the slide rule.

Early in 1913 his father decided his position as an electrical engineer required his purchase of a new Dietzgen slide rule. When the slide rule arrived in the mail, it was examined and admired by the family and promptly forgotten by everyone but John Vincent.

John Vincent read the instructions carefully, manipulated the slide rule, and was amazed that he could get correct answers. Within a matter of two or three weeks he was absorbed with the exploration of the slide rule, and baseball drifted into the background. Because John Vincent's father decided he did not have an immediate need for a slide rule to organize and repair electric motors and equipment damaged by Florida's numerous electrical storms, the new Dietzgen became the young boy's obsession.

Not satisfied with manipulation of the slide rule for correct mathematical answers, John Vincent became interested in the mathematical principles behind the operation of the slide rule and the study of logarithms, which led into studies of trigonometric functions. While he soon recognized that he could use logarithms taken from tables to solve problems, he could not himself calculate any but the most simple logarithms.

At this point he found a book in his father's library entitled *A College Algebra* by J. M. Taylor and published by Allyn and Bacon, of Boston, in 1895. A book his father had studied at Colgate, it included a beginning study on differential calculus and also had a chapter on infinite series and how to calculate logarithms, Atanasoff recalled years later.

"I suppose I was the first man – or shall I say boy – without elementary algebra who attempted to read the book," Atanasoff said later. He explained that it was his mother, Iva Purdy Atanasoff, who gave him the personal help he needed to comprehend that college algebra book because his father was too much occupied with his electrical repair work.

Iva Purdy Atanasoff had not studied college algebra, but she had studied algebra in high school and "she knew it," Atanasoff recalled years later. Within a few months her precocious nine-year-old son had progressed beyond the point of needing help, and in a short time much beyond the point that she could be of further assistance.

However, it was from one of his mother's eighth grade arithmetic textbooks that he first read a chapter on number bases other than ten. It was this early understanding of mathematical bases other than ten that led him to explore a wide range of bases, including base-two, in his early experimentation of ideas for an automatic electronic digital computer. (The use of base-two or the binary principle was a part of his 1939 plan that eventually became the Atanasoff Berry Computer. Atanasoff has searched for years to try to identify the specific eighth grade arithmetic textbook, but he has not been able to find this text.)

[*Above*] John V. Atanasoff's parents: John Atanasoff, graduate of Colgate University, 1900, and Iva Purdy Atanasoff at the time of her marriage, 1900. [*Left*] John V. Atanasoff with his mother. [*Below*] John and Iva Atanasoff in later years.

Atanasoff [*center*], Class of 1930 Ph.D. candidates, University of Wisconsin–Madison

[*Right*] The young John Vincent
Atanasoff. [*Below*] Lura
Meeks Atanasoff shortly after
her marriage in June 1926.

[*Left*] The Atanasoffs' oldest daughter, Elsie (Mrs. Richard Whistler of Rockville, Maryland), about 1940. [*Right*] The two younger children, John and Joanne (Mrs. Charles E. Gathers of Englewood, Colorado), 1940–1941. [*Below*] John V. Atanasoff and his children Elsie, Joanne, and John (later to become an Iowa State graduate in engineering).

John V. Atanasoff in his Maryland workshop, 1967.

John V. Atanasoff, Iowa State University, May 22, 1981.

Alice Crosby Atanasoff and JV at the Holley Medal ceremony, 1985.

[*Over*] Honorary Doctor of Science degree, John V. Atanasoff, 1987, University of Wisconsin–Madison.

CITATION

JOHN VINCENT ATANASOFF

John Vincent Atanasoff earned his Doctor of Philosophy degree from the University of Wisconsin-Madison in 1930. While yet a graduate student, he experienced intensifying intellectual frustration because of the cumbersome and inadequate computing machines available at the time. That benign perplexity—a condition that is not unknown to graduate students—haunted John Vincent Atanasoff during his post-doctoral years until, in one eventful evening in 1937, he had the central insights that led to one of the most momentous inventions of the century, the electronic digital computer.

His invention is transforming our world. It accelerates mathematical calculation beyond the dreams of our ancestors; it enhances our collective memory; it functions as a surrogate to human intelligence in applications so numerous that not even a computer can aggregate them all. Yet, this astonishing innovation did not exhaust John Vincent Atanasoff's ingenuity. He holds thirty-two patents for subsequent inventions in such diverse fields as agriculture, transportation and information science. His contributions to technology have been protean and abundant.

CONFERRAL

JOHN VINCENT ATANASOFF: Your technical mastery and inventiveness have yielded an instrument of transforming power. In recognition of your achievement, the University of Wisconsin-Madison confers on you its honorary degree Doctor of Science.

UNIVERSITY OF WISCONSIN-MADISON

The Board of Regents of The University of Wisconsin System,
on the nomination of the faculty, has conferred upon

JOHN VINCENT ATANASOFF

The Degree of

DOCTOR OF SCIENCE

Together with all honors, rights, and privileges belonging to that degree.
In witness whereof, this diploma is granted. Given at Madison
in The State of Wisconsin, this sixteenth day of May
in the year nineteen hundred eighty-seven, and of
The University the one hundred thirty-seventh.

President of the Board

President, University of Wisconsin System

Chancellor, University of Wisconsin-Madison

In the year John Vincent was to enter high school, the Atanasoff family moved to a farm near Old Chicora, Florida, where John Atanasoff had taken another job as an electrical engineer. Most of the 155-acre Atanasoff farm was made up of a yellow pine timberland, with only 30 acres under cultivation. The cultivated acres included a 3-acre orange grove.

John Vincent completed the Mulberry High School course in two years maintaining grades of "A" in science courses and mathematics and deciding that he wanted to be a theoretic physicist. He stayed out of school one year, working to save money to enter the University of Florida at Gainesville in 1921.

No degree in theoretic physics was as yet offered at the University of Florida and the closest thing to it was an electrical engineering course. This turned out to be a fortuitous circumstance. While taking the subjects required for an electrical engineering degree, he became interested in electronics, continued forward with higher mathematics, and was required to complete the types of practical mechanical construction projects that proved to be beneficial in his initial thinking about an automatic calculator.

When he graduated from the University of Florida in 1925 with a Bachelor of Science degree in electrical engineering, he had a straight "A" academic average. In the last semester of his senior year the offers of teaching fellowships poured in from a dozen educational institutions including Harvard. He accepted a teaching fellowship at Iowa State College because it was the first one he received and because it was an institution with a fine reputation in engineering and sciences.

Although he had not traveled extensively outside of Florida, it was a confident John Vincent Atanasoff who boarded the train at Gainesville for the trip to Ames, Iowa, the heart of the Corn Belt. He had been teaching mathematics in a Florida high school ever since his second year at the University of Florida. His "A" average (a phenomenal 97.6 average) at the University of Florida gave him confidence that he could meet the competition and excel at Iowa State College or any other institution.

Bronzed from a summer working in the Gainesville area, John Vincent Atanasoff got off the train in downtown Ames and carried his bags to the nearby Sheldon Munn Hotel for his first night in Iowa. He was tired from the long train ride and anxious to put the night behind him and get to the college to meet the faculty members who would be his associates for the next few years.

Up early the next day, John Vincent Atanasoff had breakfast at the hotel, inquired how to get to Iowa State College, and opted for taking a taxi the two miles to the campus rather than carry his bags to the nearest street railway stop and then to the administration building (later known as Beardshear Hall) where the Department of Mathematics was housed. It was an important financial decision, for his money was in short supply and he was unaccustomed to pampering himself with the accommodations of a taxi.

It was after 9:00 A.M. when he arrived at Beardshear Hall and walked into the office of Dr. E. R. Smith for his first meeting with the head of the Mathematics Department. He also met briefly with Dr. A. E. Brandt, a professor of mathematics with whom he was to work closely a few years later in his first efforts to find a mechanism that would take the drudgery out of complex mathematical computations.

After the friendly meetings with Professors Smith and Brandt, the bronzed young Floridian set out on foot to find a room to rent that would be within walking distance of Beardshear Hall—a pleasant walk that acquainted him with the winding tree-lined streets and rolling green lawns that were such a contrast to his semitropical Florida.

This was Iowa State College and the twenty-two-year-old Floridian was determined to use his teaching fellowship to make his mark in the world of mathematics and physics.

CHAPTER 3

Iowa State Years:
Fertile Field For Genius, 1926–1936

THE first morning John Vincent Atanasoff hiked from his Knapp Street rooming house to Beardshear Hall it was an invigorating walk, but within a few days the distances on the sprawling Iowa State College campus made walking a chore. It wasted time the intense young graduate assistant did not feel he could afford to waste if he was to keep up the standards he had set for himself as a student and a teaching assistant.

The $800-a-year salary he received as a graduate assistant was far from a princely sum, but he permitted himself the luxury of a bicycle for commuting to the usual tedious routine chores that went with a student's existence on the Iowa State College campus. He had a limited social life in the first weeks in Iowa but did develop a close friendship with Dr. Brandt, the amiable and wise professor of mathematics he had met in Beardshear Hall on his first day at Iowa State. He also developed a close friendship with Professor Fred Brandner, another mathematics professor who had come to Iowa State by way of the University of Chicago and the University of Iowa. On a few occasions, John Vincent was invited to Dr. Brandt's home for dinner. It was the beginning of what was to be a life-long friendship.

At Iowa State the young graduate assistant had to become accustomed to answering to "Mr. Atanasoff" from the mathematics students and to plain "John" by other faculty members. At home his mother had called him "John Vincent" or just "Vincent" to distinguish him from his father.

From September to the Thanksgiving break, John buried himself in work on his master's degree and in teaching two mathematics classes to undergraduates. Even if he had been interested in social life, he did not believe he could have afforded it. However, there were Thanksgiving parties at the fraternity houses and at the various clubs organized on the Iowa State campus that were minimal in cost. The Dixie Club was a campus club organized for southern students away from home. The slim, handsome young Floridian decided to drop by the club to see what was going on. That evening at the Dixie Club turned out to be one of the most important nights in John Atanasoff's life. He met Lura Meeks, a home economics major from Oklahoma. Lura was a farm girl from western Oklahoma who came from a large family. Hers was a family that had experienced more than its share of poverty, as Josephus C. Meeks had moved from farm to farm in the Texas Panhandle, northeastern New Mexico, and Oklahoma in search of better farmland.

Lura was a beautiful, brown-haired, blue-eyed woman of twenty-five when she met John Atanasoff. She had many boyfriends in the years she was working her way through college as a country school teacher in Oklahoma. Most of the men she had dated were young businessmen or Oklahoma farmers or ranchers in whom she had no serious interest. She enjoyed going to parties and dances with them but, as she later told her oldest daughter, she was waiting for someone who "was really going some place." She felt she had found that someone in John Vincent Atanasoff, the enthusiastic and imaginative twenty-two-year-old mathematics instructor from Florida, she told her daughters later.

John Atanasoff was initially not aware that Lura was three years his senior, but it probably wouldn't have made any difference. She was an attractive, slim, and self-assured young woman. They both came from farm homes, from large families, and both were interested in an education to improve their lot in life and to conceivably do a lot more. Their chance meeting at the Dixie Club led to another date, and then another date, and soon they were having lunch together at the Student Union and spending the winter and spring nights walking near and under the Campanile. Their friendship became an important part of his life.

In June 1926 John Atanasoff received his master's degree in mathematics from Iowa State College, and a few days later he married Lura. With his master's degree in hand, Iowa State hired him at $1,800-a-year salary to teach mathematics while continuing to take courses in physics and mathematics in preparation for study at the

University of Wisconsin for a doctorate in the field of theoretic physics.

Lura had not yet completed the work for her degree in home economics, and she had already signed a contract to teach school during the 1926–1927 school year in Montana to make enough money to complete the year of credit she needed for that degree. The marriage was a sudden decision, and she was determined to carry out her contract to teach in Montana during the 1926–1927 school year. However, midway through the school year in Montana she decided to break her teaching contract to return to Ames to be with her husband. Their oldest daughter, Elsie, was born a little over a year later, and about a year after the birth of Elsie the family moved to Madison, Wisconsin, where John had been accepted as a doctoral candidate.

Iowa State College was then on a quarter system, with the winter quarter ending in March. March was halfway through the winter semester at the University of Wisconsin, but this did not deter John Atanasoff who had planned to enroll in courses in Electrodynamics, Quantum Mechanics, and the Mathematical Theory of Elasticity. Professor Herman March, who taught the course in Elasticity, had accepted John Atanasoff on the basis of a recommendation from Prof. E. R. Smith, head of the Mathematics Department at Iowa State. He had been assured that young Atanasoff was a brilliant student and a hard worker who would have no problem catching up with the rest of the class.

The similar cooperative spirit was exhibited by Prof. Warren Weaver, who taught the course on Electricity and Magnetism. He accepted John Atanasoff as a student with a distinguished record and with the potential for outstanding achievement. Professor Weaver and John Atanasoff became acquainted, and their paths crossed many times in later years.

Professor John Hasbrouck Van Vleck, the only theoretic physicist on the University of Wisconsin staff at that time, was less obliging. He raised objections to Atanasoff entering his class on Quantum Mechanics in the middle of the second term. He said it would not be possible for Atanasoff to understand the lectures and class discussions, and to consider doing the back work and taking the examination was out of the question.

Over Professor Van Vleck's objections, Atanasoff started attending Van Vleck's class, asking questions, and taking part in the work as if he were a welcome member of the class. Van Vleck's responses to his questions were usually a cool comment that "if you had been here in the first half of the semester you wouldn't have to ask that question."

"I worked like the dickens in that class and in all my classes, but particularly in that class because I was certain after a few days that I could pass it," Atanasoff recalled recently. "I was certain that Dr. Van Vleck was going out of his way to put me down when some of the other students said that questions I asked had not been covered in earlier lectures."

"There were perhaps twenty-five graduate students in the class, and when the semester was over, only five even bothered to take the final examination," Atanasoff recalled. "I wrote for seven hours on that test, and when Dr. Van Vleck called me in later he told me my test was one of the best and indicated that it was the best but made no comment of congratulation." Professor Van Vleck exhibited no warmth, nor did he acknowledge that his assessment of Atanasoff had been in error, Atanasoff recalled.

Professor Van Vleck was listed as Atanasoff's major professor in his doctoral studies, but he took leave during the 1929–1930 year when Atanasoff was a $3,000-a-year instructor in mathematics at the University of Wisconsin while completing his doctoral thesis. Professor Gregory Wentzel, from Zurich, Switzerland, was the visiting professor replacing Van Vleck, and Atanasoff found him rather more genial and helpful as he completed his doctoral thesis, "The Dielectric Constant of Helium."

As a basis for his study of helium, Atanasoff used the wave functions for the ground state developed by E. A. Hylleraas dealing with "approximate solutions." In working out the complicated mathematical problems related to his doctoral thesis, Atanasoff spent hours of time on a Monroe calculator, one of the most advanced calculating machines of the time.

"This was my first experience in serious computing," Atanasoff recalled. "Such calculations required many weeks of hard work on a desk calculator, the Monroe, which was the only one available at that time."

It was the drudgery of the days of work on the Monroe calculator that reinforced the young professor's first serious interest in developing a better and faster computing machine, and after he received his Ph.D. as a theoretic physicist in July 1930, Atanasoff returned to Iowa State College with a determination to see what he could do about it.

As a member of the Iowa State College faculty in the fall of 1930, he was given the rank of assistant professor in mathematics and physics and a salary of $2,700 a year. It was a comfortable salary for those years, but three years later the Depression forced cuts that resulted in Atanasoff's salary being reduced to $2,305 a year. It remained at that level until 1940.

With background that included a bachelor's degree in electrical engineering, a master's degree in mathematics, and a doctorate in theoretic physics, Atanasoff believed he was as well equipped as anyone to tackle the job of developing a faster more effective way of doing complicated mathematical problems he had encountered in his doctoral thesis. As he took on a larger group of graduate students, Atanasoff saw their need for faster and more effective ways of obtaining solutions to complicated problems in higher mathematics.

First, he was interested in a close examination of existing devices for calculation, including the Monroe calculator and the International Business Machines (IBM) tabulator. He had a familiarity with the Monroe machine from the time he was nine years old when he had tinkered with one in his father's office. Atanasoff gave some consideration to obtaining several Monroe calculators and lining them up in tandem but abandoned that idea because of the limited budget and the high cost of the Monroe calculators. It was impractical to even think of requesting such an expenditure.

The Mathematics Department at Iowa State had no mechanical calculators at that time, but there was one IBM tabulator housed in the Statistics Department then headed by Atanasoff's good friend, Professor Brandt. While the IBM machine did not permit the mathematical dexterity of the Monroe calculator, it did represent the largest computer of the day and it was available.

With the assistance of Brandt, Atanasoff started looking for a problem in theoretical physics that could be solved by the IBM equipment. First, they thought of applying the IBM equipment to the analysis of complex spectra, but on close analysis they determined that the IBM equipment would not perform the job. Then Atanasoff and Brandt concluded that by using some additional devices they might enable the IBM equipment to solve the problems they had devised. "In this we succeeded," Atanasoff recalled later and noted that the *Journal of The Optical Society of America* had published their paper on this experiment in February 1936.

Although Atanasoff and Brandt ended that article with laudatory comments about their relations with IBM representatives in this experiment, they were unaware at the time of internal memorandums at IBM expressing a highly critical view of the two Iowa

State College professors meddling with the IBM tabulators and using them in ways the corporation officials had not intended that they be used.

Even as Atanasoff was engaging in the revamping of the IBM calculators with Brandt, he was examining the emerging field of electronics and doing other experimentation with vacuum tubes and radio. Despite his background as an electrical engineer and theoretic physicist, he felt deficient in electronics; hence he obtained one of the first textbooks on electronics written by Hendrik Johannes Van der Bijl of South Africa from which he learned about vacuum tubes and then built a radio set and other projects in his own workshop. (The 1912 text was entitled *The Thermionic Vacuum Tube and Its Applications.*)

During this period he was promoted from assistant professor to associate professor of both mathematics and physics and moved his office from the Mathematics Department in Beardshear Hall to the Physics Building where he had more room and an office by himself. By this time he was teaching a variety of advanced courses in theoretic physics and was envisioning more and more practical use for a faster, accurate computing machine to aid his major graduate students in their advanced experimentations and studies. He was particularly interested in experimentations aimed at developing better ways of approximating the solution of partial differential equations. Atanasoff used the word "approximation" because in most cases there was no way of solving these equations exactly, the solutions could only be expressed approximately as tables of numbers.

During this period Atanasoff had his graduate students working on a wide range of projects that were tangentially related to simplifying the task of finding suitable approximations. He hoped those projects would lead to the simple and reliable method of solving the partial differential equations.

Atanasoff's list of graduate students who worked on these various projects and made some important contributions to his own thinking in this early period were Robert T. Wilson, Philip J. Hart, Erwin W. Kammer, Roy H. Cook, and Lynn A. Hannum. Those who made more specific than general contributions were George L. Gross and C. J. Thorne, both graduate students. Gross did an unpublished thesis on "Use of Functionals in Obtaining Approximate Solutions of Linear Operational Equations." Thorne's thesis, also unpublished, was titled "The Approximate Solution of Linear Differential Equations by the Use of Functionals."

In the examination of the types of mathematical apparatus available at that time, Atanasoff concluded that the calculating devices fell into two classes – analog and digital. In his papers on the subject during the late 1930s he did speak of analog devices as "analogue" devices and contrasted them to what he called "computing machines proper." The term "digital" did not come into use until much later.

The analog computer is a machine in which a number is represented by a physical quantity as measured by some system of units, Atanasoff has explained. "That physical quality can be anything: a distance, an electric voltage, a current of electricity, air pressure, etc.," Atanasoff commented. "If we desire to determine the number more exactly, we will have to measure the quantity more exactly. We can do so either by making better physical measurements or by changing our scales."

The slide rule, with which Atanasoff was familiar from the time he was ten years old, is an analog calculator, its accuracy depending upon the precise accuracy of distances on a slide rule as related to other distances. However, it provides approximations with limitations dictated to a large degree by its length. To obtain the approximations that Atanasoff had in mind would have required a slide rule the length of a football field, or in some instances a mile or more in length. This was obviously impractical as a simple solution.

The Bush Differential Analyzer, built by Prof. Vannevar Bush at the Massachusetts Institute of Technology in 1930 and 1931, was also an analog device. The physical quality involved in the Bush Differential Analyzer was the measure of the turns of a shaft. It was useful to perform certain limited tasks, but in reading the literature related to it, Atanasoff concluded that the solution of linear algebraic equations was not within the capacity of the Bush Differential Analyzer and that it was doubtful it would be possible to adapt it to solve linear algebraic equations.

In 1936 Atanasoff engaged in his last effort to construct a small analog calculator. With Glenn Murphy, then an Iowa State College atomic physicist, Atanasoff built a small analog calculator called the "Laplaciometer." It was for use in analyzing the geometry of surfaces – and was a small device measuring about 14 inches high with its slim body measuring 3 inches by 3 inches.

While the Atanasoff-Hannum-Murphy "Laplaciometer" was regarded as a success in holding the errors down to the acceptable engineering standards of that period, Atanasoff regarded it as having the same flaws as other analog devices where the accuracy was too dependent upon the ideal performance of the parts of the machine.

The "Laplaciometer" was Atanasoff's last effort to find the solutions he sought for complicated mathematical problems in analog devices. (The work on the "Laplaciometer" was first developed by Lynn Hannum, a graduate student, with Atanasoff. Dr. Glenn Murphy did study and work related to the machine and wrote papers related to the machine that were published later.)

Atanasoff's mind then turned to using electronics and electric impulses as the power media and measuring stick for a computer and to abandoning the normal base-ten arithmetic for a base other than ten. There was a problem of stability with the use of electronics or electric power as the media which Atanasoff recognized even as he was first visualizing the use of vacuum tubes.

If he used a base other than ten in a computer device, there would be a constant problem of converting out of the traditional base-ten and then, when the solution was obtained, to convert back to base-ten. Also, he did considerable figuring on the possible use of bases above ten, but this was totally unsatisfactory from a practical standpoint.

Figuring that some base of less than ten would be the way to go, Atanasoff finally came to a tentative conclusion that perhaps base-two would be the most practical for a number of reasons.

During the last part of 1936 and most of 1937, Atanasoff puzzled. He believed he was on the brink of discovery only to lose his train of thought in the complicated field of higher mathematics and mechanisms that were beyond the line of knowledge covered in the textbooks.

The frustration of many months of work and study had built to a frenzy in the winter months of 1937 when Atanasoff felt compelled to leave his office in the Physics Building to go for a mind-clearing drive in the Iowa countryside. It was Atanasoff's habit to get in the car and drive to clear his mind when particularly baffled by a problem. He had no destination in mind and only the purpose of finding some relief from grappling with the computer problem that had become an obsession. It was a ride he would never forget and that he would have occasion to recall many times in the next fifty years.

CHAPTER 4

It All Comes Together:
A Drive, a Dive, and a Drink,
1937–1938

THE slim handsome thirty-four-year-old professor of mathematics and physics did not intend to go for a long drive as he piloted his Ford V8 out of his parking space near the Physics Building. Atanasoff had been home for an early dinner and had returned to his office to do some serious thinking about how to create a machine that would solve complicated mathematics, and it hadn't worked. He was more frustrated than ever as he pulled on a heavy coat and hat to leave Room 52 in the Physics Building.

Although there was no snow on the ground the temperature was twenty degrees below zero and the wind provided an additional bite. The motor of his car was still warm enough so he had no trouble starting it, and by the time he had driven the few blocks south to Highway 30, the Lincoln Highway, it was working smoothly. Atanasoff was pleased with the operation of the gasoline-burning South-Wind heater built by Stewart-Werner of Chicago.

At Highway 30 Atanasoff turned left to drive through the Iowa State campus shopping center and past the row of large brick fraternity houses on the south side of the highway. He had no real plan as he followed Highway 30 through Ames. He could see the Chicago North Western Railroad Station where he had stepped from the train only twelve years earlier as a young enthusiastic graduate assistant from Florida.

Although he was frustrated in his obsession with finding the key for a mechanism that could revolutionize mathematical computations, Atanasoff found some consolation in musing. He had done reasonably well for a boy from a large family who had to make his own way through college. After all, it was the depths of the Depression and many college-educated men and women were unemployed. He had a steady income and employment in an honorable and satisfying profession and in pleasant surroundings. He liked the graduate students and was stimulated by their youthful enthusiasm, and he liked most of his colleagues on the Iowa State College faculty.

Atanasoff took stock of his home life, and found it to be generally satisfactory even as he admitted he was too much absorbed with his work and his obsession with producing a new and better computing machine. He believed that if a mechanism could be created to solve linear algebraic equations, then there would be essentially no limits to the task such a mechanism could perform. Because he believed he could do it, Lura believed he could do it. Because she believed that her husband was working on something of unusual significance, she was willing to put up with the little eccentricities that went with his intense absorption in this problem of creating a new mechanism or adapting some current calculating machine to the solution of linear algebraic equations.

Although he had been unduly engrossed in thoughts about the mathematical problem, he had not neglected his graduate students, nor had he neglected the major problems at home. Atanasoff had drawn the plans for, and supervised the construction of, a new brick home about a mile west of the Iowa State College campus in 1935, the year his third child, John Vincent Atanasoff, Jr., was born.

When their oldest daughter, Elsie, developed an asthmatic condition as a result of an allergy to cows' milk, Atanasoff bought a goat and milked the goat early every morning before going to his office at the college. Because Elsie's allergy was life threatening at one stage, Atanasoff studied all of the books on the subject of allergies. He became so knowledgeable about the subject that a local medical doctor sent his patients to him for advice. Before Elsie's allergic condition was corrected, Atanasoff's herd of goats expanded to six, and by reading books on the subject of goats he had become somewhat of an expert in that area as well.

Driving east out of Ames and mulling over other things than the frustrating problem of creating a computer machine, Atanasoff drove intently and at a fast rate of speed over the dry, flat, and straight highway. The young professor reduced speed only as he drove through the small towns of Nevada and State Center, through the outskirts of Marshalltown, and through Toledo, Tama, and Gladstone. At some point east of Gladstone, Atanasoff turned south from Highway 30 and drove through Belle Plaine, Marengo, and Amana on his usual route to Highway 6. The hours passed and the miles flew by, and before he realized how far he had driven, he was crossing the broad Mississippi River and was entering Illinois.

He continued 2 or 3 miles beyond the Mississippi River before suddenly realizing that he had driven probably 200 miles from Ames. He saw the bright lights of a tavern on the right of the road and turned in the driveway as if drawn by the warm friendly glow of the garishly lighted roadhouse.

This was Illinois where he could get a drink of bourbon legally, as opposed to Iowa where it was illegal for liquor to be kept or served in taverns or restaurants. Atanasoff mused to himself that 200 miles was a long way to drive for a drink.

While it had not been his intention to drive to Illinois for a drink, he decided that since he was here he might as well get a bourbon and mixer before starting the long drive back to Ames. As he got out of the warm car, JV pulled the heavy coat around him as protection against the subzero weather. In the roadhouse he took a table in the corner away from the bar, removed his heavy coat, and asked the waitress to bring him a bourbon.

When the waitress placed the drink before him, he suddenly realized that he was no longer nervous and tense. His thoughts turned again to the creation of a computing machine, and in the cool quiet of the roadhouse he realized that his thoughts were coming together in a positive manner. Sometime between the first and second drink, all of his study and work started to pay off. His thoughts began generating ideas in a systematic way. The roadhouse was only moderately busy and it was quiet at the corner table. The waitress, occupied with other customers, did not bother him with repetitious offers of more drinks.

In the two or three hours he was in the roadhouse, JV's thoughts settled first on the use of electricity and electronics as the medium for the computer and then turned to the need for a "regenerative memory" or "jogging" of the electrical system through the use of condensers that would regenerate their own state. "If they (the condensers) were in the plus state, for instance, they would stay in the plus state; or, if they were in the negative state, they would stay in the negative state," Atanasoff explained later. "They would not blink off to zero. Or if you used two positive charges, they would retain their individual identity and would not leak across to each other."

Quietly thinking at the roadhouse, JV was able to develop his initial concept of what is now called "logic circuits." He explained this as "a non-racheting approach to the interaction between two memory units, or, as I called it the 'abaci.'" Atanasoff visualized a black box with an internal mechanism that would be moved by electric or electronic means, and would operate on a base-two system, and on the principles of an abacus, the ancient calculating device consisting of beads strung on rods in a frame.

During that evening at the Illinois roadhouse, Atanasoff made four decisions for his computer project:

1. He would use electricity and electronics as the medium for the computer.

2. In spite of custom, he would use base-two numbers (the binary system) for his computer.

3. He would use condensers for memory and would use a regenerative or "jogging" process to avoid lapses that might be caused by leakage of power.

4. He would compute by direct logical action and not by enumeration as used in analog calculating devices.

Some of the ideas he jotted down on a paper napkin, but he did not need the napkin to remind him of ideas he had thought about for such a long time.

The solution to the puzzle had been elusive, but now that the theory was in place the young professor wondered why he had not seen it earlier.

He drove slowly back to Ames, weary but satisfied that he was finally on the right track for a revolutionary new machine using the four new basic concepts he had envisioned. He realized that his concepts were, at that stage, only theories upon which to proceed and that it might be necessary to modify to some degree any or all of those theories. But his training as an electrical engineer, as a mathematician, and as a theoretic physicist gave him confidence that the testing would prove that his concepts were valid.

All of his training in electrical engineering made him certain that electricity or electronics should be the medium for his computer. His principal worry was to find a way to make electricity or electronics as stable as the measuring elements of analog calculators. Control of electricity was not as effective in 1937 and 1938 as it was to become a few years later. He reflected that he was building a digital computer rather than an analog device and concluded "that digital devices do not require absolute accuracy to yield perfect results."

Atanasoff was totally convinced because of his past experimentation and study that the use of base-two (the binary) system in his computer would have great advantages and essentially no disadvantages except that it was against the custom. However, he expected to face much criticism in a swing away from the customary base-ten.

While Atanasoff saw only tremendous advantages in a base-two computing machine, he recognized that it would to some degree be like changing the metric system, or the alphabet, or calendar reform. He gave himself courage on that point by noting that using base-two for a computer machine would be mainly for scientific purposes and that most people would not need to use it.

The final decision for the memory element for his computer did not come so easily. Years earlier Atanasoff had read about Valdemar Poulsen's magnetic wire, but he had never built such a device. However, the Poulsen logic appealed to him as the basis for a slow memory for a computing machine.

"I was convinced that if the piece of ferromagnetic material is small, the power out will be very small. Even at that time, I was planning to use vacuum tubes for computing circuits, but I could not afford too many vacuum tubes. I chose small condensers for memory because they would have the required voltage to actuate the tubes, and the plates of the tubes would give enough power to charge the condensers," Atanasoff explained. "In the past, I had been worried about loss charge in the condensers, but now with jogging (regeneration) that worry was gone." Design and construction of the actual circuit for jogging the memory required a minimum amount of time, a week or two at most, Atanasoff explained later.

The decision to compute by direct logical action and not by enumeration was much more difficult, Atanasoff found. "I had merely hypothecated a black box that would do this, and nobody knew how to make such a box," Atanasoff commented. "If I had chosen to do the job by enumeration, I would have tried to simulate by electronic means the counting processes that have always been used in computing. But here I wanted something different."

"I considered how I might add two numbers," Atanasoff continued. "I would have them enter the black box from two separate memory devices. The black box would find their sum and would signal this to a third memory device or, what is more usual, back into one of the memories that had sent the original numbers. The box would have, in each case, to compute the answers to the additions or subtractions required."

Atanasoff planned to use serial addition or subtraction; that is, to operate on numbers digit by digit. The black box, which he began to call the computing device, started at the lowest power of two and moved to the highest power, and at each power it received the two signals from the digits to be added or subtracted. At the same time it received the carry or borrow digit, if any, from the previous step. The logic of the system gave the answer and the carry or borrow, if any, for the next step, according to Atanasoff's figuring. The black box or computing device was to contain vacuum tubes to carry out these operations.

Atanasoff explained that in designing such devices today, he would use an abstract kind of mathematics called Boolean algebra (after George Boole's work published in the 1850s) and the so-called truth table. However, at the time, he did not recognize the Boolean algebra's application to the problem and obtained his results by trial and "by a kind of cognition."

"I called my logic circuit an add-subtract mechanism," Atanasoff continued. "It contained thirteen vacuum tubes, and in the end these were all triodes. Adjustment of the biases of the tubes would cause the circuit to add or to subtract as required. By arranging for the data on one of the two memory devices to be shifted, I had planned to provide for automatic multiplication and division."

Solution of these problems took many months of his spare time, and it was not finalized until the last months of 1938 and the first month of 1939. Atanasoff has explained that all of his work on the capacitor memory and the add-subtract mechanism was entirely theoretical. "No experiments were used in deriving the circuits or in checking them," he said.

Atanasoff had spent more than a year after his visit to the Illinois roadhouse working on the plans for his computer, and most of that time had been spent on jogging and the logic circuits for adding and subtracting. He now felt confident that the computer project would be a success but was also certain he could not go it alone.

In the early spring of 1939 Atanasoff made a formal application to the dean of the graduate school for a grant to provide for the hiring of an assistant and to provide a small budget for shop work and materials. That application explained the plan for an electronic digital computer that contained the four concepts Atanasoff had first visualized over a bourbon at the Illinois roadhouse a year earlier. They are the four concepts that Atanasoff found to be involved in virtually all computers forty-five years later in the 1980s when he wrote:

All computing is now done with electrical and electronic means. Base-two numbers (binary numbers) are current on all machines. To the best of my knowledge, all machines now operate with logic circuits and without enumeration. It is true that I did not invent the modern dynamic memory but this memory uses capacitors for memory and the refresh cycle directly derived from my jogging or regenerative ideas.

Atanasoff submitted his application for a grant in March 1939, and the Iowa State College committee in early May approved a grant of $650. It was a large commitment of grant funds for those depression years, and Atanasoff was delighted to be able to give consideration to hiring a particularly bright and able electrical engineering student to embark upon this exciting adventure.

CHAPTER 5

The Professor and His Protege:
Clifford Berry, 1939–1941

I T was midmorning on a cool spring day in May in 1939 when
Atanasoff walked leisurely across the Iowa State College campus toward the Physics Building. The beauty of the rolling
green lawns of the campus and the hustle of walking students
had distracted him from his thoughts about his computer-machine
project and the important decision he had to make in selecting a
graduate assistant who could be a real help on his project instead of
a drain on his energy.

As the young professor was walking north of Beardshear Hall
near the book store the approach of Prof. Harold Anderson reminded him of his project and of his intention to ask the professor to
recommend an electrical engineering student as an assistant. Harold
Anderson was one of his best friends on the Iowa State College
faculty as well as an enthusiastic supporter of his research on a
computer machine. Most important, Anderson was a professor of
electrical engineering and a man in whom Atanasoff had the
greatest confidence. He hadn't called him earlier because it was only
within the last few days that he had made a final decision that he
should choose an electrical engineer assistant since most students
doing graduate work in physics or mathematics did not possess the
required mechanical and electronic skills.

Anderson was already aware of JV's computer-machine project,
so it was unnecessary to make any explanation other than to say he
had decided he needed an electrical engineer with outstanding mechanical ability and knowledge of electronics.

"I have your man – Clifford Berry," Anderson volunteered even before Atanasoff had specifically requested a recommendation. "Berry is a brilliant student, has a tremendous grasp of mechanical construction, and is well grounded in electronics."

For the next few minutes Anderson explained that Clifford Edward Berry was to receive his bachelor's degree in electrical engineering that spring and would be attending Iowa State in the fall to start work on a master's degree. Anderson's comments on Cliff Berry's brilliance, his pleasant personality, his capacity for hard work, and his meticulous care in construction convinced Atanasoff that this young student would in all probability be his selection. He asked Anderson to have Cliff Berry call him to set a suitable time for an interview. The big question now was how the work on the computer would fit into Cliff Berry's plans.

The next day Atanasoff received a call from Cliff Berry who was interested in the job. That brief phone conversation convinced Atanasoff that he was dealing with an unusual young man – serious but pleasant, with an uncommon combination of brilliance and common sense. Atanasoff had never seen or heard of Cliff Berry before Harold Anderson mentioned his name, so he had no preconceived impression of the slight-figured young man who came into his office later and introduced himself. The slimness of Cliff Berry's five-foot, eight-inch frame made him appear fragile and even younger than his twenty-two years, and the sweater and the open neck of his shirt were both typical of the attire of undergraduates on the Iowa State campus. But there was something about the firmness of the young Berry's handshake, and the directness of his gaze that gave Atanasoff immediate confidence. He felt Berry was a graduate student who could understand his computer concepts without undue preliminary explanations. Within a few minutes, Atanasoff had taken the preliminary computer sketches from his desk drawer to explain them to the young electrical engineer. Cliff Berry asked intelligent and perceptive questions, and his relevant comments buoyed Atanasoff's enthusiasm and optimism about his computer project.

In that first meeting there was immediate rapport, both personal and professional, between Professor Atanasoff and the young man who was to be his protege and co-inventor of the first electronic digital computer. Although they were too much absorbed with talk of the planned computer project to discuss it at the time, Atanasoff and his precocious protege came from similar backgrounds. Both were the sons of self-taught electrical engineers, and both had become fascinated with the operation of electrical devices and electrical construction through the electrical tinkering of their fathers. Both were blessed with brilliant minds, curiosity, and mechanical skills, and with the confident belief that persistent work would make it possible to accomplish what no others had achieved.

Clifford Berry's parents, Fred and Grace Strohm Berry, were born on farms near Gladbrook, Iowa, and grew up with the work ethic and confidence of young farm people who shoulder an adult work load at an early age. Fred Berry was reared on the family farm near Gladbrook and had dropped out of Gladbrook High School after completing the tenth grade. He augmented the mechanical skills he had learned on the farm with work for the local telephone company and then took a job on an electrical construction project in St. Paul, Minnesota, where he became foreman over a twenty-man crew before he was twenty years of age.

When Fred Berry returned to Gladbrook to take a job with the local telephone company, he married Grace Strohm, a neighbor who was the sister of his older brother's wife. Two years later, on 19 April 1918, Clifford E. Berry was born. He was the oldest of the four children born to Fred and Grace Berry during the ten years that they lived in the little town of Gladbrook.

By the time Clifford was a small child his father had an electrical appliance and repair store in Gladbrook and was tinkering with electrical construction projects of one kind or another. The most memorable as far as Cliff and other members of the Berry family were concerned was a radio—the first radio in Gladbrook. It was equipped with earphones, and there was a constant stream of visitors at the Berry home to see Fred Berry's home-built talking machine. Fred Berry patiently explained the construction to his eldest son when Cliff was no more than six or seven years of age, and it was but a few years later that Cliff Berry started his own tinkering with electricity and radio. Cliff built his first ham radio sometime after April 1929, when the family moved about fifty miles south and east of Gladbrook to Marengo, where Fred Berry had taken a job as a division manager for the Iowa Power Company. The move took place on 18 April 1929—the day before Cliff's eleventh birthday.

Clifford Berry was precocious from the time he started first grade in the Gladbrook school at age five. Because he had such an easy time in school, the teacher and the school principal suggested that he be moved a grade ahead in his second year in school. Fred and Grace Berry resisted the suggestion for two years but finally gave in when the principal argued that unless Clifford was challenged more he might become "a loafer." Fred and Grace Berry agreed to let Clifford skip the fourth grade at Gladbrook.

When the family moved to Marengo, Cliff Berry's scholastic excellence continued even though he was one or two years younger than the other members of his class. His scholarly achievement continued despite the tragedy that struck the family during his sophomore year at Marengo High School. Fred Berry, then manager of the Marengo office for Iowa Power Company, was shot and killed by an employee who had been fired for not doing his job properly.

The death of Fred Berry left Grace Berry with the responsibility for rearing four children ranging in age from four-year-old Barbara to thirteen-year-old Cliff. Fred's death not only brought grief to the family, but also placed a dark cloud over Fred's plan to assure all four children a college education.

From as early as the Berry family members could remember, Clifford Berry had aspired to study electrical engineering at Iowa State College. Clifford and his father had decided that Iowa State was the college for Clifford even though the University of Iowa, at Iowa City, was much closer to Marengo.

At Fred Berry's death, Grace Berry decided she would remain in Marengo until Cliff was ready for Iowa State. Cliff Berry was only fifteen years old as a senior at Marengo, and although he was a top student in the class, Grace Berry concluded that he could use another year of high school classes before facing the rigors of college work at Iowa State. Cliff accepted her judgment, and he enrolled in another year of high school courses while his brother, Fred Dean Berry, completed another year of high school in Marengo. Cliff enjoyed life with his friends in the small town and he had a particularly close relationship with a few ham radio operators in the community.

From the time Cliff Berry entered Iowa State, his record as a student of electrical engineering was as impressive to students and other faculty members who knew him as it was to Prof. Harold Anderson who had recommended him to Atanasoff without reservation. That recommendation from Anderson resulted in putting together at Iowa State the Atanasoff-Berry team, a team that was later described by David Ritchie, the science writer and computer historian, as "one of the most famous teams in engineering history."

This was the background of the young man, Clifford Berry, who on that morning in the spring of 1939 engaged in the first conversations about the concepts and the basic problems they would have to solve in the construction of the prototype of an electronic digital computer. However, there were some practical matters that stood in the way of an immediate start on the project.

Atanasoff explained that the $650 grant to take care of Berry's salary, materials, and shop work would not be available until the fall term in September 1939. Berry understood the problem but did not want that to interfere with the meetings and discussions with Atanasoff that would be essential for the speedy and effective progress they wanted to achieve once the funds became available for material and shop work.

As a result of that first meeting, Atanasoff believed the choice of Cliff Berry was one of the best things that could have happened to him and to the project. The periodic meetings that he had with Cliff Berry during the summer of 1939 further solidified his faith in Harold Anderson's judgment of this young electrical engineering student. He not only had the required mechanical and electronic skills, but "he had vision and inventive skills as well."

While Atanasoff would have liked to have begun work on the computer project that summer, he accepted the financial realities with only minor frustration and made plans for the construction project that would test his theories. Although Atanasoff had worked his ideas out on paper, he recognized that his theoretical approach did not constitute proof of the feasibility of his new method of computing.

As they started work on the project in September, Atanasoff's enthusiasm often masked the skepticism and doubts that he and Cliff Berry had about bringing into physical being his theories of an electronic digital computer. As far as he knew—and he had read widely on the subject for more than a decade—he and Cliff Berry were plowing new ground in using electricity and electronics as the medium, in using base-two numbers (binary numbers) as opposed to the conventional base-ten, in using condensers for memory "jogging" or regeneration, and in using logic circuits rather than conventional enumeration.

The first problem was to find the space for construction of the prototype computer machine. Every square foot of space on the main floor of the Physics Building was in use. It would have been presumptuous at that point to assume any kind of priority would be given to his computer project by administrators at Iowa State College. He had his $650 grant, felt fortunate to have it, and did not want to call attention to his project until he had something physical to demonstrate the soundness of his theories.

Fred Berry and Grace Strohm Berry, Gladbrook natives and
parents of Clifford Berry. [*Right*] Gladbrook, Iowa, birthplace of
Clifford E. Berry, co-inventor of the first electronic digital
computer. (*Courtesy of Grace Berry*)

Clifford Berry as a baby, [*left*], and a few years later with his
brother Robert. (*Courtesy of Grace Berry*)

Clifford Berry, Eagle Scout, Marengo, Iowa. (*Courtesy of Grace Berry*) [*Below left*] Clifford Berry, Atanasoff's assistant between 1939 and 1942 when the ABC was built. (*Courtesy of J. V. Atanasoff*) [*Right*] Jean Reed, Iowa State College coed and JV's secretary, who married Clifford Berry in June 1942. (*Courtesy of Jean Reed Berry*)

Clifford and Jean Reed Berry,
June 1942. [*Below*] The Berrys,
latter part of 1940s. (*Courtesy of
Jean Reed Berry*)

Clifford Berry, 1959, Director of Engineering, Analytical and Control Instrument Division, Consolidated Electrodynamics Corporation.

Atanasoff found a less prestigious location in the cavernous basement of the Physics Building. The unfinished basement contained a student shop, and he was able to stake out an alcove about 40 feet from the workshop. This juxtaposition turned out to be advantageous to Cliff Berry. The place was heated and dry and was relatively cool in the summer.

Although neither JV with a student load, nor Cliff Berry, who was just starting his graduate work, were free to devote full time to the computer machine prototype, it moved forward with amazing speed. In that initial prototype they abandoned the idea of attacking the total problem of solving large systems of linear algebraic equations that had been an important motivational factor for Atanasoff's invention and decided it should be a simple electronic digital computer and the simpler the better.

While Atanasoff had worked out some parts of the design of the computer in meticulous detail, he had only rough sketches of some other parts of the proposed machine and with Cliff Berry worked out those details as they moved forward with the project. Within a few weeks the prototype took the shape of a breadboard-size device, with the electrical components mounted crudely on the surface. It was small enough to be moved easily, and yet it included all the essential components of a complete calculating machine and made it possible for Cliff Berry and Atanasoff to see where their ideas were leading them.

"Almost as soon as the prototype was completed, it began to work well," Atanasoff recalled. "The assembly procedure for the logic circuit which Berry had devised made them perfect." The first demonstrations of the prototype electronic computer took place in October—within two months of the time Atanasoff and Berry began their construction work. There were several other demonstrations of the machine in November. "Our visitors who understood what was going on were surprised to find so much structure giving additions and subtractions that were correct," Atanasoff reported. "Of course, our explanations to them (the visitors) had to cover base-two number theory."

The completion of that prototype Atanasoff Berry Computer was regarded as a "great success" by JV and Cliff, and they engaged in brief self-congratulations. It settled their doubts that an electronic computer could be built. This crude device could just add and subtract the binary equivalents of decimal numbers having up to eight places. However, it was a digital device rather than analog like the differential analyzer and other calculating mechanisms that had held center stage with inventor's experiments for decades.

Atanasoff enumerated the other significant advances the prototype encompassed:

> While the clock system was mechanical, all computing was electronic.
> For the first time, vacuum tubes were used in computing.
> The advantageous base-2 number system was first used.
> Logic Systems were first employed in computing.
> All computation was done in a serial manner.
> Capacitors (or condensers) were used as memory elements.
> A rotating-drum memory contained the capacitors.
> What I (Atanasoff) called jogging (others call it regeneration or refreshing) was first used in computation.

In December 1939 a demonstration of the prototype to Iowa State College officials convinced them that Atanasoff's project was worthy of a grant of $850 from the Iowa State College Research Council to construct a full-scale machine capable of solving systems of equations. Work on that full-scale machine started immediately after the Christmas holidays.

In January 1940 Atanasoff made an estimate on the size of the full-scale machine, based upon the dimensions of a few parts of the machine. He tried to keep the machine within the dimensions of a large desk. Although he had made those rough calculations, Atanasoff acknowledged later that the accuracy of his initial estimate was probably due as much to luck as to science.

Those estimates were for the angle irons for the frame that Cliff Berry was cutting to start the construction. This was the first step on what they believed could be a great innovation. It was to be constructed for the specific purpose of solving linear algebraic equations, but if it accomplished that task with any reasonable speed, there would be a wide range of uses as Atanasoff and Berry saw it.

Some of Atanasoff's academic colleagues at Iowa State were not so optimistic, and one friendly professor quipped that even if it was successful in solving linear algebraic equations, "it will not run a street car."

Disregarding the quips and sarcasm of a few of his colleagues, JV moved forward swiftly to buy the material for the construction and testing of the full-scale computer he had described in a two-page memorandum to the Iowa State College Research Corporation. The thirty-seven-year-old physics professor and his protege, Cliff Berry, were fully confident that they could construct a full-scale computer that would provide solutions with substantial accuracy for twenty-nine equations with twenty-nine unknowns. They had put the skepticism and doubts behind them with the successful construction of the prototype.

Atanasoff had a full class load of graduate students in physics and was considering involvement in a military defense project with Dr. Warren Weaver of the National Defense Research Committee (NDRC), but he did not let those interests interfere with the computer project. He simply put in a longer work day.

It was the same way with Cliff Berry, whose brilliance in electronics and mechanical innovations was vital to effective progress. Berry, at twenty-two, had enthusiasm and energy to burn despite the routine related to his work for a master's degree in physics. With several months of exposure to Atanasoff's project, he had developed his knowledge and skills to the point where he was no longer dependent upon precise instructions from Atanasoff. By the time they were a few weeks into the construction of the full-scale computer, Cliff Berry was making suggestions for improvements in Atanasoff's designs and initiating construction innovations. Cliff Berry had the full confidence of Atanasoff, and they moved forward as a smooth-working team.

By late spring it was obvious that they had the project under control and that some consideration should be given to taking steps to patent the Atanasoff Berry Computer in addition to obtaining additional funding to refine and perfect the construction. Atanasoff, with Berry's assistance, spent several weeks in writing a 35-page manuscript detailing the theories and construction ideas that were going into this first electronic digital computer.

In those days before modern duplicating machines, the copies of the 35-page manuscript, "Computing Machines for the Solution of Large Systems of Linear Algebraic Equations," were made with carbon paper on a typewriter. The accompanying sketches were drawn by hand and pasted in the booklets that were completed in early August 1940. Copies were sent to the Iowa State College Research Corporation as a preliminary to a request for a $5,000 grant, one copy was later sent to Chicago patent lawyer Richard R. Trexler, and Atanasoff retained one copy in a green cover for the use of Cliff Berry and other students who were doing the wiring, soldering, and other routine construction work on the computing machine.

The Chicago patent lawyer, Trexler, was hired by Iowa State College because officials believed they would need a patent law specialist to give them advice on how to protect the inventions that were incorporated in the Atanasoff Berry Computer. Atanasoff and

Berry met with Trexler several times to determine just what descriptions and drawings he would need to protect their work. They had hoped that the 35-page manuscript would take care of the patent requirements, since the major components of the machine had been tested immediately after construction and before being placed in the machine. It had been demonstrated that the machine would perform the function it was constructed to perform: It would solve systems of linear algebraic equations of up to thirty numbers.

However, even though the Atanasoff Berry Computer had passed many tests, it was determined that there was a flaw related to the reliability of the computer's method of punching holes in binary cards through an electric spark method. Atanasoff described the flaw in the following terms: "We had tested the base-2 card system rather carefully, but the number of tests was not sufficient to find an error which occurred once in 10,000 or 100,000 times."

"It was quite good, but not good enough," Atanasoff explained. He and Cliff Berry wanted total accuracy and they continued to work on the problem and to refine other aspects of the machine in the late fall and winter of 1940.

In December of each year it was Atanasoff's practice to attend the annual meeting of the American Association for the Advancement of Science (AAAS) that held its meetings during the week after Christmas. In 1940 the AAAS meeting was scheduled to be held in Philadelphia, and Atanasoff took his family along for a pre-Christmas visit to New York. He made arrangements to meet Cliff Berry in Washington after the AAAS meeting for some work at the patent office in the Commerce Department building.

Atanasoff attended the AAAS conference that began on 26 December 1940 and by chance dropped in on a lecture being given by Dr. John W. Mauchly, a physicist at Ursinus College, a short distance north of Philadelphia. The young physics professor, long fascinated with the collection and analysis of weather data, had constructed a harmonic analyzer that could sift through huge amounts of weather data quickly. Mauchly used this harmonic analyzer in tracing two cycles of American weather. It was an analog machine, but its functions were in the general area of Atanasoff's interests, so the Iowa State College professor stopped to listen to what was a generally entertaining lecture.

When Mauchly's lecture ended, Atanasoff went to the front of the lecture hall, introduced himself, and engaged Mauchly in conversation about his harmonic analyzer and in short order turned the discussion to Atanasoff's construction of a computer machine at

Iowa State College. The length of that conversation has been estimated by Atanasoff and by Mauchly to have taken anywhere from twenty or twenty-five minutes, but the emphasis and details of that conversation were later disputed. However, there is no dispute that there was conversation about Atanasoff's computer machine to the point that Mauchly became interested in learning more about the details.

How much detail Atanasoff disclosed in that meeting was later a subject of much dispute. It is acknowledged by both parties that at some point Mauchly's questioning on those details was blocked by Atanasoff's assertion that he had been cautioned by Iowa State College lawyers to avoid any disclosures that might jeopardize the patents they were going to seek.

However, to stop Mauchly's persistent inquires about his computer, Atanasoff told Mauchly that if he would visit him at Ames, he would show him the computer machine and explain its functions.

When he left Philadelphia, Atanasoff drove to Washington where he met Cliff Berry, and together they spent several days at the patent office. They came away reassured that the electronic digital computer and most of its concepts were entirely new and patentable, and Atanasoff obtained a recommendation for a Chicago patent attorney, Richard Trexler, from an official in the patent office.

Back at Iowa State Atanasoff passed the name of Trexler to Iowa State College officials and settled down with Cliff Berry to the last remaining problem of any consequence – designing and constructing the base-two card-punching system and the base-ten–base-two conversion table.

In early January Atanasoff was so pleased with the state of development that he gave his approval for an interview by a reporter from the *Des Moines Register,* and also approved the photographing of Cliff Berry with a section of the machine used for regenerating the memory.

On 15 January 1941 the *Des Moines Tribune* carried the following brief nontechnical story under the headline: "Machine Remembers":

An electrical computing machine said here to operate more like the human brain than any other such machine known to exist is being built by Dr. John V. Atanasoff, Iowa State College, Physics Professor.

The machine contains more than 300 vacuum tubes and will be used to compute complicated algebraic equations. Dr. Atanasoff said it will occupy about as much space as a large office desk. The instrument will be entirely electrical and will be used in research experiments.

Dr. Atanasoff said he has been working on the machine several years and probably will finish it in about a year.

The brief story was accompanied by a large picture of Cliff Berry holding the device for regenerating the memory. Atanasoff and Berry were displeased with the lack of precision in the cutline. That cutline identified the board with forty-five tubes, held by Cliff Berry, as "the memory" of the machine rather than the device for regenerating "the memory." The "memory" was in a different part of the machine.

While that story was in preparation, Atanasoff received a letter from Mauchly in which the Ursinus College professor formally accepted Atanasoff's invitation to examine his computer machine.

On 23 January 1941 Atanasoff replied and renewed his invitation to Mauchly to visit Iowa State to find out more about the computer machine. He received a quick response from Mauchly indicating that he was making plans to drive to Iowa during the spring break. Mauchly canceled that planned visit but then rescheduled it for his earliest opportunity during the summer vacation period.

Atanasoff was pleased that Mauchly was so interested in his computer that he would plan to drive halfway across the country to spend a week or more of his vacation time to examine it, but at the moment he had other things on his mind related to further funding, patent rights, and perfecting the base-ten–base-two converters.

On 24 March 1941 Iowa State College President Charles E. Friley received a letter of notification from Howard Poillon, president of Research Corporation, on the approval of a grant of $5,330 for Atanasoff to continue the research and development of the Atanasoff Berry Computer. The grant was, for that era, a large sum of money for a project such as the Atanasoff Berry Computer and caused President Friley to realize that the computer project could be worth a considerable sum of money to Iowa State College; he was determined to make sure that Iowa State was insured a lion's share. President Friley directed the Iowa State College Research Foundation (ISCRF) to take all necessary steps to assure that Atanasoff would sign an agreement making Iowa State College the recipient of 90 percent of any income from the computer ideas before releasing the $5,330 grant to him.

Up to that time, Iowa State College had no firm policy on patent rights that might flow from the work of faculty members. When Atanasoff was apprised of President Friley's proposal that he be given only 10 percent of any income from his computer ideas, he balked. He explained that he had already agreed to give Cliff Berry 10 percent of his share of any income from patents because of his substantial contribution to the development and construction of the Atanasoff Berry Computer.

Atanasoff explained that his most significant concepts were already tested and incorporated in the computer machine in place in the basement of the Physics Building, and the additional funds were simply for refinement and perfection of those basic ideas. He made it clear that he did not believe a 90/10 division was fair, and that he and Cliff Berry could not continue to work on the machine unless the $5,330 grant was released.

Although he pressed for an agreement in which Cliff Berry would be assured of a cut of the proceeds, Iowa State College administrators rejected completely the idea of the college setting a precedent by making an agreement permitting a graduate student to receive a share of income from a patent. However, in the end the college and Atanasoff agreed on a 50/50 split on any income from patents on the machine and further stated they would not interfere with any agreement he might enter into with Cliff Berry.

The patent agreement with the college was settled, the money was released, and Atanasoff and Berry continued to work on the problem of the reliability of the computer's method of punching holes in binary conversion cards. Also, Atanasoff evinced some concern about the lack of progress or the lack of communications on the computer patent applications. Patent law was not his area of expertise, but he had done some study in the area and he could not understand the delay. He had hoped that the applications would have been filed by now or that there would be some explanation as to why they had not been filed.

On 31 May 1941 Atanasoff wrote Mauchly the following letter:

Mr. J. W. Mauchly
Ursinus College
Collegeville, Pennsylvania

Dear Doctor Mauchly:
I think that it is an excellent idea for you to come west during the month of June or any other time for that matter. You might visit the Physics Colloquium at the University of Iowa if you wish. I generally do not go because the discussions are mainly in the field of physics teaching. But you could either go back by Iowa City or stop on your way west. Or, if it proves more convenient, I could drive you over. We have plenty of room and will be delighted to have you stay with us while here.

As you may surmise, I am somewhat out of the beaten track of computing machine gossip, and so I am always interested in any details you can give me. The figures on the electronic differential integraph seem absolutely startling. During Dr. Caldwell's last visit here, I suddenly obtained an idea as to how the computing machine which we are building can be converted into an integraph. Its action would be analogous to numerical integration and not like that of the Bush Integraph which is, of course, an analogue machine, but it would be very rapid, and the steps in the numerical integration could be made arbitrarily small. It should therefore equal the Bush machine in speed and excel in its accuracy.

Progress on the construction of this machine is excellent in spite of the amount of time that defense work is taking, and I am still in a high state of enthusiasm about its ultimate success. I hope to see you within two or three weeks.

> Very sincerely yours,
> J. V. ATANASOFF
> Associate Professor, Math. and Physics

Atanasoff still had not received any word on the patent applications when he received a letter dated 7 June from Mauchly stating that he would start the drive from eastern Pennsylvania to Iowa after a faculty meeting at Ursinus College scheduled for 10 June. Mauchly reported that two neighbors were accompanying him part of the way to share the costs, and that he planned a brief stop at a conference at the State University of Iowa, at Iowa City, before coming to Ames.

Atanasoff had hoped the patent applications would be on file before Mauchly's visit, but he had told Mauchly he would show him the machine and answer his questions and felt obliged to try to live up to that promise to a colleague. The warnings of caution by Iowa State's lawyers were laid aside because Atanasoff believed that Mauchly, an academic colleague, was a man who would have genuine understanding and admiration for what he and Cliff Berry had achieved. In short, he believed Mauchly to be an honorable man who would not take advantage of the confidence placed in him by a friendly colleague.

CHAPTER 6

A Visitor from Pennsylvania: Dr. John W. Mauchly, 1940–1941

IT was dusk in the evening of 13 June 1941 when John William Mauchly and his six-year-old son, Jimmy, arrived at the Atanasoff home at 3439 Woodland Avenue, Ames, Iowa. It was a day earlier than John V. Atanasoff and his wife, Lura, had anticipated, but JV was delighted that Mauchly had arrived to observe the computing machine he was constructing in the basement of the Physics Building at Iowa State College. Atanasoff believed that Mauchly really appreciated the potential of his computing machine that had become the major focal point of his life.

While he had not really been expecting Mauchly until the next day, it was with warmth and enthusiasm that Atanasoff walked to the Mauchly car and shook his visitor's hand even before the Pennsylvanian had time to get out of the car. Caught unprepared, Lura Atanasoff hurried off to the attic to get extra sheets and pillows for the spare room. Lura took an almost instant dislike of and distrust for her husband's Pennsylvania colleague because she felt it was inconsiderate to arrive after the supper hour expecting her to feed him and his son. Also, Mauchly's explanation for bringing his son was less than satisfactory from her viewpoint. "I thought my wife needed a vacation," was his apology to Lura who had the care of her own three small children. Mauchly's request for her to "baby sit with my little boy" emphasized his lack of consideration for her, Lura felt. The initial bad impression that Lura had of Mauchly was augmented by his total lack of interest in any of the children. He almost immediately engaged Atanasoff in what seemed to her a constantly prying conversation about the details of the computer project. Lura had only a general knowledge of the computer project, but she had a wife's personal interest in protecting her husband's brainchild from those who might be inclined to steal the ideas he had worked so hard to develop.

On the weekend Lura and all four children accompanied Atanasoff and Mauchly to the basement of the Physics Building for Mauchly's first examination of the Atanasoff Berry Computer. She did not hear or understand much of the conversation that took place on that occasion because the job of keeping control of four children, who were running up and down the deserted and cavernous Physics Building, kept her constant attention.

While not aware of the technical details of the conversations between her husband and Mauchly, Lura was deeply concerned that her husband was "talking too much" and might be giving away the secrets of his invention because of his enthusiastic desire to have his work appreciated. On several occasions during the four days that Mauchly was a guest in their home, she managed to pull her husband aside to caution him.

To Lura, JV had a vulnerability born of his almost boyish enthusiasm over his computer. "I think you should be careful," Lura said. Her husband said she was too suspicious of John Mauchly and responded to her criticism: "Oh, this is a fine, honorable man, you don't have to worry about him." Although Lura felt momentarily that she was too suspicious in her assessment of Mauchly and "was ashamed" at her own resentment of his "prying," she retained a distrust of this man who monopolized all of her husband's waking hours with incessant questions. Mauchly never seemed to her to be giving any information but was always taking and pressing for more, as she viewed it.

During the four days that Mauchly and his son were guests in the Atanasoff home, Lura served breakfast after which the men were off to college with briefcases in hand, talking computers. When they returned for lunch it was computer talk to the exclusion of all else, and when they returned home for the evening meal it was the same pattern. At least one or two nights of the Mauchly visit, Atanasoff and Mauchly went back to the college for an evening session, and on the other evenings the two were in Atanasoff's den talking about the computer that Atanasoff and Clifford Berry had built and were revamping.

Lura's efforts to get Atanasoff to be more cautious were unsuccessful. Atanasoff's responses were a combination of "Dr.

Mauchly is an honorable man" and repetition of the belief that Mauchly did not have sufficient understanding of electronics to construct a machine that would work. While Lura Atanasoff was alternately feeling ashamed of her suspicions of Mauchly and fretting over her husband's lack of caution, Atanasoff was enjoying himself thoroughly in explaining his brainchild to a man he believed to be an interested and trustworthy colleague. The enthusiastic interest that Mauchly showed in his computer from their first meeting in Philadelphia in December 1940 was in sharp contrast to the lack of interest that most of his Iowa State colleagues showed for his computer. Even a few of his colleagues in the Mathematics and Physics Departments had made what he considered to be bad jokes about the computer project.

Even though JV did not believe that Mauchly had sufficient background in electrical engineering and electronics, the Pennsylvania man was enthusiastic about the future that there could be for a computing machine embodying the concepts of the Atanasoff Berry. Atanasoff spent the better part of four days and five nights explaining the computer machine and answering Mauchly's questions, but he did have other duties to attend to relating to a government defense project and the supervision of graduate students.

During the time he was involved in these duties, Atanasoff turned Mauchly over to Clifford Berry. Atanasoff's instructions to Berry were to show Mauchly all parts of the computing machine, to demonstrate the operations, and to explain the philosophy of the project.

In the four-day visit at Iowa State College, there was only one request that Mauchly made that was refused. Mauchly had taken the copy of the green-covered folder on the construction and operation of the Atanasoff Berry Computer from its accustomed place on the machine and had read at least some parts of it. When he asked Atanasoff if he could have a copy of the 35-page paper to take back to Ursinus College in Pennsylvania, Atanasoff finally said "No." But to avoid hurting Mauchly's feelings, JV gently explained the sensitivity of his computer ideas prior to formal application for patents by Iowa State. However, Mauchly did keep the Atanasoff folder in his possession, carried it to his room, and even asked for paper so he could take some notes from it.

Even as Atanasoff and Lura arose early on Wednesday, 18 June 1941, to see Mauchly and his son off for their return to Ursinus College in Collegeville, Pennsylvania, Atanasoff was still feeling good about the visit of the man he considered to be both a friendly colleague and a genuine admirer of his brainchild. They parted with a warm handshake and promised to keep each other posted on developments in the computer field and to write often.

Lura Atanasoff remained skeptical about that man she later called "Old Mauchly," and she was pleased to have the visit come to an end. It had been unpleasant for her and for the children, who had endured and coped with the aggressiveness of the Mauchly child, who was two years older than young Johnny Atanasoff. All the children – Elsie, Joanne, and John – made the concession without complaint, because Mauchly was "Daddy's guest."

Letters that Dr. Atanasoff received from Mauchly in late June and in September seemed to confirm Atanasoff's belief that Mauchly was an interested and enthusiastic admirer and had no intent or desire to steal the ideas from his computer. In a letter dated 22 June 1941 Mauchly wrote Atanasoff as follows:

Dear J.V.,

The trip back here was uneventful, except for the fact that I was carrying on a mental debate with myself on the question of whether to teach at Hazleton, or to learn something of U. of Pa. My natural avarice for knowledge vied with that for money, and won out, so after obtaining assurance from Marsh White at State College that they would find some one else to take the Hazleton work, I dropped that and prepared to become a student again.

I drove to Southbridge, Mass., Friday evening, and looked through the American Optical plant on Saturday morning. They seemed quite serious in their intentions toward me, but no decision is to be made for several weeks.

On the way back east a lot of ideas came barging into my consciousness, but I haven't had time to sift them or organize them. They were on the subject of computing devices, of course. If any look promising, you may hear more later.

I do hope that your amplifier problem has been licked by some adequate design. The tubes that I ordered two weeks ago aren't here yet, so I couldn't try anything here even if I had time.

I forgot to ask what happens to Cliff Berry after he gets a master's degree – does he stay on for Ph.D. work?

Please give the enclosed note to your wife. We enjoyed our trip very much, and hope you can stop here some time.

                                                              Sincerely,
                                                              J. W. MAUCHLY

On 30 September 1941 Mauchly wrote Atanasoff as follows:

Dear J.V.,

This is to let you know that I still have the same living quarters, but a different job. During the summer I looked around a bit while sounding out the Ursinus people as to promotions and assistance; I finally gave up the idea of taking an industrial job (or a navy job) and stayed in the ranks of teaching.

The Moore School of Electrical Engineering (Univ. of Pa.) is what I have joined up with, and they have me teaching circuit theory and measurements and machinery—but only 11 hours a week of the 33 that Ursinus had developed into.

As time goes on, I expect to get a first-hand knowledge of the operation of the differential analyzer—I have already spent a bit of time watching the process of setting up and operating the thing—and with more such background I hope I can outdo the analyzer electronically.

A number of different ideas have come to me recently anent computing circuits—some of which are more or less hybrids, combining your methods with other things, and some of which are nothing like your machine. The question in my mind is this: Is there any objection, from your point of view, to my building some sort of computer which incorporates some of the features of your machine? For the time being, of course, I shall be lucky to find time and material to do more than merely make exploratory tests of some of my different ideas, with the hope of getting something very speedy, not too costly, etc.

Ultimately a second question might come up, of course and that is, in the event that your present design were to hold the field against all challengers, and I got the Moore School interested in having something of the sort, would the way be open for us to build an "Atanasoff Calculator" (a la Bush analyzer) here?

I am occupying the office of Travis, the man who designed the analyzer here (duplicated at Aberdeen); I think I told you that he is now in the Navy, so I have no opportunity of benefiting by his rich experience.

I hope your defense efforts have been successful, but not so time-consuming as to stop progress on the computer. When you are East, arrange to see us. Perhaps you would like to look over the diff. analyzer, etc.

Convey my best regards to your family and Cliff Berry and all the gang.

Sincerely, yours

JOHN W. MAUCHLY

When Atanasoff received that letter, it seemed to him to be further evidence that Mauchly was merely an eager and enthusiastic supporter and admirer who shared his own vision of the importance of an electronic computer and who was anxious to help in any way to give him full credit for any of the ideas derived from the Atanasoff Berry machine. However, while Atanasoff was pleased with Mauchly's enthusiasm, he had no interest in seeking help outside of Iowa State College or of sharing the credit with anyone except Clifford Berry, whose talents and mechanical genius had been vital to the development and testing of the electronic computer they had constructed and were perfecting together. Atanasoff and Cliff Berry had a tested electronic computer that would solve problems, and he saw no benefit to joining with Mauchly who was, at best, a beginner in the field of electronics.

In his reply to Mauchly, JV informed him of the sensitivity of the information that Mauchly had been given access to during his June visit to Iowa State College. On the whole Atanasoff's letter was a polite attempt to steer the enthusiastic Mauchly away from any unauthorized use or disclosures of the information he had been given.

Actually, Atanasoff went out of his way to assure John Mauchly that he still had "no qualms about having informed you about our device." That 7 October 1941 letter of reassurance from Atanasoff to Mauchly read as follows:

Dear Mauchly:

I am delighted to hear that you are teaching in the Department of Electrical Engineering at the University of Pennsylvania, and I will be sure to get in touch with you the next time I come east which should be in the very near future. At that time we can discuss our mutual interest in calculators.

Our attorney has emphasized the need of being careful about the dissemination of information about our device until a patent application is filed. This should not require too long, and of course, I have no qualms about having informed you about our device, but it does require that we refrain from making public any details for the time being. It is, as a matter of fact, preventing me from making an invited address to the American Statistical Association.

We greatly enjoyed your visit last spring and hope that it can be repeated in the not too distant future.

Very sincerely yours,
JOHN V. ATANASOFF

That polite and perhaps overly diplomatic warning on the sensitivity of the information that had been given to Mauchly at Iowa State College was the last written communication between the two men, although it did not end their generally cordial relationship. Atanasoff was a trusting man, and it is possible that John Mauchly at that time did not intend to engage in computer piracy and the later deceit in which he denied learning anything of value from the 1941 trip to Iowa State College and described the Atanasoff Berry Computer as "a pile of junk that wouldn't do anything."

Following the Mauchly visit in June 1941, JV and Cliff Berry continued to work on improving their computer even as Atanasoff pressed the Iowa State patent committee to move more aggressively to make application for patents on that Atanasoff Berry machine.

When the Japanese bombs fell on Pearl Harbor on 7 December 1941, it put an effective end to the work on the computer in the basement of the Physics Building. It became increasingly more difficult to obtain parts, and there was pressure on Atanasoff to complete his government project for the navy.

In May, Cliff Berry received his Master's degree in electrical engineering, married Atanasoff's secretary, Jean Reed, and left for a defense-related job with a California firm. He had helped Atanasoff prepare the papers for application for patents on the computer; Atanasoff would take care of the job of pushing the Iowa State administrators and patent lawyers to complete the filing.

After completing all of the paperwork for the patent applications, in September Atanasoff left Ames and Iowa State on leave for a defense-related position at the Naval Ordnance Laboratory in Washington, D.C. As far as he knew, he had done everything required for the formal filing of patent applications. Although Atanasoff made periodic inquiries as to the status of the patent matter, the faculty and administration at Iowa State were either off to war or involved in war-related work. It was impossible to get anything but vague answers as to the status of the patent matter.

CHAPTER 7

The War Years: Washington and a Wily Use of National Security, 1942-1945

JOHN VINCENT ATANASOFF boarded the Chicago North Western passenger train at Ames in mid-September 1942 for the trip to Washington, D.C., and a scientific job in the Naval Ordnance Laboratory. He was satisfied with his past achievements, and he was confident that Iowa State College officials would take care of the routine work related to the patent application for his computer with the Chicago patent lawyer, Richard R. Trexler.

At this point JV figured that he and Cliff Berry had done all they could by providing the drawings and explanations of the computing machine they had constructed in the basement of the Physics Building, and he had full confidence in Sam Legvold, a brilliant graduate student, who had some familiarity with the computer and had promised to keep an eye on it until he returned. While Atanasoff was looking forward with some excitement to his job in wartime Washington at the Naval Ordnance Laboratory, he was hoping to return to the faculty of Iowa State College within a short time.

As he settled in his seat for the first leg of the long trip to Washington, he was satisfied that he had finally been able to get around the Iowa State College bureaucracy to get his salary boosted above the $2,305-year-level where it had been stuck during the Depression years and until 1940. The big boosts he had received in 1940, 1941, and 1942 had brought his college salary up to $5,800 a year, which was among the highest salaries at Iowa State in that period.

Because he was an associate professor in both the Mathematics and Physics Departments, he had not been considered a member of either department and was overlooked for a time after the Depression salary lids were lifted. His appeal for a higher salary, taken over the heads of the departments, had been highly successful, and it set the stage for him to request and receive a Navy salary that was correspondingly higher than his college salary.

Atanasoff expected to spend several months, or at most a few years, in government and then to return to Iowa State where, if all went smoothly, he would probably become a department head. He was afraid to let himself imagine the bright future that might be ahead if he was granted patent rights on the computer. While he felt he had done everything necessary for the patent application to be granted, JV did not like to make that assumption before the papers were in his hands.

When he arrived in Washington, the capitol city was in turmoil with the activity that characterized the war years. He had been to Washington before; one of those times was when he and Cliff Berry had done the research at the patent office in December 1940. At that time there had been none of the headlong, frantic pace that greeted him now when he stepped off the train at Washington's Union Station and walked out to the street across the plaza from the Senate Office Building.

At the Naval Ordnance Laboratory (NOL), located in the U.S. Naval Gun Factory on the Anacostia River, Atanasoff was initially just another member of the scientific staff of researchers carrying out duties related to depth charges, mines, and various other assigned projects. However, within a few months he was made chief of the Acoustics Division operation in Building 184.

Although acoustics had never been one of his particular fields of interest, he read the major books on the subject in preparation for supervising the acoustical testing of mines and set about acquiring a technical staff that eventually included David Beecher, an Iowa State graduate who had done some work on the computer; Sam Legvold, another Iowa State graduate who as a student had worked on a defense-related project under Atanasoff's supervision; and Dr. Herman Ellingson, who had been on the faculty at Luther College, Decorah, Iowa.

In early 1943, while Atanasoff was seated at his desk in a dirty and noisy work space in Building 184, he looked up and saw John W.

Mauchly standing in front of him. The visit was unannounced, and JV exhibited surprise in rising to shake Mauchly's hand. He had not had contact with Mauchly since the fall of 1941, but Atanasoff remembered their last meeting as congenial.

Although Atanasoff's last letter to Mauchly had included a caution that he consider the information about the operation of the Atanasoff Berry Computer confidential, Atanasoff had worded that caution in terms that should not have offended his colleague from Pennsylvania.

The fact that John Mauchly had looked him up at the office in the U.S. Naval Gun Factory was evidence he had not been offended by Atanasoff's warning. Atanasoff did not find it at all strange or suspicious that, after the greeting, Mauchly turned the conversation to their mutual interest in computers, and specifically to the theories of the Atanasoff Berry Computer.

It was a brief and friendly meeting, but after Mauchly left the U.S. Naval Gun Factory, Atanasoff raised a question in his own mind, and later with others, as to how Mauchly had been able to gain access to this high security area and what business he had there. JV was never able to get an answer to this question of Mauchly's access other than a vague explanation that Mauchly had grown up in Washington, D.C., where his father had a high scientific post and a wide range of high political connections.

Mauchly's visit in early 1943 was but the first of many visits he made to the Naval Ordnance Laboratory in the next few years, and his conversations with Atanasoff followed the same pattern of casual talk and then questions about Atanasoff's computer theories.

In those numerous conversations throughout 1943 Mauchly carefully avoided any mention that he had drawn plans for an electronic digital computer in 1942, ten months after Mauchly's visit to Iowa State and only seven months after Atanasoff's caution to regard that information as confidential. Nor did Mauchly reveal to Atanasoff during those meetings in 1943 that he and electronic expert J. Presper Eckert, Jr., were, even at that time, starting to build a large computer for the army at the Moore School of Electrical Engineering at the University of Pennsylvania.

"Dr. Mauchly would drop by, and engage in casual conversation for a time and then turn the conversation to questions on my computer theories," Atanasoff explained recently. "I guess I was a little naive even then. I thought he was just interested in knowing more about the machine that he had seen, and because he just didn't fully comprehend the explanations he had read in my papers."

In one of the earliest meetings in 1943, Mauchly asked Atanasoff if he would recommend him for a part-time position at the Naval Ordnance Laboratory. Atanasoff accommodated him, believing that someone with Mauchly's education and background might make some contribution in the statistical section then headed by Dr. Herman Ellingson, an exceptionally well-qualified statistician and scientist. Atanasoff took some chiding later from Herman Ellingson about his recommendation for John Mauchly whom Ellingson characterized as "one who talked a good game" but in fact was "not worth a damn" as a statistician.

The part-time job at the Naval Ordnance Laboratory gave Mauchly a reason for making periodic visits to Washington. The clearance for the part-time position at the Naval Ordnance now permitted him easy access to Atanasoff for his persistent and continuing questioning about JV's computer theories.

In early 1944 Mauchly surprised Atanasoff with the announcement that he was building a computer for the Army at the Moore School of Electrical Engineering. Mauchly quickly assured Atanasoff that his computer "isn't anything like your machine."

"It is much better than your machine," Mauchly added and explained that he and Presper Eckert and their associates had effectively tested out all of the new theories and that it was only a matter of months before the machine would be completed.

Upon hearing Mauchly was building a machine that was "better than your machine," Atanasoff was initially suspicious that Mauchly had stolen some of his ideas, but he did not want to make any accusation nor did he want to believe that Mauchly had taken advantage of the confidences he had reposed in him. But JV was also a curious scientist who wanted to know how Mauchly had gone about solving the problem that had puzzled him and others for years without using the ideas that he and Cliff Berry had used in constructing the Atanasoff Berry Computer.

Although Atanasoff was buried in a work project at the time Mauchly made the disclosure that he was working on a new computer, he pushed his work back on his desk and turned to Mauchly to give his full attention to conversation with him.

"Sit right down there and tell me all about it," Atanasoff said, motioning to a nearby chair and indicating a deep interest in the technical details of the computer machine that Mauchly was building at the Moore School. Mauchly declined the offer to be seated and he hurriedly rejected the suggestion that he explain how he had developed a computer that was "not like" the Atanasoff Berry Computer he had seen at Iowa State.

"It is a highly classified project, and I can't say any more about it," Mauchly replied to the man who had been totally open in the disclosure of his theories and plans for the Atanasoff Berry Computer and had even allowed him to study the plans. Atanasoff protested briefly to Mauchly's refusal to disclose any details of his new computer to one who had the highest military security clearances possible and who ·had been totally open with him. However, Mauchly insisted that his failure to disclose anything about his computer was only because that policy was required by law. It was an effective stonewalling by Mauchly, who then made a quick exit and never did offer any further explanation of the theories incorporated in his computer.

While Atanasoff harbored some suspicions that perhaps Lura had been right about Mauchly, he consoled himself with the belief that the Chicago patent lawyer was proceeding with the patent applications for his machine, and that if there was any theft of ideas by Mauchly, it would be established later in some forum.

Lura Atanasoff and their three children had remained in the family home at Ames while Atanasoff rented a room and later an apartment in the southeast section of Washington near the U.S. Naval Gun Factory where he had his office. But he made frequent trips, every month or two, back to Ames.

On those trips to Ames he had made it a practice to inquire about any progress that might have been made on the processing of the patent applications. With the frequent staff changes at Iowa State College in those war years, it was impossible to get a satisfactory answer to the simplest question, and he was too weary from the 53-hour-a-week schedule at the Naval Ordnance Laboratory to press the issue. It was just not his style.

Despite the futility of his inquiries, Atanasoff had a preference for optimism and would not permit himself to believe that the computer machine that Mauchly and Eckert were building would make obsolete the ideas that he had conceived and that were built into the Atanasoff Berry machine. On his trips to Ames he would frequently go to the basement of the Physics Building just to put his hands on the contours of the computer machine that was his brainchild and that he and Cliff Berry had labored over so patiently and completed with such high enthusiasm.

While his job at the Naval Ordnance Laboratory kept him too

busy to give more than occasional thought to his computer patent problems, he did have a few moments when he believed that the Mauchly-Eckert computer could have destroyed the possibility for the success of his own machine.

Atanasoff met J. Presper Eckert on only one occasion. On 30 August 1944 Mauchly and Eckert visited him at the Gun Factory. Eckert did not have security clearances for the area, so he and Mauchly were escorted to Atanasoff's desk. Atanasoff explained the reason for their visit later:

> Through some military procedure they had obtained an army and navy agreement that I should help them with quartz transducers, a subject in which I had considerable expertise. I knew that the quartz was to be used in a delay line memory. I agreed to help them, but presumably they filled their needs elsewhere. It did not occur to me until much later that a delay line memory required a regeneration or jogging effect, just as I had previously used in (computer) memory methods.

In 1946 when the Army unveiled ENIAC (Electronic Numerical Integrator and Computer) as the first general electronic computer, the massive high speed calculation machine was hailed as the great advance in computing and John Mauchly and Presper Eckert were lauded as the co-inventors of this revolutionary new computing machine.

When Atanasoff was invited to view the ENIAC machine with some of his colleagues from NOL, neither Mauchly nor Eckert were present for the exhibition. Those invited to view the revolutionary computing machine were given only general explanations about all the magnificent things that ENIAC could do, with a few demonstrations, but there were no detailed descriptions as to the theories of how it did its computing. There was no opportunity to open it up and examine just how it functioned technically. National security classifications covered the details of the ENIAC construction and technical operation and would for years continue to block Atanasoff and others from determining the genesis for the concepts that made the giant computing machine function.

It was a depressing time for Atanasoff who had learned that somehow the application for patents on the Atanasoff Berry Computer machine had not been filed by Trexler, the Chicago patent attorney. Trexler said he believed that Iowa State officials had indicated a lack of interest in pursuing the matter. Iowa State College officials had lost track of the patent matter in the shifting of responsibilities and the turmoil of the World War II years. Atanasoff found it impossible to make a determination of the responsibility for the computer application disaster. While Atanasoff and Cliff Berry were not giving up an interest in pursuing the patents, Atanasoff recognized that ENIAC had grabbed the spotlight and that Mauchly and Eckert were receiving the acclaim and taking the bows that he and Clifford Berry might have been taking.

In 1946 Atanasoff was invited to return to Iowa State College to head the Physics Department, a post that a few years earlier he would have grabbed at a moment's notice. But there were political currents flowing in the Chemistry and Physics Departments that he did not like, and in addition, his government job with the navy was paying him a sum that was considerably above the $10,000 cap on government salaries at that time.

Atanasoff, as Chief of the Acoustics Division at the Naval Ordnance Laboratory in Washington, was one of those individuals with unique scientific skills and talents who could be paid more than the highest ranking civil servants and more than congressmen and senators. He turned down the offer to head the Department of Physics at Iowa State College and continued his post in the navy with the faint hope that he would be able to pursue his computer ideas and further experimentation on a project for the navy.

For a few months Atanasoff was placed in charge of developing a computer for the U.S. Navy. On the surface it looked like the great opportunity to achieve what he had been seeking for years, but as it turned out it was worse than no opportunity at all. Although JV agreed to take on the computer project for the Bureau of Ordnance only if he would be relieved of his other responsibilities with the Acoustics Division, the unwritten agreement was not kept.

At this same time he became involved in another project that was time consuming and exciting—the first atomic test after World War II at Bikini Atoll in the Pacific. This was fascinating to him because he believed it would play a large part in determining the effect of the sound generated by the atomic blast in the water and in the air.

"Perhaps I should have insisted that I could not do both projects competently at the same time; on the other hand [Lynn H.] Rambaugh [Atanasoff's superior at NOL] did not have anyone else to do either job," Atanasoff said later in explaining why he had not been more forceful in insisting that he be relieved of the Acoustics Division job.

Over a period of months he started accumulating a staff for the Bureau of Ordnance Computer project by robbing his Acoustics

Division staff of David Beecher, David Bobroff, Robert Elbourne, and Ernest Kolsrud. He was also able to obtain the service of Calvin Mooers from another part of NOL as well as the services of Dr. A. E. Brandt, the statistician with whom he had worked years earlier at Iowa State College.

While Atanasoff was in this staff dilemma in 1945, Mauchly came to see him for the first time in several months, and they had some conversations about the Bureau of Ordnance Computer project and the writing of job descriptions for personnel. At the time Atanasoff was fussing over the bureaucratic problem of writing job descriptions for the computer project that would fulfill civil service requirements. He was also involved in making plans for participation in the atomic tests at Bikini in June and July of 1946.

However, a short time after Atanasoff returned from the atomic tests at Bikini, the Bureau of Ordnance made a sudden and unexplained decision to halt the navy's computer development program. It was a sharp disappointment to Atanasoff; despite understaffing and constant interruptions he felt he was finally making some progress. Also, he had just set in motion in the navy "a need to know" request to gain access to the detailed explanations of how the Mauchly-Eckert machine, ENIAC, was operated and was constructed, which at that time was highly classified information.

Cancellation of the navy computer project ended the possibility of Atanasoff being alerted in 1946 that Mauchly had used many ideas similar to the Atanasoff Berry Computer concepts in ENIAC. It was to be years before he was to examine some of the ENIAC patents and to learn that they were almost identical with the concepts in the computer he and Berry had constructed at Iowa State.

In typical bureaucratic fashion, the navy gave no explanation for its decision to terminate Atanasoff's computer research just as it was getting well started. Thus ended Atanasoff's last chance for producing a computer for the navy and of finding out for years how many of his own ideas were a part of the Mauchly-Eckert computer.

CHAPTER 8

ENIAC "The First Computer": Frustrations and Cover-up, 1946–1954

THE invention of ENIAC and the patents claimed by Mauchly and Eckert dominated the computer discussions of the post–World War II era. They were disappointing years for John Atanasoff. He still believed the concepts he had developed in the Atanasoff Berry Computer were of considerable significance, and Mauchly's secretive and deceptive conduct made him believe some of his computer ideas might have been incorporated in ENIAC.

As long as the national security classification covered the ENIAC construction and patents, there was no way he could prove his ideas were stolen. He would not let himself destroy the rest of his life with an obsession for getting to the roots of whether Mauchly had stolen some of his computer ideas.

If Atanasoff had known the chronology of all Mauchly's activities in the months following his 1941 trip to Iowa State, he would probably have been less open and cooperative in his conversations with the University of Pennsylvania colleague. Mauchly had written several letters praising the Atanasoff Berry Computer as being able to "solve within a few minutes any system of linear equations involving no more than thirty variables." In one of those letters he had stated that the Atanasoff Berry Computer "can be adapted to do the job of the Bush differential analyzer more rapidly than the Bush machine does, and it costs a lot less."

In those same letters Mauchly related that his own computing device used a different principle than the electronic device he had seen at Iowa State College. He had written to a friend that he had become a student in an Emergency Defense Training Course at the University of Pennsylvania and was working in electrical engineering and electronics in the hope "it will be helpful in connection with electronic computing devices."

The letters were written after his trip to Iowa State and prior to Atanasoff's letter of 7 October 1941 rejecting the idea of a joint computer project with Mauchly and cautioning the Pennsylvania mathematician to treat the information about the Atanasoff Berry Computer in the greatest of confidence until the patent applications could be filed.

Mauchly did not respond to that Atanasoff letter but within a few months had written a short memorandum describing what he referred to as his idea of an "electronic device operating solely on the principle of counting" and outlining what he believed its great advantages would be over the mechanical operations of a differential analyzer in solving differential equations. Mauchly had consulted with J. Presper Eckert, a particularly apt student at electronics, before putting his first memorandum together in August 1942. Eckert had earned a bachelor's degree at the Moore School in 1941 and was engaged in work on his master's degree. Although this memorandum was intended to be used to stimulate interest and support from the government in building such a computer, it was not given immediate support by John Gist Brainerd, then director of war research at the Moore School. In fact it was misplaced for several weeks by either Mauchly or Brainerd.

In September 1942 Dr. Herman H. Goldstine, then an Army first lieutenant at the Aberdeen Ballistic Research Laboratory, was assigned to the Moore School research program. In the following weeks Lieutenant Goldstine learned of Mauchly's idea of using an electronic digital computer for rapid calculation of trajectory firing tables. He arranged to bring Mauchly and Eckert together with Brainerd for formal preparation of a proposal that was to be submitted to the Ballistic Research Laboratory at Aberdeen.

By the following April 1943 Mauchly and Eckert and Brainerd had written a proposal for an electronic digital computer. In the proposal they made reference to computers in a wide range of terms such as "electronic analyzer," "a difference analyzer," and "electronic differential analyzer."

The proposal's final draft of 8 April 1943 was entitled "Report on an Electronic Diff. Analyzer, submitted to the Ballistic Research Laboratory, Aberdeen Proving Grounds by the Moore School of Electrical Engineering, University of Pennsylvania." It was this proposal that resulted in the construction of the Electronic Numerical Integrator and Computer known as ENIAC. The proposal was presented to Aberdeen on 9 April and was approved a few days later and work was started on 31 May 1943.

It was during the preparation for the writing of this April 1943 proposal that Mauchly started calling on Atanasoff in a pattern of periodic visits, questioning him without giving any hint he was building an electronic digital computer until sometime in 1944. Even then, Mauchly used "national security classification" as his reason for refusing to tell Atanasoff anything about the nature of the computer being constructed at the Moore School. Atanasoff was barred from access to this information by Mauchly's refusal to discuss ENIAC and the national security classification that covered the planning, construction, and operational procedure of ENIAC.

Thoroughly frustrated in his efforts to find out the secrets of the ENIAC plans, Atanasoff was further depressed to learn that Iowa State College officials and Richard Trexler, the Chicago patent attorney, had not yet filed the application for patents on the Atanasoff Berry Computer.

Atanasoff buried himself in the work of the Acoustic Division of the Research Department of the Naval Ordnance Laboratory where there was much exciting and useful work to be done. In the spring of 1947 he was contacted by a naval officer from the staff of the Chief of Naval Operations with the proposal that he consider as a project monitoring some large explosive detonations the British planned a few weeks later on Helgoland Island.

The island of Helgoland, off the north coast of Germany, had been used by the Germans in World War II as a depository for conventional ammunition of every kind. Much of it was regarded as too old and too unstable to use. The British who were in charge of the island planned to blow it up in a single blast.

The Office of the Chief of Naval Operations suggested that this detonation might be used to monitor the explosive waves through the earth in hopes that the findings might be useful in laying the foundation for long-range detection of atomic explosions. The British exercise was to take place in only eight weeks, Atanasoff was told, and he soon learned that a number of organizations that could normally have been expected to do such monitoring had rejected the project because the relatively short time for preparation provided little or no chance of the project being successful.

Atanasoff quoted a good friend of his, Merle Tuve, of the Carnegie Institution's Department of Terrestrial Magnetism, as warning him: "You shouldn't agree to do it. No one else would take on the job when the time to prepare was longer. You will lose your reputation."

Despite such warnings, Atanasoff surveyed the situation carefully and notified the Chief of Naval Operations that he would take on the job "if you get me the highest priority in the Navy." He was given that priority and went to work in building the seismographs and other electronic gadgets needed to do the monitoring from twenty-four locations. Working overtime, JV and his staff had the equipment constructed on time and in place and the staff of monitors trained in time for the massive explosion. He was delighted with the success of the project as twenty-three of the twenty-four monitoring stations brought back seismic and microbarographic data. The data came from Penemunde in North Germany to Gorizia in North Italy, a distance of over 1000 kilometers. An accident involving an Army jeep prevented one of Atanasoff's operators from getting to his data site.

That successful monitoring operation laid the foundation for long-range detection of explosions, and the chief of the Bureau of Ordnance gave Atanasoff a citation for his work. Still another citation was awarded Atanasoff by the Seismological Society of America. Shortly thereafter, Dr. Atanasoff's division was given the responsibility for projects dealing with the detection of atomic explosions.

It was an exhilarating experience that he needed to sustain him through several disappointing experiences in this period. In 1948 Atanasoff returned to Iowa State College for a visit, and was surprised, shocked, and saddened to find that the Atanasoff Berry Computer had been removed from the basement of the Physics Building and demolished. The action had been taken by a graduate student at the suggestion of Dr. G. W. Fox, who was named to head the Physics Department after Atanasoff had declined the position.

Neither Atanasoff nor Clifford E. Berry, then a department head with Consolidated Engineering Corporation in Pasadena, California, had been given notice that the Atanasoff Berry Computer was to be removed, dismembered, and destroyed. To JV the arbitrary action to destroy his brainchild was inexcusable from a standpoint of common decency. Only a few parts of that historic Atanasoff Berry Computer were saved by Dr. Sam Legvold and other close friends of Atanasoff, and the inventor was unable at that time to get any explanation of what had happened to his brainchild or to even find out who had disassembled it or authorized the destruction. All professed ignorance of the thoughtless or cruel act, and Atanasoff was too saddened and hurt to press the issue even among his friends who were deeply embarrassed at what they considered a tragedy. More than twenty-five years later, Dr. Robert M. Stewart, then head of the Department of Computer Science at Iowa State University, revealed that in 1948, when he was a graduate student at Iowa State University, he dismantled the computer on instruction from G. W. Fox, then head of the Physics Department. Writing in *Annals of the History of Computing* for July 1984, he explained that he had no idea what the unusual equipment was he dismantled at the direction of Professor Fox to make room for an office and laboratory in the basement of the Physics Building.

"I asked Fox what should be done with it, and he said, 'Dismantle it.' He said that it was John V. Atanasoff's calculator and would never be used again—that Atanasoff was not going to return to the department, and we needed the space."

While Atanasoff had more than his share of success at forty-five, 1948 was a year of many disappointments in addition to the dismantling of the Atanasoff Berry Computer at Iowa State. There were problems and turmoil in his personal family life that had been building up for some time. John Atanasoff and Lura had drifted apart during the time he was in Washington and Lura was continuing to live in their family home in Ames with the three children. In the first years Atanasoff tried to get back to Ames every month or so, but in later years the visits had been more irregular and tensions between them had mounted. During this period Lura had made the decision to move to Florida for Elsie's health and later had moved to Denver, Colorado, again on the theory that it was a better climate for Elsie's continuing asthmatic problems. In 1949 they were divorced and shortly thereafter John Atanasoff married Alice Crosby, a girl from Webster City, Iowa, who had gone to Washington to work in the war years.

At about the same time as the divorce and the remarriage, Atanasoff changed jobs. He became chief scientist for the Army Field Forces in Fort Monroe, Virginia. He stayed in that position for only about a year before returning to Washington as director of the Navy Fuse Program at the Naval Ordnance Laboratory in late 1950 and throughout 1951.

In 1952 Atanasoff decided to strike out into the field of private

Atanasoff and Murphy's Laplaciometer, an instrument for nondigital calculation. [*Below*] Prototype of the Atanasoff Berry Computer.

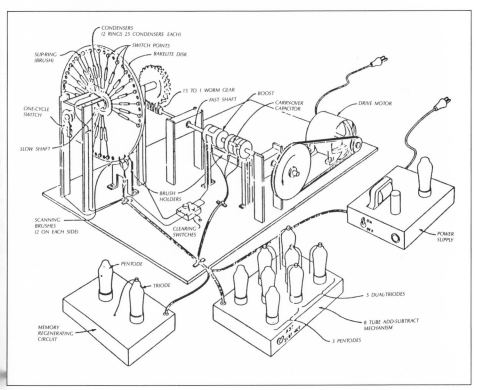

CONDENSERS
(2 RINGS 25 CONDENSERS EACH)

SWITCH POINTS

SLIP-RING
(BRUSH)

BAKELITE DISK

15 TO 1 WORM GEAR

FAST SHAFT

BOOST

CARRY-OVER
CAPACITOR

DRIVE MOTOR

ONE-CYCLE
SWITCH

SLOW SHAFT

BRUSH
HOLDERS

SCANNING
BRUSHES
(2 ON EACH SIDE)

CLEARING
SWITCHES

POWER
SUPPLY

PENTODE

TRIODE

5 DUAL-TRIODES

8 TUBE ADD-SUBTRACT
MECHANISM

MEMORY
REGENERATING
CIRCUIT

3 PENTODES

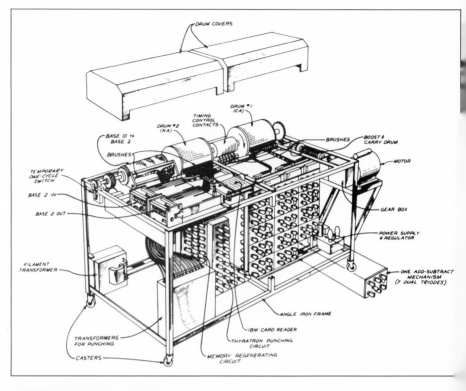

DRUM COVERS

DRUM #1
(CA)

TIMING
CONTROL
CONTACTS

DRUM #2
(KA)

BASE 10 TO
BASE 2

BRUSHES

BRUSHES

BOOST &
CARRY DRUM

MOTOR

TEMPORARY
ONE-CYCLE
SWITCH

BASE 2 IN

BASE 2 OUT

GEAR BOX

FILAMENT
TRANSFORMER

POWER SUPPLY
& REGULATOR

ONE ADD-SUBTRACT
MECHANISM
(7 DUAL TRIODES)

ANGLE IRON FRAME

IBM CARD READER

TRANSFORMERS
FOR PUNCHING

THYRATRON PUNCHING
CIRCUIT

CASTERS

MEMORY REGENERATING
CIRCUIT

[*Above*] Drawing of the Atanasoff Berry Computer, 1941. [*Left*] The Physics Building, Iowa State College, where the ABC was built and stored. [*Opposite*] Clifford Berry holding vacuum tubes that were part of the ABC's memory bank, 1941.

A side view of the Atanasoff Berry Computer, 1942.

An end view of one of
the ABC's memory
drums.

All that remains at
Iowa State University
of the Atanasoff Berry
Computer.

John V. Atanasoff and the rebuilt breadboard of the Atanasoff Berry Computer at the Digital Computer Museum in 1980.

enterprise, leaving his government job to establish The Ordnance Engineering Corporation, initially with offices in Rockville, Maryland, and later in Frederick, Maryland. Atanasoff was president of the corporation, and he took with him from the Naval Ordnance Laboratory his old friend and former student, David Beecher, and others. They funded the corporation with the money they could pull together. It was a sufficient amount to do contract research and development work for various government agencies without ever borrowing any money.

He buried himself in the work of making The Ordnance Engineering Corporation a success and had not given serious thought to the Atanasoff Berry Computer for several years. He knew that Mauchly and Eckert had filed for patent rights and had entered into some agreement to sell those patent rights to what was then the Remington Rand Corporation. He also had learned that the Moore School of Electrical Engineering had gone forward with the next step of the computer – a machine known as EDVAC (Electronic Discrete Variable Computer).

EDVAC, employing many of the electronic digital computer concepts of ENIAC, was recognized as moving far beyond the technology of ENIAC, particularly in the utilization of mercury delay storage lines in the computer memory. It also made use of the stored program concept that was not a part of ENIAC.

That was the situation in the spring of 1954 when Atanasoff received the first allegation, from a source he considered reliable, that Mauchly might have used some of the Atanasoff Berry Computer theories in planning and designing ENIAC. He received this information from a lawyer for IBM who said that with Atanasoff's help he believed that the Mauchly-Eckert patent claims for ENIAC could be broken. It was a disillusioning experience for JV, who after agreeing to help the IBM lawyer, learned months later that IBM had entered into a patent-sharing agreement with Sperry Rand and was no longer interested in breaking the Mauchly-Eckert patent claims.

CHAPTER 9

First Allegation of Piracy— Then a Long Silence, 1954-1961

D URING 1953 and 1954 Atanasoff spent little or no time brooding about the lost chance on the Atanasoff Berry Computer and the combination of unfortunate circumstances that had resulted in the failure to file patent applications. He and his friend and colleague, Dave Beecher, were at work in the Rockville, Maryland, offices of their new business, The Ordnance Engineering Corporation (TOEC).

However, unknown at the time to Atanasoff, others were interested. The executives of some of the biggest business machine firms in the country were showing a lively interest in the precise nature of some of the ideas that had gone into the Atanasoff Berry Computer in the 1939-1942 period. Among the firms showing a quiet but intensive interest was the giant International Business Machines (IBM) firm. The IBM Patent Office manager had run across information that a Dr. Clifford Edward Berry, the head of a research division for Consolidated Engineering Corporation (CEC) had worked on a project at Iowa State College in about 1940 that involved "a capacitor drum (memory) storage device incorporating the revolver principle for storing information."

The IBM Patent Department manager, A. Robert Noll, wrote a memorandum for the IBM file in which he identified the source of his information as a James B. Christie, secretary and patent counsel for Consolidated Engineering Corporation and a working associate of Dr. Berry. Noll stated in the 30 September 1953 memorandum that he and two other IBM patent executives, H. R. Keith and John

Shipman, met with Christie to discuss magnetic drum patents, with particular reference to the magnetic drum patent situation surrounding the digital computer then under consideration by Consolidated Engineering.

In the memorandum Noll reported Christie said that Consolidated Engineering planned to market commercially a digital computer having a magnetic drum storage, and that CEC was not concerned about patent rights on two of the machines they had installed at government agencies. They were concerned about the computers they planned to market commercially because of patents held on magnetic drums by Cohen and Coombs and revolver drum patents held by Eckert and Mauchly.

"Apparently there was no question in Mr. Christie's mind that licenses will have to be obtained under the Cohen and Coombs patents," Noll wrote in his memorandum. "He is planning, according to his statement, to see Mr. [George V.] Eltgroth [a patent attorney who helped Mauchly and Eckert on the patents] of Rem-Rand [Remington-Rand] today in this connection and also the Eckert Mauchly patents."

"A general discussion was held regarding the Eckert Mauchly patents and we pointed out to Mr. Christie that we have been unable to find the necessary prior art to satisfy us in order to limit the scope of this patent," Noll wrote and added: "Mr. Christie ventured information that their [CEC's] Dr. Clifford E. Berry . . . formerly a graduate student, . . . while at the University worked on a capacitor drum storage device incorporating the revolver principle for storing information. He believed this work was done around 1940 at the University."

Noll, in his memorandum, stated that he told Christie: "We explored every avenue (for prior art) we have heard about and that this was news to us and that we definitely would check into this matter."

"Mr. Christie mentioned that he was planning, through Dr. Berry, to do the same thing. We suggested in order not to create too much confusion at the University [Iowa State College] that it might be well for one or the other of us to conduct this investigation. Mr. Christie suggested that since Dr. Berry knew the various people who worked on this project . . . , that Dr. Berry could be helpful in this connection and he would appreciate it if we could have one of the experts join Dr. Berry during the investigation. We indicated that we would be pleased to cooperate in this matter. Mr. Christie will keep us informed of his plans in this connection."

In his file memorandum, the IBM Patent Department manager

added a final paragraph dealing with what was rumored to be an industrywide concern over the Eckert-Mauchly patents: "Mr. Christie also mentioned that he had heard rumors that Burroughs, National Cash and IBM were planning, as part of a team, to form a patent pool, particularly with a view of fighting the Eckert-Mauchly patents, whereupon we informed Mr. Christie that we knew nothing of this matter and certainly IBM was not involved in any such arrangement as rumored."

A few weeks after Noll wrote that memorandum for the IBM file which started research on the Atanasoff Berry Computer, an article written by J. Presper Eckert appeared in the published proceedings (October 1953) of the Institute of Radio Engineers (IRE) stating:

> Probably the first example of what might generally be termed regenerative memory was developed earlier than 1942 by Atanasoff in Iowa. He [Atanasoff] used a drum with many capacitors mounted on it, and with a commutative method of connecting the capacitors with brushes for reading-in, reading-out and regenerating. The principal feature of the capacitor memory was the use of cheap, reusable elements.
>
> The capacitors could be charged, discharged and recharged as often as desired, and they were common and readily available components. The characteristics of small initial expense and almost unlimited reusability have guided the development of memory systems since, and remain two important criteria of the merit of any system at any time. There may have been similar systems prior to Atanasoff's but none was as inexpensive to construct. Unfortunately his development was interrupted by the war and never completed.

Those few sentences by Eckert on pages 1393–1406 of his article "A Survey of Digital Computer Memory Systems" were published in October 1953, but it was not called to Atanasoff's attention for many years. Atanasoff said he did not know where Eckert could have received such detailed information about the regenerative memory of his computer in 1953 except through Mauchly.

Within a few weeks after the publication, it was called to the attention of Joseph C. Sweet, Jr., of the IBM Patent Department, by A. J. Etienne, an IBM patent attorney. On 8 February 1954 Sweet wrote to Etienne stating that he had reviewed the article and found it relevant to the Eckert-Mauchly patent number 2,629,827 involving the use of revolving drums in the regenerative memory of electronic digital computers. Sweet noted that on page 1394 of the Eckert article the author had stated: "Probably the first example of what might generally be termed regenerative memory was developed ear-

lier than 1942 by Atanasoff in Iowa." Sweet called attention to the
"brief description of the system" developed by "Atanasoff in Iowa"
and to the fact that there was no further identification of Atanasoff
in the article "or further mention of this work in the bibliography of
the article."

Officials of IBM's Patent Department were now deeply interested in the details of the history of the Atanasoff Berry Computer as "prior art" in the area of patents held by Eckert and
Mauchly. Arrangements were made for James B. Christie, the outside counsel for Consolidated Engineering Corporation, to move
forward with plans to "interview Dr. Berry in the near future to
uncover any and all additional facts or leads which might be available which would be useful in proving prior art relative to the [Eck-
ert-Mauchly] patent."

Those plans were laid out in a 30 April 1954 memorandum by
John R. Shipman, of the IBM Patent Department, on the subject of
the "Eckert-Mauchly Revolver Patent." That memorandum was
written for the direction of the West Coast office of IBM. In that
memorandum, Shipman called attention to the article by Eckert in
the IRE proceedings published in October 1953. Shipman stated
that Berry was employed by Consolidated Engineering in Pasadena
and that he [Shipman] had the following information: "Present plans
call for him [Berry] to be in Pasadena for the next few months
except for the week of May 24."

Shipman, with the thoroughness and efficiency characteristic of
the IBM Patent Department, included a list of sixteen questions he
wanted answered in the interview Christie was to arrange with Clifford Berry, but added: "However, your interview should not be limited to these questions but should pursue all aspects of the matter
which become apparent in your discussions." The memorandum included a postscript: "For your information, we are arranging to interview Atanasoff and are having searches made through newspapers (the *Des Moines Register,* the *Des Moines Tribune,* and *Ames
Tribune*) for the articles [on the Atanasoff Berry Computer] referred
to by Christie."

On 14 May 1954 John B. Sponsler, of IBM's San Jose, California, office, gave to Shipman the answers to the sixteen questions
and a report on the interview with Berry. The interview with Atanasoff was as yet unfinished business.

In June of 1954 Atanasoff was at work in the office of The
Ordnance Engineering Corporation in Rockville, Maryland, when
he received a telephone call from a lawyer who said he represented

the International Business Machine Corporation. It was Atanasoff's first indication that IBM, or any other giant business equipment corporation, had an interest in the Atanasoff Berry Computer. His last contact with IBM was in 1941 or 1942 when an IBM official had written that IBM had no interest in his computer unless he would sign papers that would give IBM the right to appropriate the ideas of his brainchild and set the price. He had wanted no part of such a one-sided arrangement.

The IBM lawyer who called him in June 1954 gave his name as A. J. Etienne. He said he would like to talk with Atanasoff on an important matter as soon as possible. Etienne came to the office a short time later, identified himself, and said he wished to engage in patent talks. Upon learning that the IBM lawyer wanted to discuss details of his computer development, Atanasoff called for his associate David Beecher, who was his company vice-president, to join in the conference. He wanted a witness. Atanasoff said that Etienne opened the conversation with the statement: "If you will help us, we will break the Mauchly-Eckert computer patent; it was derived from you." (This is corroborated by David Beecher.)

While Etienne says he does not recall making that specific statement, he did acknowledge making the visit to Atanasoff's office on 14 June 1954 and entering into exploratory conversations concerning the cooperation he could expect from Atanasoff if IBM were to attack the Mauchly-Eckert patents.

Initially, Atanasoff hesitated to reply with a specific commitment. His mind flashed back to the time when Mauchly told him that he and Eckert had invented a "new method of computing, different from yours." He had wanted to believe Mauchly even as Mauchly had rejected his request to explain the difference. Although he had harbored a deep suspicion about Mauchly in recent years, he had kept those suspicions to himself. Now, here was Etienne, a patent lawyer for the corporate giant IBM, indicating that IBM had obtained evidence that made officials of the corporation believe they could prove that Mauchly "had derived" some of the patented concepts from the Atanasoff Berry Computer.

This was pretty heady stuff after all the years of hope and frustration, but JV did not want his inner excitement to show. Certainly he wanted to cooperate in any action that might bring some measure of credit to him and to Cliff Berry for the invention of the electronic digital computer. However, he did not want to express those views to the IBM lawyer until he knew more about what Etienne was proposing. Inwardly he was elated over the prospects that there was a chance that he and Cliff Berry might finally receive a bit of the acclaim and perhaps even some of the monetary rewards that would flow from the recognition of their significant contribution to computer history.

In answer to Atanasoff's questions, Etienne said the patent he was referring to was the Memory System patent number 2,629,827 that had been issued in 1953. (The general ENIAC patent, applied for in 1947, was not actually issued until 1964.) Atanasoff had not kept up on the details of the patent applications filed by Mauchly and Eckert, nor those that had been granted. He told the patent lawyer that he had not seen the Memory System patent and would of course have to see it before arriving at any conclusion in his own mind as to whether he could be helpful to IBM or even whether he wanted to be helpful.

Although Atanasoff indicated he was pleased that the IBM attorney's research had demonstrated that the Atanasoff Berry Computer had some merit, he added that he was just starting a small corporation, had little financial reserve, and that he and his friends had their "all" invested in making TOEC a success.

The meeting with Etienne ended in a friendly fashion with Atanasoff saying he would try to help by searching his records to review his contacts with Mauchly but adding that he had to devote most of his time to making the corporation a success. Although he was elated about the evidence indicating that Mauchly's inventions had been derived from the Atanasoff Berry Computer, Atanasoff knew that the outcome would depend upon how serious IBM was in pursuing the genesis of ENIAC's concepts. He hoped that IBM would find it in the interest of the corporation to prove that Mauchly had stolen some of his ideas. Atanasoff mused about the fact that it would take a giant corporation like IBM to finance the litigation to break the Mauchly-Eckert patents, but on the other hand if IBM couldn't break the Mauchly-Eckert patents, then it would probably be impossible to break them.

Although Atanasoff had kept reasonably complete files on his correspondence related to the Atanasoff Berry Computer, he could not remember exactly what that correspondence was or where those particular files were now located since his separation and divorce and the confusion involved in setting up a new corporation.

On 21 June, Etienne wrote Atanasoff enclosing a copy of the Mauchly-Eckert patent number 2,629,827 along with other related patents. The IBM lawyer said he hoped that Atanasoff would turn all of the files on his computer over to him. Atanasoff made a brief and unsuccessful search for the files. He then wrote to Etienne stating he would search further and explaining that the press of work at the corporation made it impossible to do more at that time.

He heard no more from the IBM lawyer and assumed that the IBM officials who had been so enthusiastic about breaking the Mauchly-Eckert patent had concluded that it was not worth pursuing. In the months later, when he thought about Etienne's visit, he became depressed over the possibility of ever breaking the Mauchly-Eckert patents. If a big corporation like IBM couldn't do it, it would probably be impossible. (Unknown to Atanasoff until years later was the fact that IBM had used its information on prior art to negotiate a patent-sharing arrangement with Sperry Rand that benefited both computer giants.)

There was no question that the visit from Etienne had sparked his imagination with the hope that his computer might be generally recognized as having historic significance. His cursory examination of the Memory System patent 2,629,827 confirmed his own suspicion that Mauchly might have derived his ideas from examination of the Atanasoff Berry Computer and from related conversations. But certainly it would be impractical for him to give any serious thought of taking on the task of investigation while he was having a financial struggle just to keep The Ordnance Engineering Corporation moving on a successful course.

Atanasoff did keep his corporation on course with successful research projects for the Department of Defense, the Post Office Department, and other government agencies. In 1956 he sold The Ordnance Engineering Corporation to Aerojet General Corporation and emerged as vice-president and manager of the Atlantic Division of that corporation with offices in Frederick, Maryland.

While Atanasoff was submerged in the work of running the Atlantic Division of Aerojet General, he had little time to concern himself with the things that were past. Certainly his experience with the Atanasoff Berry Computer was not a sweet memory that he wished to dwell upon, and in the years between 1954 and 1959 there were few events to remind him of the sorry experience of his relationship with Mauchly.

In 1957 a representative of Datamatic had contacted him for a brief visit about his early experiences in building the Atanasoff Berry Computer, and in the 1954–1959 year span he learned that Remington Rand had merged with the Sperry Corporation becoming the Sperry Rand Corporation and the holder of the Eckert and

Mauchly patents evolving out of the ENIAC and EDVAC projects. At some point after 1957 he also learned that IBM had entered into a patent-sharing arrangement with Sperry Rand which constituted what many in the industry felt represented a near monopoly on some of the basic computer patents. He wondered about the process through which that had been achieved; the last time he had contact with Etienne, the IBM patent attorney officials of that firm had been in hot pursuit of evidence that they hoped would break the Mauchly-Eckert patents.

What he did not know in 1959 was that officials of IBM and Sperry Rand were now concerned about possible challenges to the patents that had been granted to Mauchly and Eckert and about other patent applications on ENIAC that were still pending. On 19 February 1959 J. B. Forman, an IBM official, sent an intracompany communication to C. A. Norton, of Sperry Rand, asking for a copy of the master's thesis that Clifford Berry had written as Atanasoff's student. The 1941 thesis, written by Berry when he was working on the Atanasoff computer, was entitled "Design of Electrical Data Recording and Reading Mechanisms."

This was only part of a quiet but intensive activity by Sperry Rand related to learning what records were in existence and what other evidence might be available to challenge the Mauchly-Eckert patents that had been issued and the ENIAC patents that were still pending. R. H. Sorensen, assistant to the vice-president, engineering, at Sperry Rand contacted Dr. Howard Aiken of Harvard, Dr. Erling Jensen, head of the Physics Department at Iowa State, and others.

On 14 April 1959 Sorensen wrote to Howard Aiken at Harvard to express appreciation for his willingness to visit the Iowa State campus to do some research on the work done by Atanasoff and his graduate student Clifford Berry in 1941 and 1942. Blind copies of that letter were also sent to Dr. Engstrom, F. J. McNamara, and T. C. Fry.

On the same day, 14 April 1959, Sorensen wrote to Erling Jensen at Iowa State. In this "Dear Dane" letter, Sorensen expressed his thanks to Jensen for his help on the Remington Rand inquiries about the early work of Atanasoff. Sorensen wrote Jensen that "although the visit [to Iowa State] did not prove too productive regarding project records, it was, at least, helpful to find more about the background of this early project." He avoided revealing reference to the possible patent problem potential, the financial reason for Sperry

Rand's interest in the work of Atanasoff and Cliff Berry. He indicated the Sperry Rand curiosity was based upon a general interest in the history of computing.

"The work of Dr. Atanasoff continues to be of interest to us since it constitutes early and creative work on re-circulating memories. For that reason, I have arranged to visit with him [Atanasoff] in Washington on Thursday of this week, and I am hopeful of finding more written evidence of the work he conducted at Iowa State," Sorensen wrote Jensen.

He noted that he had requested, but had not yet received, photographs of the Atanasoff Berry Computer from the Iowa State Photo Service. On 15 April 1959 Sorensen wrote to E. J. Light of Sperry Rand on the subject of the "Iowa State Computer Project" stating that on 13 April he had reported to the Sperry Rand "Patent Advisory Committee relative to my visit at Iowa State on April 7." Sorensen related that the project was known as "Physics Project Number 35" and was sponsored by the Research Corporation that invested $5,000 in its furtherance.

Sorensen listed three people other than Atanasoff and Cliff Berry as having been involved in Project Number 35. Those listed were Robert Mather, Norman Fulmer, and Harry F. Frissel.

On 16 April 1959 Sorensen and Engstrom took Atanasoff to lunch at the Cosmos Club in Washington. Atanasoff recorded the event as one in which he was "entertained and cross-examined by two people from Sperry Rand." Sorensen wrote the following cautious note to Atanasoff on 17 April to thank him for visiting with the Sperry Rand representatives:

It was very helpful to us to get your first-hand recollections of the early work which you had done at Iowa State College on re-circulating memories. I was also interested to find that you had originally proposed sponsorship of this work by our company prior to undertaking it on behalf of the Research Corporation. If you have copies of any of the correspondence which you had with us at that time, I would be appreciative of any of its details, or at least an indication of whom you contacted at that time.

This carefully worded letter was written to make certain that Sperry Rand was not financially committed to Atanasoff in any manner for anything that its officials had learned at the Washington lunch. "Our meeting yesterday was particularly helpful in orienting your work in both its technical and time perspective," Sorensen wrote. "It likewise increased our understanding of your thinking regarding analogous magnetic memory devices and their utility in high speed memory systems."

The lunch was held for the purpose of cleverly picking Atanasoff's brains to find out what documents he might have that would be adverse to Sperry Rand interests, and for testing his attitude toward helping litigants who might want to challenge Sperry Rand's interest in the Eckert and Mauchly patents.

Apparently Atanasoff had used the lunch to raise a question as to whether Sperry Rand might be in the market for a computer machine with operating functional characteristics that would be somewhere between a desk calculator and a punch card electronic tabulator.

"I can assure you that your suggestions would be given careful review, if and when you finalize them and are prepared to submit them," Sorensen wrote and routinely enclosed the standard booklet of instructions for those wishing to submit proposals. He had questioned Atanasoff at length as far as it was useful for Sperry Rand's interests and wished to brush him off in a polite and formal manner.

On 30 April 1959 Sorensen wrote a memorandum on the "Visit With Dr. J. Atanasoff" for a Sperry Rand distribution list that included C. A. Norton, T. C. Fry, F. J. McNamara, and Engstrom. In that memorandum he set out more than two pages of information that his cross-examination of Atanasoff purportedly yielded. From a standpoint of "prior art," Sorensen noted, "Dr. Atanasoff claims the 'conception,' as early as 1937 or 1938, of a recirculating digital memory as part of a proposed electronic calculating machine." Sorensen related, "The capacitor-type recirculating memory, which I saw at Iowa State College, was built by Dr. Atanasoff and Dr. Berry."

"Dr. Atanasoff confirmed that he has made no publication of this recirculating memory work in technical journals or other records available to the public," Sorensen stated. "He considered the magnetic drum an obvious extension of his original capacitor-type storage and claims to have discussed this analogous memory with his co-workers, as well as with John Mauchly during his visit to Iowa State campus."

"Dr. Atanasoff did not choose to elaborate on why the development project was abandoned, or why patent applications were not filed, except to say that there were 'administrative difficulties' which caused the project to be abandoned after the first working model was built," Sorensen noted.

Then Sorensen wrote what was probably the most important

point in his memorandum as far as any possible challenge to the patent rights that Sperry Rand held through contracts with Eckert and Mauchly. "For personal reasons, Atanasoff seems anxious not to become embroiled in any legal entanglements on behalf of ourselves or others." He related that Atanasoff said he had been approached earlier for help in contesting the position which Sperry Rand has established in the field of recirculating memories, and that Atanasoff said he had declined to help in that budding challenge to Sperry Rand. The Sperry Rand executive characterized Atanasoff as "cordial to us, but [he] resisted any further discussion which might require the review or copying of his own records."

Atanasoff was now cool and cautious to those making inquiries about the Atanasoff Berry Computer and its genesis. He believed he had rather complete records on the correspondence and reports dealing with the planning and construction of the Atanasoff Berry Computer, but he was busy with, and tiring of, the life of an executive in a big corporation like Aerojet General.

In 1961 he rejected a position with greater responsibilities at Aerojet and resigned to start his own firm, Cybernetics, Incorporated, in Frederick, Maryland. In the next year he started the planning and construction of a new home near New Market, Maryland, just a few miles west of Frederick.

While that large country home was under construction, Atanasoff did not have the time or the inclination to find and sort the records dealing with either the planning and construction of the computer or reports and correspondence, including his correspondence with Mauchly in 1941. Those letters were now more than twenty years old, and Atanasoff had only the most general recollection of what those letters contained or where they were in his vast accumulation of business and research files.

CHAPTER 10

Dr. R. K. Richards Researches a Book, 1962–1966

I N late 1962 and the early months of 1963, Dr. R. K. Richards, an Iowa State graduate in electrical engineering, started in-depth research for a book on the history of the booming field of electronic digital computer systems. Richards, formerly employed by IBM in New York, had written several successful computer books and in 1962 had returned to Ames, Iowa, to concentrate on a writing career. His many books included *Arithmetic Operations in Digital Computers,* published in 1955, and *Digital Computer Components and Circuits,* published in 1957.

Reflecting upon the history of the electronic digital systems, Richards recalled his undergraduate days at Iowa State College and a visit he had made to the Physics Building to see a graduate student about some ham radio problem. The graduate student, an enthusiastic ham radio buff, was Clifford Berry. Richards remembered that he had gone to see Cliff Berry in the basement of the Physics Building, where Berry had been working with a Professor Atanasoff on some kind of computer machine. There had been little or no discussion of the machine, but Richards surmised that Berry thought it was an important development. Richards had a vague recollection that there had been a story in a newspaper about this computer. Now it intrigued him that he might have, quite by accident, seen a computer machine with some significance in computer history.

By strange coincidence, Dick Richards's neighbor in Ames, Harry Burrell, recalled that he had actually written the press release about the computer that had been constructed by Atanasoff and Berry. However, at the Iowa State University Library, Richards drew a blank on any reference to the computing machine he had seen twenty years earlier in the Physics Building. He also drew a blank in his inquiries at the Engineering Publications Office.

A visit to the office of Professor Sam Legvold resulted in the first assurance from an eyewitness that Atanasoff and Berry had constructed a computing machine in the basement of the Physics Building. Sam Legvold had been a friend of Cliff Berry's and had been one of Atanasoff's students during the 1939–1942 period. Legvold had a drum in his office that he said he had salvaged when the original Atanasoff Berry computer was dismantled in the late 1940s.

Sam Legvold told Richards he had seen the machine in operation, and had discussed it with Cliff Berry over a period of months but had no recollection of the circuitry involved in the electronic system's logic circuits and regenerative memory.

Sam Legvold explained that he had been working with Atanasoff on a highly classified defense project during the same time period and had confined his discussions with Atanasoff to the defense project. What he had learned about the Atanasoff computer was from observation and from informal discussions with his friend, Cliff Berry.

However, because of his high regard for the abilities of Atanasoff and Cliff Berry, Legvold was certain that the machine they had constructed in the Physics Building had some significance at the time it was built in the late 1930s, but he frankly admitted he had no idea how it fit into the overall history of digital computers. A handful of Iowa State professors had vague recollections of the Atanasoff-Berry project, but none could remember any of the vital details of the construction and technical operations that Richards believed were essential if he was to make any assessment of the place the Atanasoff Berry machine should have in computer history.

In mid-February 1963 Richards made inquiry at the Iowa State Alumni Office to find out where he could contact Atanasoff and Cliff Berry. He called Atanasoff at his home in Maryland. Since he had never been in any of Atanasoff's classes and never met him, Richards introduced himself as an Iowa State alumnus and an acquaintance of Cliff Berry, who was interested in exploring and documenting the place of the Atanasoff Berry Computer in history.

Richards confessed he had been amazed at the lack of any written records at the Iowa State Library. He said he believed it important that the Iowa State Library take steps to acquire and preserve any available papers related to the construction and philosophy of the Atanasoff Berry project. Richards told Atanasoff that Robert W. Orr, then director of the Iowa State University Library, agreed with him and had indicated a willingness to bind and catalogue any material that might be found.

Atanasoff, who had long believed that the Atanasoff Berry Computer deserved more attention than it had received, expressed enthusiasm for the initiative Richards was taking in researching his brainchild. While Atanasoff talked eagerly about why he thought that he and Cliff Berry had actually built the first electronic digital computer on the Iowa State campus, he communicated few of the details that Richards was seeking. He did indicate that he had some records scattered around in various offices and in his home that might be helpful in a reconstruction of the machine. He made reference to a specific paper he had written in August 1940 that had the technical details of the Atanasoff Berry Computer they used in applying for grants to a research corporation and in planning for patent applications.

Atanasoff and Cliff Berry had been disappointed and a little bitter to discover in late 1948 that the Atanasoff Berry Computer, which they had slaved to build, had been dismantled and discarded for junk by a thoughtless decision by a department head. They felt the administrator should have consulted them before authorizing destruction of the strange-looking machine. If he didn't understand the value of the computer machine, they felt he should have asked.

Now Atanasoff was at least momentarily stimulated by the conversations with Richards who appeared to have some real appreciation of what he and Cliff Berry had accomplished in their months of dedicated work. Atanasoff knew that Sam Legvold had salvaged one of the rotating memory drums from the original Atanasoff Berry machine and had it in his university office. He understood that a few other professors—friends of his or Cliff Berry—might have salvaged a few smaller parts of the machine. Recalling with some sadness that the machine had been dismantled, Atanasoff suggested that Richards talk with Clifford Berry. He assured Richards that Berry was as knowledgeable as he about most technical aspects of the machine and being younger would probably have a clearer, more specific recollection of the fine technical details.

Atanasoff also suggested that Richards might try to contact John Mauchly, one of the inventors of ENIAC, who he said had been to Iowa State in 1941 to examine the Atanasoff Berry Computer.

Although Atanasoff was suspicious that Mauchly might have pirated some of his ideas for ENIAC, Atanasoff had been too busy to conduct an investigation of the ENIAC patents to arrive at any conclusive judgment that there had been such a piracy. Even if his suspicions were valid and Mauchly had stolen some of his ideas for ENIAC, it would cost millions of dollars to fight the Sperry Rand Corporation, and there was no assurance of winning in the tangled field of patent litigation. Even as he suggested that Richards question Mauchly, Atanasoff wondered what Mauchly's reaction would be to direct questions about what he had seen and what he had learned in his examination of the Atanasoff Berry Computer.

On 12 March 1963 Richards wrote a follow-up letter to Atanasoff to give him the address of Robert W. Orr, director of the Iowa State University Library, and to suggest that Atanasoff send any material related to the Atanasoff Berry machine to Orr's "personal attention." Richards informed Atanasoff that since their telephone conversation he had been able to find a copy of 7 April 1942 Iowa State College press release that included much general but little specific information about the Atanasoff Berry Computer.

Richards enclosed a copy of the press release for Atanasoff and noted that up to that point this "is the one thing I have found in black and white that the computer existed. I think the material was published in the Ames and Des Moines papers," Richards wrote. "The man who wrote this, Harry Burrell, lives across the street from me and that is how I happened to learn about it."

Richards requested that Atanasoff write to "the patent lawyer, Mr. Richard Trexler" of Chicago "because he said he would want to hear from you before turning anything over. I don't really want the material myself, but having him send it to Mr. Orr at the Library would be a fine thing, as we talked about."

Richards continued in his letter:

I certainly hope you will be able to uncover a write-up of the computer, because as yet I have been able to learn very little about it. The people now on the campus, even those who saw it, seem to know very little about it. Even such basic information as how the data was entered, what the computer did with the data, and the results that were presented is lacking.

About all that anyone knows is that it was digital, binary, and had a capacitor storage drum. I have not, as yet, learned anything at all about the circuits, speeds, number length, and many other basic things.

On the same 12 March Richards wrote to Clifford Berry, then director of Engineering Analytical and Control Division of Consolidated Electrodynamics Corporation in Pasadena, California. He made no reference to their prior relationship as ham radio operators in getting to the point:

This letter is to inquire about an electronic computer built under the direction of Dr. John V. Atanasoff at ISU during the period of about 1939 to 1942. I understand from a recent telephone conversation with Dr. Atanasoff that you not only did much of the work on the construction of this computer, but also added much to the ideas in it.

In particular, I would like to know if you have any written material describing that computer?

I might explain that I am writing a book on computers, and I have learned of the Atanasoff machine, and I would like to include a bit about it in the historical chapter of the book.

Richards said up to that time the only written material he had been able to locate was the 7 April 1942 press release, which he enclosed. He listed his two books on computers that were published in 1955 and 1957. He explained his rationale for this request as follows:

Dr. Atanasoff and I think that it would be a good idea to have stored for historical purposes in the archives of the ISU Library anything that can be found about that computer. Mr. Robert W. Orr . . . agrees and indicates a willingness to bind and otherwise care for any material that might be found.

Accordingly, I wonder – if you do still have anything about the computer – if you would be willing to send it (or a copy) to Mr. Orr, whose address is Library Building, Iowa State University, Ames, Iowa?

On that same day, Richards posted a letter to the UNIVAC Division of the Sperry Rand Corporation in New York City requesting an address where he could contact John W. Mauchly, a former employee of UNIVAC, on "a matter of historical interest in connection with a new book I am writing."

Within a few days he received a letter saying Mauchly could be contacted at an address in Ambler, Pennsylvania, and on 19 March 1963 Richards made the first of several efforts to contact Mauchly:

"This letter is to request information about a computer built by Dr. John V. Atanasoff at Iowa State University (then Iowa State College) at Ames, Iowa, during the period of about 1938 to 1942."

That first paragraph was a blunt reminder to Mauchly of the trip to Iowa in June 1941. It was a trip he had probably forgotten or wished to forget. That paragraph was followed by what was probably even more disturbing news to Mauchly. Richards explained:

I am writing a new book on digital computers, and I would like to include a bit about Dr. Atanasoff's computer in the historical section. As yet, however, I have been unable to locate any written material describing it. Although a number of people here in Ames saw the computer, none of them seems to know much about how it worked or even what it did. Even Dr. Atanasoff, whom I talked to on the telephone recently, has not come up with anything written.

According to Dr. Atanasoff, you visited the college a few days during the construction of the computer and made a study of it. (One of the professors, who at the time had his desk in the room where the calculator was, also remembers you.) I am wondering if you might still have some notes or drawings made at the time. If you do, would you be willing to send me a copy, or perhaps preferably be willing to send a copy to Mr. Robert W. Orr, Director of the Library, Library Building, Iowa State University, at Ames for placement in the archives for historical purposes?

I can offer to pay expenses of obtaining photocopies.

Incidentally, perhaps you are aware of the two previous books I wrote, as they have been widely used. They are "Arithmetic Operations in Digital Computers" and "Digital Components and Circuits" published by Van Nostrand in 1955 and 1957, respectively."

It is now only possible to speculate the thoughts that crossed Mauchly's mind when he received that letter if he did not wish to be reminded of his visit with Atanasoff at Iowa State. It was notice to him that Richards, a respected author, was searching the background history of the electronic digital computer and had come across Mauchly's 1941 visit to the Physics Building at Iowa State.

Mauchly more than anyone must have recognized what Richards's inquiry represented to his vulnerable patent rights. Although Atanasoff had been unable to supply Richards with "anything written" about the Atanasoff Berry machine, there were others around Iowa State, including a present professor, who could testify on various aspects of that visit.

For whatever reason, Mauchly did not reply to the request by Richards, nor did he write to encourage Richards in his historic research on the origins of the electronic digital computer. Nor did Mauchly follow the alternate route of sending information to the Iowa State University Library.

While Atanasoff did not reply directly to Richards, he did write to the patent attorney, Richard Trexler, authorizing him to send a copy of his August 1940 report on the computer to the Iowa State University Library.

Fortunately, Richards's letter to Berry was much more productive. On 22 March Berry wrote a single-spaced, two-page letter to

Richards giving verbal and material support to the historic research on the place of the Atanasoff Berry machine in computer history. He wrote:

I have often regretted that the work in which I assisted Dr. Atanasoff during 1939–42 was never publicized, and I certainly support your idea of retrieving and storing for historical purposes what information still exists. In fact, I have suggested this to Dr. Atanasoff on several occasions when we have met during the past few years.

Unfortunately, my own records are extremely scanty; I have only two newspaper clippings (one based on the copy of the press release which you included with your letter), a few photographs, and a copy of my Master's Thesis. The latter, entitled "Design of Electrical Data Recording and Reading Mechanism" (1941) should be on file in the ISU Library. I am enclosing the photographs and one press clipping; since these are my only copies, I trust you will treat them with care and return them promptly.

As to other sources of documented information, Dr. Atanasoff may have forgotten to tell you that (1) we wrote a series of detailed reports to the Research Corporation, which funded much of our work, and (2) we prepared several patent applications (which were never filed) with the aid of a firm of patent attorneys in Chicago. Copies of these may still exist.

An interesting sidelight is that in 1940 or 1941 we had a visit from John Mauchly who spent a week learning all of the details of our computer and the philosophy of its design. He was the only person outside of the Research Corporation and the patent counsel who was given this opportunity, and he may still have notes of what he learned from us.

The very methodical and precise Berry concluded his letter to Richards with the following paragraph filled with the kind of detail that the scientist-author was seeking:

I am not sure what Dr. Atanasoff told you about the machine so I will describe it briefly. The machine was designed specifically to solve sets of linear simultaneous algebraic equations up to 30 × 30. All internal operations were carried on in binary arithmetic; the size of the numbers handled was up to 50 binary places (about 15 decimal places). Initial input of data was by means of standard IBM cards, with five 15-place numbers per card; the machine translated these numbers to binary numbers. The machine's "memory" consisted of two rotating drums filled with small capacitors. The polarity of the charge on a given capacitor represented the binary digit standing in that position. A "clock" frequency of 60 cycles per second was used, the mechanical parts of the machine being driven with a synchronous motor. Storage of intermediate results was by means of a special binary card punch, with which 30 binary numbers, each 50 digits long, could be punched on one card. The mathematical method employed to solve sets of equations was that of systematic elimination of coefficients through linear combinations of pairs of equations.

Dr. Berry's very helpful letter ended with an offer of any further help he could give and an expression of being "very interested in reading your book when it is published."

Delighted with Berry's letter, Richards wrote a note of thanks on 10 April 1963, stating he was making copies of the material sent by Berry and would return it shortly. He also noted that he had already written the Research Corporation, whose officials had indicated they might have some material on the Atanasoff Berry Computer but that "it was not in readily accessible files" and that "it might be a matter of a month or more before they would be able to get it, if at all. I also wrote to Dr. Mauchly, but he has not as yet replied. Dr. Atanasoff has not sent anything yet either (I checked with the library yesterday). So far, your paragraph about the computer is the only written description that I have."

On 30 April 1963 Richards wrote Berry another letter and returned the six pictures and the copies of news stories, and also some extra prints of the pictures that were made at the Iowa State University Photo Service. "It is my plan to place these in the ISU Library with whatever else about the computer that I am able to locate.

"As yet, however, the information you sent represents most of what I have been able to learn about the computer. None of the other possible sources of information has responded," Richards wrote with considerable disappointment and then continued to request further help from Dr. Berry:

For historical purposes, I would like to know more about the computer, and I have the following principal questions, which I am hopeful that you can answer for me:

1. Roughly how was the machine organized? That is, what would a block diagram of its major functions look like?

2. Briefly, how was the machine operated? That is, what needed to be done about input and output, and what controls did the machine have?

3. When did work on the machine start? (Prof. Legvold remembers that a one-digit version of the machine was working when he came to Iowa State in 1939.)

4. Was the machine completed? If not, what remained to be done, or if so, to what extent was the machine used?

5. What were some of the basic or most important circuits?

6. Other than general electronic technology, what important prior art, if any, contributed to the development of the computer? Did you know of any other electronic computers at that time? (I have not learned of any.) Were you familiar with Babbage's work of the nineteenth century on large mechanical computers?

7. Do you recall which newspaper the clippings were from? I plan to look up the exact dates in the microfilm records because these clippings apparently represent the only published information and therefore are the most concrete evidence that the machine existed at the indicated time.

8. Could you, by any chance, recall the names of the patent attorneys in Chicago?

Richards's final paragraph, casually written into his letter, brought some new information to Berry's attention.

Richards replied: "Your remark about Dr. Mauchly was particularly interesting. In a 1945 government report on the ENIAC, there is the statement that the project originated in a memo by Dr. Mauchly, and the date of this memo was given as 1942."

By this time Berry was deeply interested in helping Richards complete his historic research on the Atanasoff Berry Computer. He had consistently believed that the concepts that he and Atanasoff had built into the computer reflected pioneer work of considerable significance, but up to now he had been busy with his own computer inventions for Consolidated Electrodynamics Corporation and had assumed that Atanasoff was following up all leads to keep the historic record straight.

From his correspondence with Richards, Berry suddenly realized that little had been done to document the record of the Atanasoff Berry Computer at Iowa State and that he would have to take the initiative to help Richards piece together the record for computer historians. It had become a labor of love for Berry, who now took a deep interest in reconstruction of the unbelievably sparse record at Iowa State.

For two months Berry worked at the job of methodically answering Richards's questions by trying to reconstruct from memory the details he had known so well twenty years earlier.

On 12 July 1963 Berry wrote a three-page single-spaced letter to Richards with an apology for being so long in replying and with an expression of disappointment that Atanasoff had not replied to Richards's letter.

"It is unfortunate that Dr. Atanasoff has not responded, since he must have stored away somewhere my notebooks, various reports, and drafts of his patent applications (I do not recall the names of the attorneys)," Berry wrote. "I shall try to answer your questions as best I can from memory."

In that detailed three-page letter, Berry gave a careful accounting of the development of the machine from the design and construction phase that started in September 1939 through the last work in 1942, when he and then Atanasoff left the Iowa State College campus to take positions dealing with World War II military research. He included a sketch of the circuitry of the "memory capacitors," the "charging brushes," and the "reading brushes" that worked in the "memory drums" of the Atanasoff Berry Computer. He even recalled that "several years ago Sam Legvold had one of the memory drums under his desk."

In his reply on 18 July 1963 Richards thanked Berry for the 12 July letter. "The information it contains will be very helpful to me in preparing a suitable account of the computer in the historical section of my book."

Richards informed Berry that he "did find that capacitor drum (in Legvold's office), and I have a photograph of it." None of the other computer parts could be located. However, he told Berry he had all of the information he needed about the Atanasoff Berry Computer although he had not yet heard from Atanasoff. Richards reported he would be working on the book for the remainder of 1963 and hoped to have it ready for publication and market by the end of 1964.

While Berry's help had made it possible to state with certainty that the first electronic digital computer had been developed by Atanasoff and Berry in the 1939–1942 period, the 1941 visit of Mauchly to Iowa State opened the possibility that some of the concepts of the Atanasoff Berry Computer might have been used by Mauchly in the 1942 proposal that led to construction of ENIAC.

Even as the broad facts indicated that Mauchly could have learned something from his examination of the Atanasoff Berry machine and from his discussions with Atanasoff and Berry, Richards did not want to leave any unfair inferences. He wanted to find out what Mauchly had to say about what he had learned on that visit to Iowa State.

When months passed without a response to his letter, Richards made several attempts to reach Mauchly by telephone and finally succeeded in getting Mauchly on the line in the late summer.

Richards spelled out the purpose of his call and briefly summarized the fact that Berry recalled the "week-long visit by Mauchly which was spent . . . learning all of the details of our computer and the philosophy of its design."

Mauchly said he did not want to discuss the details of his visit at Iowa State because he did not remember having learned anything of consequence on that trip. He said he remembered Atanasoff, but did not really remember Berry or having any discussion as exten-

sive as Berry described. Mauchly said he was certain of one thing—
Berry was wrong in saying he had been at Iowa State for a full
week.

While Mauchly's reluctance to talk and his contentions that he
couldn't remember much about the trip frustrated Richards, he did
gain admissions from Mauchly on two important points:

1. Mauchly acknowledged that he was at Iowa State for
several days' discussions with Atanasoff in the summer of 1940 or
1941.
2. Mauchly acknowledged that he had viewed the Atanasoff
Berry machine at that time and had some discussions with Atanasoff
about its operation.

For Richards's purposes those two admissions were enough for
him to conclude that "the Atanasoff-Berry electronic computer . . .
does . . . appear to predate every other electronic digital system by
a matter of years."

But before he had completed work on the manuscript of his
history of electronic digital systems, he received a letter on 13 November 1963 from Clifford Berry's wife, Jean, telling of the untimely
sudden death of Berry two weeks earlier. "My husband passed away
two weeks ago," Jean Berry wrote. "I came across some correspondence from you, and thought that Sammy Legvold might not have
told you of Cliff's death. I gather from the letters that you may be
writing a book. If there is any reference to Cliff in it, I would appreciate your telling me, so that I may look it up at that time, as there is
nothing left but my memories and my tremendous pride in him and
his ability. I mean—tell me when the book is available and published. Thank you." It was signed "Jean Berry."

As she wrote the letter, Jean Berry did not relate that Cliff's
death was listed as a "possible suicide" by suffocation. She didn't
understand how it could be suicide, for he had been in the best of
spirits in his almost daily telephone calls and in his letters.

On 1 October Berry had gone on the payroll of Vacuum Electronics Corporation, in Huntington, New York. It was a comparable
job to the one he resigned as director of the Engineering Analytical
Control Division of Consolidated Electrodynamics Corporation, and
there had been a small salary increase. Although he had been on the
job only a few weeks, he had been delighted with the way he had
been treated by the company and the prospects for the future.

In his most recent telephone calls and letters he had told her of
buying a new car and that he had found two homes that were even

nicer than the very fine home they had recently sold in Altadena, California. The new company had agreed to pay her transportation costs to New York so she could take part in the final decision on which home to buy. She had already made plans to come to New York on 6 November to make the decision on the new home when she was notified of Cliff's death. All of those specific plans, and all of the enthusiasm for the move and the new job somehow did not add up to suicide in Jean Berry's mind.

On 19 November 1963 Richards wrote Jean Berry that he was "shocked and saddened to hear of Cliff's death" and assured her that Cliff Berry would be mentioned very prominently in his book on electronic digital systems. He related that Atanasoff had told him on the telephone "that many of the ideas in the machine, as well as the actual construction should be credited to Cliff."

"As you can probably tell from the correspondence you have, this computer was never described publicly in any detail; very few people in the now large computer industry know of it. Therefore Cliff and Atanasoff have never been given the recognition they deserve." Richards promised to send Jean Berry a copy of the book when it was published, and then he engaged in the following personal note about his relations with Berry: "Although I lived away from Ames for many years, I did live here as a boy, and I remember meeting Cliff on two occasions. He was a few years older than I. Both meetings were in connection with amateur radio, in which we had a common interest. One meeting was in his home and the other was at the college in the room where the computer was located. I thought highly of him as did everyone else here that knew him."

In her 25 November 1963 reply to Richards, Jean said she had not yet "heard from J.V. [Atanasoff], so he must not have heard about Cliff's death." In closing, she told Richards that if she found anything in Cliff's papers that she felt would be helpful in the book, she would get in touch with him. Again she made no reference to Cliff's death being noted on the death certificate as a "possible suicide" nor that the police were keeping the premises under lock and key pending an investigation.

When she called Atanasoff a few days later to give him news of Cliff's death, she again avoided mentioning the "possible suicide" and indicated that the death was related to epilepticlike seizures Cliff had experienced periodically since suffering severe head injuries in an automobile accident in 1956. She did not want to accept even the possibility that he had taken his own life. It seemed so implausible. It was months later that Atanasoff heard suicide mentioned, and years before he learned enough to raise serious questions in his mind about whether Clifford Berry had taken his own life.

When R. K. Richards's book, *Electronic Digital Systems,* was finally published by John Wiley and Sons in 1966, it was the first book to challenge the long-accepted claim that ENIAC was the first electronic digital computer. Richards referred to the Atanasoff Berry Computer in the preface of the book as the first electronic digital computer, then included two and one-half pages in the first chapter restating his conclusion with documentation.

Dr. Richards concluded: "The ancestry of all electronic digital systems appears to be traceable to a computer which will be called 'the Atanasoff-Berry Computer.' This computer was built during the period from about 1938 to 1942 under the direction of Dr. John V. Atanasoff, who was a professor of physics and mathematics at Iowa State University (then Iowa State College) at Ames, Iowa. He had the assistance of Dr. Clifford E. Berry, who was at the time a graduate student at the university."

Richards remarked about the lack of publicity concerning "the Atanasoff-Berry machine" being responsible for it "having relatively little influence on subsequent developments," but he went on to explain: "There was, however, one interesting link between the machine and later work. One of the few people to study the machine in detail was Dr. John Mauchly, who at the time was on the faculty of Ursinus College in Pennsylvania. According to oral reports from Dr. Atanasoff and Dr. Mauchly, the two met at an American Association for the Advancement of Science meeting. As a result of conversations at this meeting, Dr. Mauchly made a visit to ISU in 1941 for the specific purpose of studying the computer. As mentioned later, Dr. Mauchly is given credit for subsequently initiating the ENIAC project."

With the publication of the book by Richards in 1966, there was the public linking of Mauchly's observation of the Atanasoff Berry machine in June 1941 and Mauchly's writing in 1942 of the initial ENIAC program for which he and J. Presper Eckert were granted the valuable patent rights that were subsequently sold to Sperry Rand.

Those few pages written by Richards and published in 1966 were the leads that patent attorneys followed in 1967 in initiating the successful federal court challenges to the Sperry Rand patents. But there were thousands of hours of investigations and hundreds of hours of depositions to be taken before the federal court decision could be handed down on 19 October 1973.

CHAPTER 11

Piracy Evidence Emerges: Charles Call Goes to Work, 1967

I N the last month of 1966 or in the first month of 1967, patent lawyer Charles G. Call was summoned to the office of senior partner D. Dennis Allegretti. The initial question was asked with a smile, but it was a serious question: "Have you got ten years of your life to give to one case?"

At twenty-eight, Charles Call said he had that kind of time for one big patent case if Dennis Allegretti figured it was worthwhile for the law firm. Call, an electrical engineering graduate of Purdue University, had worked at Bell Laboratories while attending New York University Law School and for several years after being awarded his law degree and being admitted to the practice of law in New York. He had only been with the Chicago patent law firm of Bair, Freeman and Molinar since November 1965, and was eager to get into a case where he could demonstrate his talents.

Allegretti explained that the client was the Honeywell Company of Minneapolis and the case involved a controversy with the Sperry Rand Corporation over what was called generally "the ENIAC patents." Sperry Rand and its subsidiary corporation, Illinois Scientific Development, Incorporated, had purchased those patent rights from John W. Mauchly and J. Presper Eckert, Jr. Call was somewhat familiar with the earlier litigation involving the ENIAC patents, for that patent challenge had been brought and fought by Bell Telephone Laboratories against Sperry Rand at a time when Call was employed by Bell. Although he was employed as a patent attorney, he had not been directly involved in investigations or trial preparations for the case, *Sperry Rand Corporation et al. v. Bell Telephone Laboratories, Inc.*

U.S. District Judge Archie Dawson had upheld the validity of Sperry Rand's ENIAC patents in his 1962 decision on grounds that Bell Telephone Laboratories had failed to produce sufficient evidence of "prior public use" of ENIAC ideas. It would be an uphill battle for Honeywell to get another court to take any action that would upset Judge Dawson's decision, and Call and Allegretti recognized that point.

Dennis Allegretti said Honeywell's lawyers had some new evidence that was related to the ENIAC patents and also some antitrust theories for attacking Sperry Rand under the Sherman Act and Clayton Act. He explained that Honeywell lawyers felt that Sperry Rand was demanding "discriminatory royalties" and that irrespective of the ENIAC patent's validity, it was unlawful for Sperry Rand to enter into a total cross-licensing arrangement with IBM and Bell Telephone Laboratories to create a virtual monopoly in many electronic digital computer processes.

It was a tremendous challenge in the face of Judge Dawson's decision for Sperry Rand, but Honeywell lawyers had assured Allegretti that there would be virtually no limitation on the expenditures they could make in following leads that might unearth facts or law to break the ENIAC patents. Honeywell lawyers did come across new evidence and new arguments that they hoped would persuade Sperry Rand to negotiate rather than litigate.

The first task was to do the research and investigations necessary to put together a position paper for Honeywell lawyers and executives to use in their effort to negotiate a settlement of the patent problem without having to resort to a long and costly trial. To that end the work in early 1967 was focused on producing a persuasive position paper for Honeywell executives.

General counsel for Honeywell's patent division was Henry L. Hanson, who had received a B.S. degree in electrical engineering at Iowa State College before earning his law degree at the Willis Mitchell Law School in Minneapolis. He was an Iowa State electrical engineering classmate of R. K. Richards, author of the computer textbook giving initial public notice that John Atanasoff and Cliff Berry had constructed the first electronic digital computer at Iowa State. Because of this Iowa State College connection he learned of the Richards book and mentioned it to the lawyers who were doing the patent work for Honeywell. However, Hanson did not put any particular stress on the importance of the conclusion that Iowa State

was the birthplace of the first electronic digital computer. If it was
as conclusive as the Richards book indicated, Iowa State publications probably would have made a big thing of it in alumni publications, Hanson assumed.

Having mentioned the existence of the Richards book to the
patent law firms, Henry Hanson let the matter drop as unimportant
or unrelated to the position paper that was being put together for
Honeywell Chairman James Henry Binger to use in his efforts to
negotiate with Sperry Rand.

If the Honeywell position paper did not persuade Sperry Rand
officials to negotiate a reasonable settlement, Honeywell wanted to
be prepared to file a suit in the U.S. District Court in Minneapolis –
the federal jurisdiction where the precedents seemed less inclined
than in some others to uphold established patent rights.

In the first month of work on the case Call and Dennis Allegretti were working on matters related to Honeywell's negotiating
position paper. Call did not remember ever hearing the names of
John V. Atanasoff or Clifford Berry or of a computing machine that
they reportedly constructed at Iowa State College in the late 1930s.
Charles Call had his head buried in research and reading on the
ENIAC patents. He combed through the voluminous archives of the
Moore School of Electrical Engineering at the University of Pennsylvania. The records for the 1940s were stored under the Franklin
Field Stadium and did not have an effective index for research.
Call's job was to find all papers that were in any way related to the
planning and construction of ENIAC that started with plans drawn
by Mauchly in 1942. It was a boring and time-consuming task as
was the reading and rereading of the standard histories of computing that all ended with the same conclusion: The first electronic
digital computer was invented by John W. Mauchly and J. Presper
Eckert, Jr., at the University of Pennsylvania.

The only challenges to Mauchly and Eckert's claim were from
some of their Moore School colleagues who believed that Mauchly
and Eckert had wrongfully claimed credit for inventions and innovations that had gone into the construction of ENIAC and had been
the work of others on the staff. Those who felt that Mauchly and
Eckert had wrongfully grabbed the credit belonging to them were
eager to be helpful and obviously hoped to establish credit for themselves in the process.

Well before a negotiating impasse was reached between Honeywell and Sperry Rand in May, Honeywell lawyers had authorized

the preparation of a suit against Sperry Rand to be filed in the U.S. District Court in Minneapolis. The Dorsey and Whitney law firm, with offices only two blocks from the federal courthouse, had the papers drawn and had a runner alerted in case lawyers received word from Honeywell that negotiations had ended.

When the impasse was reached on 26 May 1967, and a Honeywell lawyer passed the word to Dorsey and Whitney "to file the Son of a Bitch," the Honeywell officials learned that what they suspected was true. Sperry Rand's subsidiary, Illinois Scientific Development, had a Washington law firm alerted for a competing race to the courthouse to try to gain the initiative in a suit charging Honeywell with violations of Sperry Rand patents. They wished to be the ones raising the issues to be litigated, and they believed that the U.S. District Court for the District of Columbia represented a jurisdiction more favorable to their position.

It was a footrace to the courthouse in Minneapolis and to the courthouse in the District of Columbia. Honeywell lawyers won in Minneapolis by about fifteen minutes. It was months before that battle over jurisdiction was settled by U.S. District Judge John J. Sirica, then chief judge in the District of Columbia. He simply declared that the courts in the District of Columbia were too busy to consider taking on a case that was likely to tie up one judge for several years.

Even before that jurisdictional tug-of-war was settled, Allen Kirkpatrick, a lawyer for Control Data Corporation, had run across the Richards book and the reference to the first electronic digital computer being constructed by Atanasoff and Berry. Control Data was involved in litigation with Sperry Rand with regard to patent rights in the "regenerative memory" of EDVAC (Electronic Discrete Variable Automatic Computer).

EDVAC was the second generation of electronic digital computers that had flowed from ENIAC, and Mauchly and Eckert claimed and obtained patent rights to the "regenerative memory" ideas that represented one of several improvements over ENIAC.

The Richards book said that no technical description of the Atanasoff Berry Computer was ever published, but it did allude to two brief and obscure newspaper accounts that made reference to the concept of the "machine remembering." Call and Allegretti noted that Richards had quoted from a *Des Moines Tribune* story that was headlined "Machine Remembers." That story of 15 January 1941 stated:

An electrical computing machine said to operate more like the human brain than any other such machine known to exist is being built here by Dr. John V. Atanasoff, Iowa State College Physics Professor.

In his book, Richards, writing from the explanation he received in Cliff Berry's letters, stated:

The machine's storage unit, or 'memory', was formed with a drum about 9 inches in diameter and 11 inches in length in which were mounted 1632 capacitors in 32 tracks with 51 capacitors per track, but with a blank sector so that at a rotational speed of one revolution per second the "clock" pulse rate was 60 cycles per second. A corresponding array of brass studs were mounted on the drum for making connection to the computer circuits as the drum rotated. A binary digit was represented by the polarity of the charge on a capacitor, with the charge being regenerated or reversed, as called for in the computations, once each drum revolution. Intermediate results were stored in binary form on punched cards through the use of specially designed punch and reader.

That paragraph would have been meaningless scientific jargon to the average lawyer, but to lawyer Kirkpatrick and his younger assistant, Kevin Joyce, it was a language they understood for both were electrical engineering graduates before they became lawyers. It set them in motion to find out where they might locate Atanasoff. Through Iowa State College they found he was living at New Market, Maryland, a short drive from their law offices in Washington, D.C. Allen Kirkpatrick and Kevin Joyce made an initial drive to Atanasoff's home to set the stage for later visits by lawyers for Control Data and Honeywell.

When they drove to Atanasoff's country home, they found him friendly and willing to explain enough about the "regenerative memory" of the Atanasoff Berry Computer to make them interested in hearing more. Atanasoff said he had some records around that would corroborate his brief account of Mauchly's visit to Iowa State and Mauchly's access to the secrets of the Atanasoff Berry Computer. However, he was unwilling at that time to permit them to see his papers and they did not push the issue.

During the same time frame that Allen Kirkpatrick and Kevin Joyce, as lawyers for Control Data, were becoming deeply interested in John Atanasoff and Cliff Berry and the history of the Atanasoff Berry Computer, Allegretti and Call were taking their first steps to explore what this Atanasoff Berry Computer was all about and whether it had any relevancy to their efforts to break the ENIAC patents.

Charles Call had been a ham radio operator from his boyhood, had built his own radio sets in the days before transistors, and he knew what vacuum tubes were all about even before he started his electrical engineering courses at Purdue. The descriptions of the Atanasoff Berry Computer in the Richards book intrigued him. He obtained a copy of Cliff Berry's thesis from Iowa State and he was more interested. Before even trying to contact Atanasoff, Call obtained and studied a copy of the 35-page memorandum that Atanasoff had written in August 1940.

Studying Atanasoff's 1940 memorandum against the background of his months of study of the ENIAC, EDVAC, and UNIVAC patents, Charles Call became convinced that Atanasoff's concepts at the time of Mauchly's visit were far ahead of his time. Also they went beyond ENIAC and included many of the most important concepts of such second-generation of computers as EDVAC.

By the time Call and Allegretti decided to talk to Atanasoff, Call was certain that many of the concepts in the ENIAC patents had been derived from the Atanasoff Berry machine. By late July, Call and Allegretti believed that the strength of the Honeywell case depended for the most part on the degree of cooperation they could get from Atanasoff, the state of his memory, and the records and witnesses who could be found to confirm and corroborate the claim that Mauchly had full access to the Atanasoff Berry Computer and the comprehensive August 1940 memorandum.

By that time, lawyers for General Electric (another of the computer firms threatened by the Mauchly-Eckert patents) had already talked to Atanasoff to explore his knowledge and assess his value and attitude relative to cooperating in an attack on the Sperry Rand patents. Atanasoff treated the lawyers for General Electric courteously. He particularly enjoyed the conversations with one of the lawyers, Norman Fulmer, an Iowa State graduate and one of the electrical engineering majors who had done some of the wiring and soldering work on the Atanasoff Berry Computer. Another of the General Electric lawyers was George V. Eltgroth, who identified himself as one of the patent lawyers who had filed the patent applications for Mauchly and Eckert. Eltgroth commented that neither Mauchly nor Eckert had mentioned Atanasoff, Cliff Berry, or Mauchly's visit to Iowa. This appeared to be a possible violation of the full disclosure required of patent applicants.

When John Atanasoff did not rush out with enthusiasm to greet the succeeding groups of corporation lawyers, it was not because he lacked a deep interest in an aggressive investigation of the ENIAC patents. He was simply suspicious and wary of corporate lawyers since his experience with the IBM patent lawyer, A. J. Etienne, in 1954.

Etienne had come to Atanasoff's company office in Frederick, Maryland, and had asked for his cooperation and files. The IBM lawyer had stated optimistically that with his active cooperation and his files on the Atanasoff Berry machine, he was certain he could break the patents that Sperry Rand held through Mauchly and Eckert.

In 1954, there had even been some correspondence with Etienne in which Dr. Atanasoff received copies of the ENIAC patent. It was the first time he had seen the patent. That was the last he heard from Etienne. There hadn't been so much as a telephone call or a brief note to explain Etienne's sudden lack of interest in pursuing the leads "to break the Sperry Rand patents." Later, Atanasoff learned that IBM officials had used the information they had obtained through Etienne and others to persuade Sperry Rand to enter into a patent exchange that created the virtual monopoly alleged in the Honeywell suit.

Atanasoff felt he had been used by Etienne and IBM and concluded that the IBM corporation lawyers were not interested in aggressive search for the truth about the origins of the automatic electronic digital computer but were only interested in monopoly and greater profits for the corporation.

That unhappy experience with Etienne made him cautious and skeptical about cooperating with lawyers for these big corporations until he was assured that they were serious about the search for the truth on the history of electronic digital computers. He concluded that the only way he could assure himself of their depth of interest in following the leads he believed should be followed was to have a clear agreement. They should pay him for his services as an expert consultant. This would give him a degree of control over how his leads should be followed. His degree of cooperation could be modified in line with his perception of their seriousness and diligence in pursuit of his interests as well as their own.

In July 1967 Atanasoff had several meetings and conversations with lawyers for Honeywell and lawyers for Control Data before he was able to conclude that his interests and those of Honeywell and Control Data were pretty much the same in establishing the full record of what Mauchly had learned on his 1941 visit at Iowa State and in conversations with Atanasoff on later occasions.

There had been several abortive efforts by the Honeywell lawyers to meet with Atanasoff for a full discussion of an agreement in late July and early August, but those meetings did not take place. Finally, a mutually agreeable time was found.

The morning of 29 August 1967 Dennis Allegretti, Charles Call, and Minneapolis trial lawyer Henry Halladay drove to Atanasoff's farm home in Maryland. By the time they arrived, JV and his wife, Alice, had brought all of his files together and had made a thorough search for all correspondence and records that they felt might be useful in corroborating the story of Mauchly's 1941 visit to Iowa State.

Atanasoff was fascinated with Charles Call's grasp of technical aspects of the Atanasoff Berry Computer and his understanding of the concepts embodied in his 35-page memorandum and in Cliff Berry's thesis. He was also impressed with Dennis Allegretti's grasp of technical detail and with the manner in which Henry Halladay, who was to be the trial lawyer, worked at converting these technical concepts into terms that could be understood by those not schooled in electrical engineering.

Relaxed and in the company of knowledgeable, likeable, and interested lawyers, Atanasoff told the Honeywell lawyers that he and Alice had pulled together a two-foot stack of correspondence and other documents they believed were relevant to the litigation. Copies were available in a small steel filing cabinet in the large room in which they were seated.

Atanasoff said he had spent more than 2,000 hours in the study of patent law and felt qualified to offer the opinion that the Control Data case involving his "regenerative memory" ideas would be simpler to prove than the ENIAC case. He explained that the Eckert and Mauchly regenerative memory patent specifically stated that various arrangements disclosed and claimed were "equivalent to employing a capacitor drum."

By contrast, Atanasoff said it would be more difficult to trace specific parts of the Atanasoff Berry Computer to ENIAC, even though he had no doubt in his own mind that the overall concept of an automatic electronic digital computer was derived from Mauchly's study of the Atanasoff Berry machine and related papers.

According to Call's memorandum of that meeting:

Atanasoff played a recording of a conversation with his (former) wife relating to the Mauchly (1941) visit (to Iowa State). Mrs. (Lura) Atanasoff, when told that her ex-husband was becoming involved in a controversy over the first computer inventions, recalled asking immediately "Who's causing the trouble—that Mauchly?" She related that Mauchly was interested in the computer, he couldn't talk of anything else while he was there, hardly knowing he had a hostess, and did not acknowledge her at all (even though she took care of his little boy who had accompanied him on the visit). She remembered telling her husband, "Vincent, I don't think he's honest."

Dr. Atanasoff responded that Mauchly was not going to steal his inventions and that he was a man of honor. Mrs. (Lura) Atanasoff specifically recalled Mauchly thanking Dr. Atanasoff for his help at the time he was leaving and further stating that he had learned a great deal.

According to Mrs. Atanasoff, Mauchly was there for three days — possibly four. She stated that it must have been "very fruitful for Mauchly to spend his vacation at Ames, all the while parking his little boy" in her house.

In talking with the Honeywell lawyers, Atanasoff recalled briefly the overtures he had from the IBM lawyer, Etienne, in 1954, and the visit with the General Electric attorney, George Eltgroth, at a later stage.

Atanasoff explained that he had prepared copies of his correspondence in 1941 with Mauchly and with others. He pointed out that he had two letters from Mauchly after his visit that were highly enthusiastic about the Atanasoff Berry Computer, a sharp contrast to Mauchly's later assertion that he had learned nothing from Atanasoff or from Cliff Berry or from his brief examination of the computer machine.

Atanasoff said that the typed September letter from Mauchly was not signed, but that it included some handwritten changes that appeared to be Mauchly's handwriting. Atanasoff also pointed out that the September letter appeared to be typed on the same typewriter as the letter in late June that Mauchly had signed.

Henry Halladay expressed his view, as the trial lawyer in the case, that the authorship of this unsigned letter could probably be proven in court by an expert examiner of questioned documents in Chicago. It was agreed immediately that the Mauchly letter should be submitted for study by this expert in the event that Mauchly would try to deny authorship and Sperry Rand lawyers seek to bar its admission into evidence.

After Alice Atanasoff served lunch, she assisted Atanasoff in laying out entire file of documents for review by Call, Allegretti, and Halladay. Even in their first casual review of the documents, the Honeywell lawyers realized they had hit a bonanza. Atanasoff was a record pack rat and had saved all of his correspondence with Mauchly as well as nearly every other paper related to the planning, construction, and attempts to get Iowa State to patent his ideas.

There was immediate agreement that the Atanasoff documents would be physically turned over to the Honeywell lawyers and the Control Data lawyers at Allen Kirkpatrick's law office in the firm of Cushman, Darby, and Cushman in Washington. However, Call went to work immediately with his camera to copy all of the key documents in the Atanasoff file, for with so many millions riding on the case it was essential to take immediate steps to preserve all relevant records.

In addition to the value of those documents in the multimillion dollar patent litigation, the Honeywell lawyers had to take Atanasoff's age and health into account. While Atanasoff appeared vigorous, he had a history of health problems that could end or destroy his availability as a credible and persuasive witness. Even if Atanasoff died or was incapacitated, the paper record he had accumulated could speak volumes.

Call photographed more than thirty-five of the key documents in the Atanasoff file and compiled a list of forty persons who might be able to corroborate Atanasoff's testimony in some respect or other. It was a banner day for Honeywell and for Atanasoff. At JV's suggestion, the lawyers drew up a list of ten priority things to do, including efforts "to locate the remains of the [original Atanasoff Berry] computer . . . and to determine the feasibility of rebuilding all or part of the computer for purposes of a trial."

The list also included the assurance that "Allen Kirkpatrick [Control Data Corporation] is to have the benefit of all the knowledge that J.V.A. [Dr. Atanasoff] generates or receives from Honeywell with respect to this suit—except that our 'ELF' [Electronic Litigation File] is to remain confidential."

Although the Honeywell lawyers had put in a highly productive day with Atanasoff, Charles Call's day was not finished. He had learned that Mauchly was to appear on a computer science panel, and he was curious to see and hear anything the "inventor of the first automatic electronic digital computer" might be saying about the origins of ENIAC.

Call got more than he had hoped to gain in his first observation of Mauchly, for the moderator of the session was Dr. Isaac Auerbach, who had worked on the ENIAC.

Auerbach's introduction started with a simple recitation of Mauchly's educational record and some of the awards related to the "invention of ENIAC," and then he tossed in a comment about R. K. Richards's book, *Electronic Digital Systems,* and suggested that Mauchly might want to comment on the assertion by Richards that the "first automatic digital computer" was the Atanasoff Berry Computer constructed at Iowa State prior to 1941.

To Call's delight, Mauchly responded to Auerbach's suggestion by launching into an admission of his visit to Iowa State, his talks with Atanasoff, and the fact that he had seen the Atanasoff Berry Computer. But Mauchly then characterized the Atanasoff Berry machine as an incomplete device "that wouldn't do anything." He went to some lengths to minimize the time he had examined the machine, and to state that he had learned nothing from his conversations with Atanasoff.

To Call, who only a few hours earlier had read the text of Mauchly's 1941 letters to Atanasoff, it was an amazing performance. Mauchly had either forgotten what he had written to Atanasoff or believed that those 1941 letters had been lost or destroyed. Call knew then that if Mauchly told the same story under oath in pretrial depositions and during the trial, he would lose his credibility. Now that he knew where Mauchly stood and had viewed his performance on the crucial point, he was more eager than ever to get on with the interviews through which they should be able to confirm and corroborate the story told by Atanasoff.

CHAPTER 12

The Search for Truth:
Depositions and Deceptions

N September 1967 the lawyers for Honeywell and Control Data made plans to follow up the leads they had obtained from Atanasoff's file. At the time it was uncertain which trial would start first, but it was to the advantage of both computer firms to get a swift and comprehensive analysis of the best available witnesses concerning the precise state of the Atanasoff Berry Computer in June 1941.

Atanasoff declared that he did not want "a herd of corporate lawyers" following him around as he contacted his former students and associates who he believed might be able to confirm his own recollections. It was decided that Charles Call would be the lawyer representative for Honeywell and that Allen Kirkpatrick would do the early interview and deposition work for Control Data.

Honeywell placed a priority on interviews with Dr. Robert Mather, of Berkeley, California, and Dr. Sam Legvold, a Professor at Iowa State University. In the 29 August meeting with the Honeywell lawyers, Atanasoff said that Robert Mather, as a student at Iowa State, had worked on the Atanasoff Berry Computer and "probably remembers more about the machine than anyone else alive" except himself now that Cliff Berry was dead. Atanasoff told the Honeywell lawyers that Mather was not articulate and did not speak in a "collected way." He also stated that Robert Mather had no knowledge of the visit of Mauchly to Iowa State.

Sam Legvold was identified as having "a good memory" but little technical knowledge of the Atanasoff Berry Computer. Atanasoff said Legvold was present at a lunch with Mauchly. He would have a good memory of other people involved in the planning and construction of the Atanasoff Berry Computer.

The interviews Call and Kirkpatrick conducted with Mather were a big disappointment because, contrary to Dr. Atanasoff's prediction, he had little memory of the Atanasoff Berry machine's construction details and could not even recall whether Cliff Berry had demonstrated the machine to him. Although Robert Mather worked full-time on the computer from June 1941 and had some memory of various individuals coming to examine the machine with regard to grants, he declared, "I just wasn't sophisticated enough to particularly notice who they were."

"You see, Cliff did most of this – he did the more complicated things, the more routine things were turned over to me," Mather explained. "I was soldering the wires to brushes and the terminal board in the binary-to-decimal converter."

The disappointment over Mather's lack of specific memory was overcome by the results of the interview that Atanasoff and Call conducted with Sam Legvold on 10 September 1967. Legvold met Atanasoff and Call at the Fleur De Lis Motor Hotel, on Fleur Drive in Des Moines, for the tape-recorded session. He was a close friend and confidant of Cliff Berry in the 1939 to 1942 period when they were both heading research projects for Atanasoff and had been much more observant about the computer project than Atanasoff had thought.

Sam Legvold recalled that it was his job, under Atanasoff's direction, to design apparatus for tracking aircraft for military gunnery. "We worked on this project in the basement of the Physics Building in a room adjoining the room where the computer work had been underway since the fall of 1939," Legvold explained to Call.

Legvold said that he believed it was in the fall of 1939, the year he entered Iowa State, that he saw the first computing element that Clifford Berry had built under Atanasoff's direction. He was able to recall considerable details of the machine's operation and the technical mechanisms through which it could add and subtract, multiply and divide. He remembered the visits of Dr. Warren Weaver, a research representative of the Rockefeller Foundation, and Dr. Sam Caldwell, of MIT and the National Defense Research Corporation. Both had made examinations and evaluations of the project.

Most important, Sam Legvold recalled Mauchly's visit to Iowa State in June 1941, remembered going to lunch with him, and remembered that Atanasoff and Cliff Berry had spent quite a bit of time with him discussing the features of the computer that was being constructed.

"At the time Mauchly visited Ames, he struck me as being a rather delightful fellow, pretty bright and stimulating, and . . . [I] remember him being there with his shirt sleeves rolled up, pitching in to help do some things on the computer as we sat and talked about it.

"I was just in and out enough so that I saw him in the room where the computer was being assembled and I heard a number of the discussions . . . I do remember that he was over to the laboratory and those recollections are sound and vivid," Legvold told Call.

When Call asked him if he remembered how long Mauchly was around the Physics Building laboratory, he responded that "It seems something like three days—it was an extended visit—it was more than just a drop-in-for-an-afternoon kind of thing because he spent quite a little time there."

"Do you remember whether Mauchly seemed surprised by what he learned?" Call asked.

"All I remember was that he had a real sharp interest and was delighted with what he saw," Legvold responded.

"In your opinion—was he able to understand everything he saw?" Call asked.

"Oh, I think he could understand all the functioning characteristics of the machine, and I'm sure the discussions were free and open," Dr. Legvold replied. ". . . There were no holds barred in the discussion. It was free and open."

When the interview with Legvold was over, Charles Call telephoned Dennis Allegretti and Allen Kirkpatrick to inform them that Legvold would corroborate Atanasoff's testimony with regard to the length of Mauchly's visit and with regard to Mauchly being given free and open access to the machine.

The next order of business for the Honeywell and Control Data lawyers was to get a deposition from Mauchly and to get him pinned down under oath as to what he contended he had seen and learned in his 1941 visit at Iowa State College. Allen Kirkpatrick, the lead lawyer for Control Data, was selected to have the first crack at Mauchly to see if, when he was under oath, he would continue to minimize the length of his stay in Ames, to minimize the access he had to the machine, and to characterize the Atanasoff Berry Computer as "a pile of junk"—"a pile of junk" that was never demonstrated to him as operational.

When Allen Kirkpatrick started taking the deposition of Mauchly on 13 October 1967, Mauchly had no knowledge that the lawyer for Control Data had obtained his 1941 letters to Atanasoff. In that deposition Kirkpatrick brought up the subject of the 30 September 1941 letter to Atanasoff that had only a typed signature, and obtained Mauchly's acknowledgment that he had written such a letter to Atanasoff in the fall of 1941 in which he had commented in highly favorable terms about the Atanasoff Berry Computer.

Kirkpatrick read him the portion in which Mauchly had asked Atanasoff: "Is there any objection, from your point of view, to my building some sort of computer which incorporates some of the features of your machine?"

That question from the 1941 letter and the lengthy question that followed appeared to be totally contradictory to Mauchly's present contention that he had learned little in his visit at Iowa State and considered the Atanasoff Berry Computer to be useless junk. In a lengthy sentence in his letter Mauchly asked:

Ultimately, a second question might come up, of course, and that is, in the event that your present design were to hold the field against all challengers, and I got the Moore School interested in having something of the sort, would the way be opened for us to build an "Atanasoff Calculator" (a la Bush Analyzer) here?

In response to Kirkpatrick's question as to what he meant by his questions in that letter to Atanasoff, a flustered Mauchly responded:

The center portion of this letter indicates that I was probing whether there would be any objection to using some of his (Atanasoff's) ideas. This is not quite as strong as saying that I had a strong desire to, but at that point, on September 30, 1941, I think the letter makes it clear that I was still seeking a good way of implementing an electronic calculator, and this is the same interest which I displayed with respect to many other ideas with respect to computation, such as those which I saw at the World's Fair in 1939.

Without pushing Mauchly in an aggressive manner, Kirkpatrick asked further questions and permitted him to make whatever explanations he chose, gently asking him to explain his words without calling attention to the significance of his contradictions or the gaping holes in the logic.

Kirkpatrick let Mauchly make his statement minimizing his time in Iowa and his lack of access to the Atanasoff Berry Computer with full knowledge that he would be contradicted on those key points by several witnesses as well as corroborative documents.

It was Laurence B. Dodds, representing Sperry Rand, who with his cross-examination of Mauchly opened the way for a most damaging response in which Mauchly testified under oath that he "might have spent an hour or an hour and a half" at the Physics Building at Iowa State and he spent only "more than a day" in Ames.

While Kirkpatrick and Call were busy preparing to take depositions from Lura Atanasoff in Denver and from Sam Legvold and R. K. Richards in Ames, Atanasoff was able to persuade the lawyers to help him conduct his own little investigation of what he considered the "suspicious circumstances" surrounding the October 1963 death of Cliff Berry in Huntington, New York. The lawyers viewed the mysterious death of Cliff Berry pragmatically. Cliff Berry alive would have been a vital witness in their case, but Cliff Berry had been dead for four years. It was a long, long shot at best whether an investigation of his death could be useful in their case even if it proved Cliff Berry was murdered by some unknown assailant.

However, Atanasoff was cooperating fully with them, and Kevin Joyce, the young lawyer from the Cushman, Darby, and Cushman firm, was authorized by Kirkpatrick to meet Atanasoff and accompany him on his interviews with the coroner, the police, and with the owner of the rooming house who had found Cliff Berry dead in his bed.

In Huntington, Atanasoff and Joyce drove by the rooming house where Berry had been living while waiting for his wife to come to New York to select their new home from two fine places he had scouted. The owner of the rooming house was not at home, so Atanasoff and Joyce went to the police station where Atanasoff read the official investigation reports of the "possible suicide."

Those reports said that the owner of the rooming house noticed Berry's car was in the parking lot and that there was no sign of activity in Berry's room, so he had investigated. He found Berry dead in his bed with a plastic clothing bag over his head, the covers pulled up to his chin, and his hands lying by his sides. Atanasoff pointed out that both he and Berry's wife, Jean, had doubts that Berry was the type who would commit suicide and that he had no reason to take his own life.

The detective who had been in charge of the investigation of Berry's death said there were some liquor bottles in the room, and indications that Dr. Berry had been drinking. However, the amount of liquor in Berry's blood was not high enough to have convicted him of drunken driving during those years, Atanasoff noted.

The detective said there had been a rash of deaths of people in that Long Island area who had died with plastic clothing bags over their heads. Some were unexplained, but the police officer said one of those who had died from suffocation from a clothing bag had been a college student who had wanted to experiment and record how it felt to die, but did not actually intend to take his own life.

At the rooming house Atanasoff found the owner, who very carefully spelled out how he had entered the room and found Berry in bed with the plastic bag over his head. He said he had grabbed the bag from Berry's head, found that Berry was already dead, and had called the police. He described how Berry was lying in bed with the blankets pulled up to his chin and his hands at his sides. Atanasoff said he found it strange that there would be no signs that Dr. Berry had been threshing about as would be expected in the body's instinctive defense against such a suffocation.

After getting an expert medical opinion supportive of his own assumption that a certain amount of threshing about is the body's instinctive defense against suffocation, Atanasoff sought to convince the police to reopen the investigation of Berry's death. "I convinced the investigator that there was merit in reopening the investigation of Cliff Berry's death, but he was overruled by his boss who said there was no point in going back into it after so many years had passed."

Because of the inconclusive nature of the investigation of Cliff Berry's death, Atanasoff remained convinced that there might have been "foul play" involved in the death, and Jean Berry was of a similar mind.

There were still more fruitful points to be pinned down in the efforts of the Control Data and Honeywell lawyers to try to break the Sperry Rand patents on the "regenerative memory" in EDVAC and in the group of patents known as "The ENIAC patents."

On 1 November 1967 Call wrote a memorandum in which he tried to sum up the importance of "Atanasoff's disclosures to Mauchly of the concept of an 'Electronic Numerical Integrator and Computer.'" That memorandum was written to D. D. Allegretti, Henry Halladay, and Henry Hanson to brief them on his analysis of the evidence now that Mauchly's first deposition had been taken, and after the interviews with Sam Legvold, Dr. Robert Mather, and Lura Atanasoff.

It now appears that Dr. Atanasoff's ideas extended well beyond those which were embodied in the computer which was under construction at the same time John Mauchly visited the Iowa State campus in June of 1941. Of particular significance, Dr. Atanasoff had developed a plan by which he could modify his computer to accomplish "electronic numerical integration." Those ideas appear to have been disclosed to Dr. Mauchly. Significantly, Mauchly's August, 1942 memorandum (which suggested the so-called "original idea" for ENIAC) is apparently patterned closely after this additional scheme which Dr. Atanasoff had in mind.

In that memorandum, Call analyzed the exchanges of correspondence between Atanasoff and Mauchly in 1942, and what they might indicate relative to the breadth of the "free and open" discussions that Atanasoff said took place with Mauchly. Call said his deductions were supported by specific details in Mauchly's letters to Atanasoff after the June 1941 visit. He spelled them out:

It should first be noted that Mauchly, in asking permission to use Atanasoff's ideas, differentiated between (1) computers which would incorporate only some of the features of Atanasoff's machine and (2) the "Atanasoff Calculator (a la Bush Analyzer)." Mauchly (at the time) apparently considered the latter device to be Atanasoff's property in its entirety.

Moreover, it is noteworthy that Mauchly apparently felt that the shorthand expression "Atanasoff Calculator (a la Bush Analyzer)" would be fully understood by Atanasoff without further explanation. Thus, the conclusion is unescapable that Atanasoff in fact had something rather definite in mind, that Mauchly understood it well enough to believe that he could build one at the Moore School with further information, and that Mauchly felt that Atanasoff's permission would be definitely required if the Moore School was to build such a device.

Call concluded his eight-page memorandum:

It is quite clear that the modification which Atanasoff proposed for his existing machine would yield a device which could quite accurately be called an "Electronic Numerical Integrator and Computer"—an ENIAC. Although few (if any) claims in the ENIAC patent are directed to the concept of numerical integration, the facts surrounding this concept provide a convincing illustration of the remarkable scope of Atanasoff's work and the manner in which this work so strongly influenced the development of the ENIAC machine.

It was only about two weeks later that the Honeywell lawyers received a telephone call from Atanasoff informing them that he had received a call from Mauchly. It was the first Atanasoff had heard from Mauchly in years, and he was surprised and inwardly annoyed when Mauchly first identified himself.

The purpose of Mauchly's call was to ask Atanasoff to see him and a lawyer for Sperry Rand. Atanasoff was cautious in his conversation, and had his wife, Alice, get on the extension to take notes as they talked. Atanasoff was curious as to the purpose of the request, but said he would be willing to meet with Mauchly and the lawyer. At some time that was mutually convenient, Mauchly and his lawyer could come out to the Atanasoff country home in Maryland, JV told Mauchly.

As soon as he completed the conversation with Mauchly, JV and Alice talked over the possible purpose of the call and decided that the wise course was to consult with lawyers for Honeywell and Control Data and let them decide if the tentative meeting plans should proceed.

After brief consultation, the lawyers agreed that if Atanasoff did not reveal the details of the file of correspondence or other documents he had there was nothing to be lost in trying to find out what the Sperry Rand lawyer had on his mind. Atanasoff assured the Honeywell and Control Data lawyers he would play his cards close to his vest, but he, too, was curious about what Mauchly and the Sperry Rand lawyer had on their minds.

CHAPTER 13

Dr. Mauchly Calls—Pleads a Poor Memory

O N the afternoon of 10 November 1967 John Mauchly called to ask if Atanasoff could see Laurence B. Dodds, the Sperry Rand lawyer, "some time after Thanksgiving." It was agreed that Mauchly would try to set up a time to accommodate the schedules of both men. Mauchly explained that Dodds represented Sperry Rand in litigation involving Control Data and that his was a busy schedule.

In an effort to remove any apprehensions that Atanasoff might have, Mauchly assured him that Dodds "seems to be a very nice man." Then as an afterthought he told Atanasoff that he had believed that Control Data lawyer Allen Kirkpatrick "was a nice man . . . then later he put on the thumbscrews, and then he tightened them."

Mauchly explained that he had been subpoenaed in the *Control Data v. Sperry Rand* case and had been asked to bring all of his correspondence and records from the Moore School.

"To my surprise I was shown correspondence with you and of course I identified them although I had completely forgotten their existence," Mauchly said.

Atanasoff replied that perhaps he should get a copy of Mauchly's deposition and read it, not letting on to Mauchly that he had already read the Mauchly deposition with alternating currents of amusement at Kirkpatrick's questions and irritation at Mauchly's evasions and misrepresentations about his Iowa trip.

"Maybe you should, if you have time to waste," Mauchly commented and continued, "Maybe you will be mad at me when you see what I said."

At first Atanasoff was going to overlook this remark, but thought better of it. "What did you say to make me mad?" he asked.

"Several things," Mauchly responded. "Perhaps the worst was that when you got into administrative work you lost interest in computers."

"Well, maybe I did seem to, perforce," Atanasoff sparred gently and Mauchly replied: "Well yes, maybe perforce."

Mauchly then remarked that he had seen a long list of witnesses in the Honeywell case and that "fully half were from Ames."

"This Ames business interests me," Atanasoff said, feigning ignorance of the list. "Something seems to have happened out at Ames."

"Something must have," Mauchly commented and added that "Mrs. Berry was on the list and not Clifford," and said he "assumed Clifford is dead." Mauchly speculated that Clifford's death must have been recent since he had seen a letter that Clifford had written to Richards stating that Mauchly was the only one whom he and Atanasoff had told about the computer machine "in full."

"Clifford must have forgotten about Caldwell," Mauchly said, and Atanasoff interrupted to declare that Caldwell was one of many people with grant committees or within the Research Foundation who "had been told something about the machine, but that very few were given a full disclosure."

Atanasoff responded pointedly, and with the knowledge that Mauchly had denied under oath that he had been given the "full disclosure" to the Atanasoff Berry Computer.

Most of the conversation was of a polite, even an overly polite, nature with Mauchly trying to exude a friendly interest in Atanasoff after more than twenty years of no communication. There was one sharply critical comment by Mauchly. He complained that Control Data attorney Kirkpatrick "practically accused me of plagiarizing everything I've done."

Atanasoff didn't believe that Mauchly's complaint deserved any sympathetic comment, and the conversation ended.

The meeting with Dodds was set for Saturday, 16 December, at 10 A.M. Mauchly arrived at 10:05 A.M. and they visited pleasantly enough until Laurence B. Dodds arrived a full hour late.

As the conversation with Dodds started, Atanasoff informed him he was willing to talk in general about the case but would not discuss the details of what he intended to say in deposition. Then

Atanasoff gave Dodds and Mauchly a brief direct summary of Mauchly's visit to Ames.

"Dr. Mauchly came to Ames on approximately June 15, 1941. He spent considerable time with the machine; he understood it fully, and in substantially every detail," Atanasoff declared. "If you don't like it, that is just too bad because those were the facts. The court must decide if this is derivation."

Mauchly sat silent and made no specific challenge, but said quietly: "You are taking a very positive posture which I cannot take. Your memory must be better than mine."

Somewhat later in the conversation, Mauchly asked: "Do you contend I read the booklet?"

Atanasoff replied at first that he would reserve the answer to that question for the deposition, and then snapped; "However, the answer is yes, and also you asked me if you could take a copy home with you. I denied that request and so you did not take a copy away."

"Will you treat us as well as our opponents?" Dodds asked in an effort to change the subject but Atanasoff's answer to that question was hardly what he was seeking.

"I do not see why I should place you and your opponents on exactly the same footing," Atanasoff replied. "It is obviously to your advantage to prove that there was no development of a computing machine at Ames, Iowa. Your opponents contend the contrary and my interests must lie in that direction."

Dodds tried to make the best of a bad situation by asking: "Do our opponents know exactly what testimony you will give on deposition?"

"They may know some testimony that I will give," Atanasoff replied avoiding specifics. "In part I will have to say a great many things they know to be true. However, in general they do not know what I will say on deposition and to some degree my own mind is not completely made up as to what happened. It will require research and refreshment of my memory to determine what is said in deposition."

"Are there other people alive who read the manuscript at the time at which it was first issued?" Dodds fished for details.

"Well, you know that the manuscript was not only sent to the Research Corporation, but was also sent to the Scientific Aids for Learning, a subsidiary of the Carnegie Corporation, and to the Natural Science Division of the Rockefeller Foundation," Atanasoff replied. "Presumably, these organizations read the manuscript at that time and they may have referred the manuscript to other persons who read it. I have tried to retrieve files from these other places and would be happy if you could succeed where I could not."

Atanasoff said he had not known "what was contained in the '827' patent (on regenerative memory) and in the ENIAC patent until this last summer."

"I must admit that when I read these patents I was somewhat appalled to find that these patents duplicated my own efforts in their claims. In particular, the '827' patent almost exactly described my own apparatus in its specifications," Atanasoff said.

Dodds interrupted to declare: "Well specifications do not matter, it is what is contained in the claims that count. We contend that that patent does not touch upon the work that you did in its claims, that its claims are much more specific and much different from what you actually accomplished."

"Alice," Atanasoff called to his wife. "Get me a copy of patent '827.' "

While Alice Atanasoff was going to the files, Mauchly asked which patent was covered by "827," and added: "You see how bad my memory is."

When Alice Atanasoff returned with the so-called 827 patent, Atanasoff read it aloud to Dodds and Mauchly with Dodds following it on his copy, and when he finished Atanasoff declared: "That is exactly what I constructed."

"What is the difference between that claim and what I had in my material possession at the time Mauchly visited me?" Atanasoff addressed the question to Dodds and Mauchly and neither gave an answer to that question.

Dodds asked Atanasoff if it was his contention "that your work bears upon the ENIAC patent?"

Atanasoff responded that he had worked upon the ENIAC patents for "a number of days, and I do not pretend to understand it."

When Dodds commented that he did not understand it either, Atanasoff continued: "The answer to your question is 'yes,' I really believe that there are claims in there related to the work which I did."

"I believe there was no regenerative memory in the ENIAC patent," Dodds commented and Atanasoff responded:

"Yes, but there was interaction of logic circuits in the computing elements and that is an item which is derived from my work."

Dodds, the lawyer, quietly answered: "Yes, there are logic circuits in the ENIAC patents." Mauchly remained a silent observer. It was the posture he took through most of the morning.

As they were breaking the serious business for lunch, Mauchly commented on Atanasoff's keen memory, and Atanasoff commented that the lawyers he was working with had urged him to try to remember all the reports, correspondence, and witnesses who might refresh or confirm his recollections of the period when he was working on the Atanasoff Berry Computer and particularly about Mauchly's visit.

"Our lawyers don't want me to remember anything," Mauchly declared.

During the conversation with Dodds, Atanasoff said that he had spent over 2,000 hours in the study of patent law, and during the lunch break he asked in an earnest way: "Mr. Dodds, in the face of the facts, how do you expect to win this case?"

A suddenly irritated Dodds answered sharply: "There are some things which are not contained in your 2,000 hours of study [of patent law]. You don't know anything about how federal judges are likely to act. They may decide that question upon their own impulse instead of fact, law or reason."

Atanasoff did not respond, and sat quietly musing over Dodds's explanation of why Sperry Rand might win the case. Dodds reconsidered his comments on the judicial process and explained his comments further.

"However, I should say that the judge at Baltimore, Judge Watkins, is a very learned and able judge and I do not believe that will happen," Dodds said in an effort to appear more lawyerlike in responding to Atanasoff's question without really answering him.

When Dodds later stated as a matter of fact that "there is no testimony except yours," Atanasoff let it pass without mention of the corroboration he knew would be forthcoming from Professor Sam Legvold, from Lura Atanasoff, and others, as well as the dozens of letters and documents that would confirm the status of the Atanasoff Berry Computer at the time of Mauchly's visit to Ames.

Atanasoff was privately amused as he imagined the surprise and shock when Dodds and Mauchly would first hear Sam Legvold testify that he had seen Mauchly working on the Atanasoff Berry Computer "for two days with his sleeves rolled up."

Obviously disturbing to Dodds and Mauchly was Atanasoff's comment that Norman Fulmer, then a member of the computing patent staff for General Electric, was a graduate of Iowa State College and had been employed for a time on the construction of the Atanasoff Berry Computer. General Electric was one of the large computer firms involved in patent disputes with Sperry Rand.

The gentle sparring continued between Dodds and Atanasoff for about two hours after lunch. Shortly before 3 P.M. Dodds said he had to catch a plane in Baltimore and would have to leave. Atanasoff and Alice had expected Mauchly to depart with him, and they were somewhat surprised that he lingered on without explanation.

Mauchly did comment that Sperry Rand was paying him handsomely as "a consultant" for his work in preparing for the patent litigation, and indicated that Atanasoff might be able to make similar arrangements.

Atanasoff passed by the opportunity to ask just what Mauchly's arrangements were because it could lead rather naturally to a question of his own financial arrangements with Control Data and Honeywell.

As Atanasoff, in a pleasant enough manner, continued to stress his own clear memory of events related to Mauchly's 1941 visit to Iowa State, Mauchly stated that his instructions from Sperry Rand lawyers had been that he should not concern himself with attempting to reconstruct any details of that visit to Ames, but to remember only casually what he could and otherwise to simply state that he had forgotten. Earlier, with Dodds still present, Mauchly had mentioned in a half-facetious comment to Atanasoff that his lawyers didn't "want me to remember anything."

With Dodds gone, Mauchly related the suggestion that he make no great effort to remember details of the Iowa State visit "as exhibiting a rather casual attitude on Dodds's part." To Atanasoff these comments by Mauchly indicated a poor communication between Dodds and Mauchly for he read it as a subtle invitation for Mauchly to forget as much as possible about the Ames visit. "If this was his [Dodds's] design he failed to take Dr. Mauchly fully aboard because he [Dr. Mauchly] was openly stating that Dodds had invited him not to remember," Atanasoff said later.

Throughout the late afternoon the conversation wandered in and out of Mauchly's memory problem. On at least two occasions he, Mauchly, made reference to the letter that Clifford Berry had written to Richards in which he said "Dr. Mauchly . . . who spent a week (at Iowa State) learning all of the details of our computer and the philosophy of its design. . . ."

That one paragraph in Berry's letter of 22 March 1963 was testimony from the grave that haunted Mauchly and troubled Attorney Dodds. The factual and nonaccusatory tone of that letter made it an extremely difficult hurdle to jump, for it was written long before the litigation started, with no apparent motive other than to help Richards write an accurate history of the Atanasoff Berry machine.

During the afternoon, the conversation rambled and Mauchly told Atanasoff that the Mauchly-Eckert Corporation had received a half million dollars at the time IBM settled with Sperry Rand for the sum of 10 million dollars. Mauchly complained that the contract with Sperry Rand required that all of the royalties he and Eckert received be regarded as "personal services" so the corporation could write it off as expenses, but this meant Mauchly and Eckert had to pay taxes on the money they received as ordinary income.

While Atanasoff did not grieve for Mauchly or Eckert, he was interested in all the financial details that Mauchly was willing to give him. The tone of the conversation was friendly enough with Atanasoff chiding him about his three-pack-a-day smoking habit and berating him with his often-repeated "quit smoking" lecture.

All in all, it was not an unpleasant afternoon and dinner hour. Mauchly expressed his pleasure at the hospitality he received, and Atanasoff had "the impression that Dr. Mauchly was genuinely pleased to find that he had not entirely deprived me of living substance."

After Mauchly left, Atanasoff had an uneasy feeling that he might have said something in the conversations with Dodds or Mauchly that he would regret when he testified in depositions or at the trial. However, he could not think of what it might be, and lawyers for Honeywell and Control Data were not at all displeased with the report on his exchanges with Dodds and Mauchly.

Atanasoff was pleased with the reports of the depositions taken in the first week of December from Sam Legvold, Lura Atanasoff, and R. K. Richards, the author whose research on computer history had produced the important correspondence from Berry. Under oath, Professor Legvold and Lura Atanasoff had been even better than in the earlier interviews.

While Richards was a generally reluctant witness, the record of his correspondence with Berry was an invaluable window on the past that would have been otherwise closed with Berry's mysterious death.

In December 1967 Allen Kirkpatrick decided that it would be helpful to Control Data's case against Sperry Rand if Atanasoff could take the computer papers he had drawn up in 1940 and 1941 and build a prototype of the electronic digital computer machine similar to the one he and Cliff Berry had constructed in the basement of the Physics Building at Iowa State.

Atanasoff said he would go Kirkpatrick one better. He said he and Alice would order the material needed, and then he would let two or three of his electronics technicians in his Rockville, Maryland, shop do the construction job with a minimum of guidance from him.

"It will demonstrate that the plans we had then and have today would construct an operational automatic electronic digital computer," Atanasoff said. He and Alice started work immediately to assemble the material for the reconstruction of the major parts of the Atanasoff Berry machine, and they were even able to get some of the hard-to-find 1930 vintage tubes that were used in the original machine.

Call, Allegretti, and Halladay, the lawyers for Honeywell, applauded the Control Data project, which they hoped they might be able to use when their case came up for trial. But there were still months of jurisdictional fights, depositions, and other legal jockeying before the trial would start in U.S. District Court in Minneapolis.

CHAPTER 14

Jockeying of Computer Giants: Pretrial, 1968–1969

I N January 1968 Atanasoff proceeded with the pretrial project of having his electronics experts at his Frederick, Maryland, plant construct a replica of the prototype computer he and Cliff Berry had constructed more than twenty-five years earlier at Iowa State College. They were to use the project plans that Atanasoff and his graduate student, Berry, had drawn, and Atanasoff decided to give his workmen only a minimum of guidance to see if they could build a successful operational electronic digital computer from his plans.

Control Data officials had suggested the project, and had plans to use it in their suit against Sperry Rand in the U.S. District Court in Baltimore. However, it was understood that the replica of the Atanasoff prototype could be used in connection with Atanasoff's testimony in the Honeywell litigation against Sperry Rand in the U.S. District Court in Minneapolis. Because of Atanasoff's age and health problems, the deposition was videotaped with agreement that it could be used in trial if Atanasoff was unavailable.

Atanasoff was excited about the project in which he could establish clearly that sketches, ideas, and plans he had made available to Mauchly in June 1941 could be used to construct a prototype electronic digital computer. Presentation of such a machine in court should, with finality, demolish Mauchly's contention that he didn't learn anything from his examination of the Atanasoff Berry Computer, his examination of the plans, or his conversations with Atanasoff or Cliff Berry.

Alice Atanasoff did considerable shopping around before she was able to acquire the rather antiquated 1939–1940 era tubes that were used in the original Atanasoff Berry Computer. Both JV and Alice were highly enthusiastic about what they considered the grand opportunity to establish the falsity of Mauchly's contention that the machine he saw and studied at Iowa State College was "a little pile of junk that wouldn't do anything."

The Control Data litigation in Baltimore involved the so-called 827 patent dealing with the regenerative memory patents in ED-VAC. The Honeywell litigation against Sperry Rand in Minneapolis involved the more general ENIAC patents involved in the construction of ENIAC at the Moore School of Electrical Engineering and also the follow-on, EDVAC, which also was built at the Moore School.

As is usually true in complicated litigations in federal courts, it was impossible to make any judgment as to which case would go first and as to which one would be decided first. So lawyers for Control Data and lawyers for Honeywell were making their plans independently, cooperating on many aspects of the challenges to Sperry Rand.

Atanasoff was working with lawyers for Control Data and for Honeywell, but he believed that the Control Data case involving the regenerative memory 827 patent would be the easiest to challenge directly and conclusively. The Honeywell case involved a multiplicity of complicated claims of concepts in the ENIAC machine, and they would be much more difficult to prove if Mauchly was able to establish any degree of credibility.

Since the U.S. Patent Office had issued the ENIAC patents only after years of examination of the information available involving "prior art" and other claims, the burden of proof would be on the challengers to establish fraud or misrepresentations. Sperry Rand's defense was based upon Mauchly's claim that he had been thinking about the concepts involved in ENIAC at Ursinus College in 1938 and 1939, prior to the December day in 1940 when he met Atanasoff for the first time. Until Mauchly was questioned in a discovery deposition, it would not be possible to determine if he had documents or witnesses to corroborate his claims of work on electronic digital computer concepts prior to December 1940.

As long as there was no reason to disbelieve Mauchly, or to believe that he was intentionally telling a false story, the Sperry Rand patents would probably withstand the challenge regardless of the brilliance of the work done by Atanasoff and Cliff Berry at Iowa State College.

The task for the Honeywell and Control Data lawyers was to prove that the Atanasoff Berry Computer represented a pioneer development in electronic digital computing, and also to prove that Atanasoff was such a credible witness that the judge or jury would believe his testimony even when it contradicted the story told by Mauchly. In brief, it meant that lawyers for Honeywell, Control Data, or any other challengers had to prove that Mauchly was a willful liar, or so mixed up, confused, and unreliable as to lack credibility.

With that substantial task in front of them, Honeywell lawyers were in search of every scrap of evidence that would support Atanasoff generally and that would corroborate his testimony specifically on the points at odds with Mauchly's statements of fact or even Mauchly's general recollections of what he knew and when he knew it.

In the summer of 1968 lawyers for Honeywell and Control Data issued subpoenas for all the relevant records from the files of Sperry Rand, IBM, and the Moore School of Electrical Engineering, as well as any personal records that might be in the possession of Mauchly or Eckert related to the ENIAC or EDVAC projects. They also sought to depose all witnesses whose testimony would support the credibility of Atanasoff or challenge or contradict Mauchly.

The construction of the replica of the prototype of the Atanasoff Berry Computer was completed in the summer, and it worked so well that Atanasoff went into his own pocket to finance construction of a second one. To some degree it patched up the wound his soul and pride had suffered when he was told of the thoughtless dismantling of the original Atanasoff Berry Computer at Iowa State.

Late in October 1968 lawyers for Honeywell had a momentary disappointment when they subpoenaed Mauchly for three days of discovery testimony. When Mauchly showed up for the deposition, he had only a few records explaining that those scanty records were all he could find. The Honeywell lawyers were certain that he had not looked very hard and warned him that the procedures required that he search more diligently for all the relevant records.

Although they were disappointed with the small amount of records produced by Mauchly, they used the opportunity to put him through an intensive three days of questioning of every aspect of his story trying to pin him down on some important details and to establish his claimed lack of recollection relative to his assertion that he had thought of the ENIAC patent concepts before his December 1941 meeting with Atanasoff in Philadelphia. They also questioned him about his visit to Iowa State in June 1941, and to some extent about his correspondence with Atanasoff before and after that 1941 visit to Iowa State.

There was no intensive effort by Honeywell lawyers to challenge Mauchly or to question him in other than a totally civilized manner. They realized that his professed lack of memory on many highly relevant points was a potential vulnerability that might be exploited at trial. That professed lack of memory in many instances involved a claim that he could not recall the names of persons who he said had heard his views on electronic digital computing concepts prior to December 1940.

The Honeywell lawyers recognized that such a professed lack of memory might be a skillful trap. Mauchly's consistent and persistent comments about his faulty memory could be his response to his lawyers' suggestion that he had once related to Atanasoff that "the less you remember the better."

The man who claimed to be the co-inventor of the first electronic digital computer still contended that he had not stolen, or inadvertently copied, any of those concepts from Atanasoff. In making that claim, Mauchly continued to make derogatory remarks about the Atanasoff Berry Computer and to contend he had learned nothing from conversations with Atanasoff or Berry. It was "an incomplete machine," Mauchly said. It "would not do" the things that Atanasoff said it would do.

Mauchly fumbled to some degree when he tried to explain how he knew that the machine was incomplete and useless after having paid as little attention to it as he contended he did. The Honeywell lawyers did not push the issue on the contradiction of his testimony and his letters to Atanasoff in which he praised the computer he had seen at Iowa State.

When Mauchly's deposition was concluded on 31 October 1968, Honeywell lawyers were optimistic that they could win the case even if Mauchly had either intentionally, or inadvertently, destroyed correspondence and other records that they knew had existed at some time. However, their case was to a large degree contingent upon the availability of Atanasoff as a witness.

While Atanasoff was an eager and well-corroborated witness, he had turned sixty-five years of age in October, and he did have a history of some nagging health problems that could incapacitate him or otherwise make him unavailable for testimony in the trial. Steps were taken immediately to obtain his deposition under arrangements that his sworn testimony would be available for use in the trial if for any reason Atanasoff was unavailable.

In keeping with that arrangement, Atanasoff's deposition started on 11 November 1968 and proceeded for five days of that week. The second section of Atanasoff's deposition commenced on 3 December and concluded 6 December.

That long and tiring deposition was a good trial run for Atanasoff, but under conditions that were considerably less formal than in the courtroom of a U.S. courthouse.

The direct examination carried him through the story of his life; his early aptitude for mathematics, his education in electrical engineering at the University of Florida, his education at Iowa State College and at the University of Wisconsin.

In setting out his qualifications and background for his invention of the first electronic digital computer, the Honeywell lawyers filled the record with his papers on related mathematical projects and with the theses of his many students in the period from 1930 to his story of the long drive to the Illinois roadhouse. While there was no corroboration for the trip itself, there were bushels of documents to support his testimony on his work in 1938 and 1939 that laid the groundwork for his first application for a grant to build the prototype computer.

On the whole, Atanasoff's deposition was a huge success. It had demonstrated his comprehensive background and long-time interest in obtaining a mechanism that would speed up complicated mathematical computations, and it pinned down his testimony under oath in a form that could be used by lawyers for Honeywell in the event their key witness would be stricken ill. It had also demonstrated areas where Atanasoff had to be more careful in his choice of rhetoric to avoid confusing the picture.

Atanasoff was fast becoming a precocious student of the ways of the courtroom. In the nine days of deposition in mid-November and the first week of December, he became more sensitive to the kind of information the Honeywell lawyers were seeking, and he became wise in anticipating the traps the Sperry Rand lawyers might be setting with seemingly innocuous lines of questioning.

For the Honeywell lawyers, the nine days of deposition were helpful in pinpointing areas in which they should do further investigations to provide even more corroboration for their key witness – John Atanasoff – and to iron out the little seeming inconsistencies that might exist between his testimony and other witnesses.

The deposition testimony of Atanasoff set the stage for the Honeywell lawyers to put Mauchly under oath for further questioning, and to see if it might be possible to persuade him to produce more of the correspondence and other records that they were certain had existed at some time.

On 28 April 1969, when Mauchly appeared for that second session of questioning under oath, he produced a trunk full of records and correspondence. While Henry Halladay, the Minneapolis trial lawyer, proceeded with extensive questioning, Charles Call started to go through Mauchly's trunk of documents.

It was a bonanza of relevant documents that was nearly as important as the documents they found at Atanasoff's home in August 1967. Some of Mauchly's letters to friends and colleagues in 1941 had made reference to his trip to Iowa State and his discovery of the Atanasoff Berry Computer that would perform all kinds of complicated mathematical feats.

Call handed some of these documents to Henry Halladay, who used the information skillfully to get Mauchly to make admissions beyond what the documents themselves would clearly establish. The questioning of Mauchly went on through 28, 29, and 30 April 1969, and then was resumed again on 6 May for four more days. When this deposing of Mauchly was concluded on 9 May, attorneys Halladay and Call were immensely pleased. The documents from Mauchly's trunk were helpful in answering many unanswered questions and in establishing that the Pennsylvania physicist and mathematician had expressed enthusiasm about Atanasoff's computer machine and had commented specifically about the feats it would perform.

Some of these documents were used by Halladay in his questioning of Mauchly, but others were simply copied for further investigation and study and for possible use at the trial. There was a lot of work to be done by Call to integrate those documents chronologically into the massive files that were being prepared for the trial. The Honeywell challenge to the Sperry Rand patents was being put together in a computerized record called "ELF" for Electronic Legal Files. ELF made it possible for the Honeywell litigation team to call up and print out vast amounts of chronological information on hundreds of different subjects.

That huge computerized record permitted the Honeywell litigation team to retrieve almost instantaneously the testimony of any witness with regard to any transaction or document, but before that computerized record could do these marvelous tricks, someone had to organize the material and get it into the computer in a usable fashion. That was Call's job, with the help of several secretaries.

As marvelous as the computer was at retrieving vast amounts of specific information upon demand, the trial lawyer, Henry Halladay, had to have a grasp of the totality of the picture in his own mind, including the detailed phrases in the letters, the conversations between Atanasoff and Mauchly, and specific chronological details that were relevant. In the examination or cross-examination of witnesses a trial lawyer could rely to some degree upon reference to papers and large charts, but, except in unusual circumstances, total effectiveness was contingent upon a fast and systematic flow of questions.

The Honeywell lawyers knew they had to be prepared for every possible development and strategy by the Sperry Rand Corporation lawyers, for hundreds of millions of dollars were at stake in the patents Sperry Rand acquired from Mauchly and Eckert. When the trial was concluded, it would be too late to look back and wish that there had been more research done on the background of witnesses, and it would be too late to wish that some lead had been explored.

Although they had spent more than two years in the investigation by the time they obtained the trunk of records at Mauchly's April 1969 deposition, there was still much more work to be done before the case would go to trial before the U.S. District Judge Earl R. Larson in Minneapolis, Minnesota.

CHAPTER 15

Judge Earl R. Larson: Making the Computer History Record

U NITED STATES District Judge Earl Richard Larson came to an early conclusion that the Honeywell case against Sperry Rand would be a long and complicated one, and that it would consume essentially all of the time of one of the U.S. District judges in Minnesota for a period of at least a year. However, at the time the case jurisdiction was finally established in Minnesota, Judge Larson did not suspect that the litigation would continue for nearly five years and be one of the longest cases in the history of the federal courts in the United States.

For months Sperry Rand and Honeywell had engaged in a tug-of-war over whether the case should be tried in Washington, D.C., or Minneapolis. While Honeywell had won the race to the court-house by a few minutes, the Sperry Rand lawyers kept the dispute alive for several months because of their desire to have the plaintiff's initiative in setting the issues and because Washington, D.C., was regarded as a jurisdiction that was more favorable to established patent rights.

The jurisdiction was finally placed in Minnesota when U.S. Judge John Sirica, the Chief Judge in the District of Columbia, ruled that Honeywell had won the jurisdictional footrace by a few minutes. He also stated that the federal court dockets in the nation's capitol were so crowded that it would be impractical to find a judge who could give the case the time it merited.

From the outset, it was apparent to Judge Larson that this was an important case involving patent rights worth hundreds of millions of dollars and perhaps several billion dollars over a period of years. Both Sperry Rand and Honeywell already had spent several million dollars on investigations and preliminary legal jockeying, and there would be no lack of funds for further investigations and legal maneuvers by both sides.

Lawyers for Sperry Rand had been successful in defeating the patent challenges by Bell Laboratories only a few years earlier, and that decision in the U.S. Court in New York stood as a barrier for Honeywell. Also, the patents owned by Sperry Rand had been issued by the U.S. Patent Office, and there was a legal presumption that they were valid patents. The presumption on the validity of the patents could be defeated only if there was a substantial amount of new evidence demonstrating that the claims made were false or fraudulent or were derived from the inventions of others.

With the huge financial resources available to both parties to this dispute, it was almost certain that any decision would be appealed if any error could be pinpointed. The spotlighting of error in such an important case could do serious permanent damage to a judge's reputation. Judge Larson knew it would be a great challenge, and it would also take a tremendous amount of hard work over an extended period of time.

Judge Larson, fifty-eight years old at the time he took jurisdiction of the case, was accustomed to hard work and to making tough and difficult decisions. His excellent physical condition and his whole background made him an almost ideal judge to try this long and complicated case. As the oldest of four children of Swedish immigrant parents, Axel and Hannah Johnson Larson, Earl Larson was strongly disciplined by his childhood work experiences.

His father, a janitor in a downtown Minneapolis office building, died during a flu epidemic when Earl was only seven years old. Earl then carried newspapers and did odd jobs to help his mother support the three younger children, and a few years later he and his brother started working as caddies at a Minneapolis golf course.

The job as a caddy and the easy access to the golf course set the stage for him to be self-sufficient financially and to help put himself and his two brothers and sister through high school and college. He was Caddy Master during the six years he was at the University of Minnesota as an undergraduate and as a law student at the University of Minnesota Law School.

He won his varsity letter in golf in 1931, 1932, and 1933, and was captain of the golf team in 1932 and in 1933. Although he was an outstanding athlete, he did not let that interfere with his work in the classroom or in other college activities.

Earl was an "A" student during his years at North High School in Minneapolis and was graduated from the University of Minnesota cum laude with an L.L.B. degree in 1935. At the University of Minnesota he was chairman of Homecoming in 1933 and president of All University Student Council in 1934–1935. But Earl Larson's proudest achievement at the university was his leadership role in establishing a campus political group outside of the fraternity system that was known as the Jacobins Club (named for the French Revolutionary group). In that group, Larson was associated with CBS News Analyst Eric Sevareid; Richard Scammon, later an outstanding nationally known political analyst; and Lee Loevinger, a Minnesota Supreme Court Judge and U.S. Federal Communications Commission member.

Upon graduating from law school, Earl Larson practiced law in Minneapolis for four years before being named an Assistant U.S. Attorney in St. Paul in 1940. While in the U.S. Attorney's office in St. Paul, he successfully prosecuted a group of Minnesota Trotsky-ites on federal charges of subversive activities. During this period he was selected to be a trial attorney for the Justice Department and was involved in the investigation and the successful prosecution of Boston Mayor James Michael Curley on fraud charges related to government contracts.

He was in service in the U.S. Navy between 1943 and 1946 as a lieutenant (senior grade) in Naval Air Intelligence. In 1946 he established a law firm with Leonard Lindquist, who later became a state legislator and a Minnesota Railroad and Warehouse Commission member, and Lee Loevinger, later a member of the Federal Communications Commission. Later on, former Vice-President Walter Mondale, former Agriculture Secretary Orville Freeman, and former Congressman Donald Frasier were members of that firm as they were starting up the political ladder. Earl Larson was also a lecturer in Business Law at the School of Business Administration at the University of Minnesota (1946–1953). He remained in the law firm until 1961 when he was nominated to be a U.S. District Judge by President John F. Kennedy. That nomination was on the recommendation of Senators Hubert H. Humphrey and Eugene McCarthy. In 1968 Judge Larson was named by Chief Justice Earl Warren to the Judicial Conference Committee on the Administration of the Criminal Law.

By the time he took on the Honeywell-Sperry Rand case he had

[*Left*] Judge Earl R. Larson, U.S. District Judge in Minnesota who presided in the Honeywell case, ruling that Atanasoff and Berry invented the first electronic digital computer. [*Below*] John W. Mauchly holding a section of the BINAC circuitry. (*Courtesy of the Hagley Museum and Library, Wilmington, Delaware*)

[*Above*] J. Presper Eckert with the BINAC memory bank. (*Courtesy of the Hagley Museum and Library, Wilmington, Delaware*)

R. K. Richards of Ames, Iowa, in 1964, an inventor of various computers, components, and circuits and author of a number of books on computers.

Allan R. Mackintosh, distinguished theoretic physicist.

Dr. Sam Legvold, distinguished former Iowa State University professor and key corroborative witness for JV. (*Courtesy of Lavona Legvold*)

Henry L. Hanson, Iowa State College graduate of 1943 and later general counsel for Honeywell. (*From 1943* Bomb)

Henry Halladay, Honeywell trial lawyer, January 1959. (*Courtesy of Dorsey and Whitney, Minneapolis, Minnesota*)

Kevin Joyce, Control Data lawyer, who accompanied JV to New York to investigate the death of Clifford Berry.

Allen Kirkpatrick, Control Data lawyer, who first contacted JV in the spring of 1967.

Charles Call, Honeywell lawyer.

D. Dennis Allegretti, Honeywell lawyer.

Bernard Galler, editor, *Annals of the History of Computing.*

earned a reputation as a hardworking and serious judge who started his day in the office at 7:30 A.M. and rarely left before 6:00 P.M. Earl Larson was just the kind of judge that this patent litigation required. Although he had no scientific background or computer expertise, he was highly intelligent, patient, work oriented, and had experience with complicated investigations and business problems.

Within a few weeks of the time Judge Larson became involved in the Honeywell–Sperry Rand case, he saw that the organization of the bulky pleadings, depositions, and exhibits that would be a part of the record would represent a major problem. Simply keeping these records straight and accessible was a major task for Gerald Bergquist, the clerk of the U.S. District Court in Minneapolis. Eventually it was necessary for Judge Larson to set aside the office space that had been used by a former federal judge just to house the patent case records. Judge Larson and the personnel in Clerk Bergquist's office referred to this space as the "Honeywell–Sperry Rand Room."

Judge Larson served notice on lawyers for Honeywell and Sperry Rand that he would rely upon them to provide the expert witnesses, charts, and devices necessary to educate him about the technical problems involved in the litigation. He was confident he had the years of experience in general practice and as an adviser to corporate business clients to understand essentially any problem. Successful investigations and prosecutions and a half-dozen years as a federal judge had added to his experience and his reputation as a good judge who made a solid record.

Judge Larson was rarely reversed on appeal, and he knew that if there was any hint of reversible error in the Honeywell–Sperry Rand case, it was likely his decision would be appealed. His pride in his record as a federal judge meant that he must spare no work on the pretrial motions and proceedings, on the trial itself, or on the decision once the trial was ended and arguments made.

One of the major problems for Judge Larson was to familiarize himself with the complicated computer terminology. It was essential to understand the history of the development of the various concepts in the planning and construction of ENIAC and the contribution that Mauchly and Eckert made to that electronic digital computer. The so-called memory patent involving the follow-on EDVAC machine was not directly at issue in the Minneapolis trial, but understanding and tracing that development was important as it related to the credibility of Mauchly.

Judge Larson acknowledged his lack of technical expertise to lawyers for Honeywell and Sperry Rand, and for that reason he placed upon them the burden and the responsibility of providing expert witnesses, charts, and devices to clarify technical matters not only for the court but also to make certain that the witnesses understood and agreed on the meaning of words and concepts and the importance of certain specific dates.

Before Judge Larson had moved very far along in reading the pleadings, ruling on motions, and keeping pace with key depositions and documents, he realized that the case could involve a decision as to whether Atanasoff was the real father of the electronic digital computer – one of the most important inventions of the century.

From the standpoint of computer history, the court record of this case, including the depositions, pleadings, and trial testimony, would be as important as the hundreds of millions of dollars at stake for Sperry Rand in the challenge to the Mauchly-Eckert patents. It was a grave responsibility and Judge Earl R. Larson did not take it lightly as he spent hours and days reading the transcripts of depositions, examining exhibits, ruling on motions, and plowing through other papers that piled up in the Honeywell–Sperry Rand Room on the sixth floor of the U.S. Court House in Minneapolis.

Becoming familiar with computer history was a new and fascinating experience for Judge Larson, and the job of keeping the voluminous records organized and accessible to Judge Larson was a never ending and tedious chore for Clerk of Court Bergquist and his staff.

CHAPTER 16

Trial Preparation and
Bulgarian Interlude, 1970

OLLOWING up on their responsibility to produce witnesses and evidence to aid Judge Larson in understanding the technical concepts and the computer jargon, the Honeywell lawyers looked for expert witnesses with solid credentials. Charles G. Call consulted with the law firm's senior partner, D. Dennis Allegretti, and the Minneapolis trial lawyer, Henry Halladay, and it was decided that they should hire the Philadelphia computer consultant's firm, Auerbach Associates.

Auerbach Associates was headed by Isaac Auerbach, who was the chairman of the panel that Charles Call had seen put Mauchly on the spot in August 1967 by suggesting that Mauchly explain his trip to Iowa State College in 1941 to examine the Atanasoff Berry Computer. Isaac Auerbach had worked with Mauchly and Eckert on ENIAC and EDVAC and had considerable personal knowledge about those computer projects. However, just as important to the Honeywell lawyers was the fact that Auerbach Associates included three other highly talented computer experts – Paul Winsor III, Louis D. Wilson, and Kenneth Rose.

Winsor, Wilson, and Rose had worked on BINAC (Binary Automatic Computer), the follow-on computer to EDVAC that Mauchly and Eckert had constructed through their own firm shortly after they left the Moore School of Engineering.

The Honeywell lawyers believed they had found the ideal team to serve as expert witnesses for the following purposes:

1. To corroborate Atanasoff on various aspects of his testimony that involved highly technical explanations.

2. To educate Judge Larson with a glossary of technical computer terms.

3. To spell out the relevant history of computer development and the difference between the "analogue computer" devices that were in use before 1940 and the automatic electronic digital computer concepts in the Atanasoff Berry Computer.

4. To explain the electronic digital concepts that were embodied in the Atanasoff Berry Computer, and to demonstrate how those same concepts were present in the ENIAC and EDVAC machines that Mauchly helped construct at Moore School of Electrical Engineering.

5. To corroborate Atanasoff's explanations of the prototype of the Atanasoff Berry Computer that had been constructed at Atanasoff's company at Fredericksburg, Maryland.

6. To examine the plans for the Atanasoff Berry Computer that Atanasoff had put together in August 1940 and to explain to Judge Larson whether they believed those plans could have produced an operational and effective electronic digital computer.

7. To explain to the court what, if any, of the concepts in the Atanasoff Berry plans that Mauchly had examined in 1941 were incorporated in the ENIAC and EDVAC machines Mauchly and his associates at the Moore School had drawn in 1942 and 1943.

While the Honeywell lawyers were working with his associates Winsor, Wilson, and Rose, Isaac Auerbach went to London to attend an international conference of mathematicians. By unusual coincidence he met Dr. Blagovest Sendov, a Bulgarian mathematician who was a member of the Bulgarian Academy of Sciences. That chance meeting set the stage for events that were to be a tremendous morale booster for John Atanasoff and his wife, Alice, who were often discouraged and restive over the seemingly interminable delays involved in complicated litigation in the federal courts.

Auerbach told Sendov about the Atanasoff Berry Computer, and called his attention to the computer history by Richards that stated John Atanasoff and his graduate assistant, Cliff Berry, had constructed an electronic digital computer at Iowa State College in the 1939 to 1941 period.

When Sendov heard the name Atanasoff he became more interested. The name Atanasoff was possibly of Bulgarian origin, for names of Atanas, Atanasov and Atanasoff were as common in Bulgaria as Smith or Jones in the United States.

Blagovest Sendov, a professor of mathematics at the University of Sofia, noted that the construction of the Atanasoff Berry Computer at Iowa State predated the unveiling of ENIAC by more than five years, and that Richards had reported John W. Mauchly's visit to Iowa State to examine the Atanasoff Berry Computer in June 1941.

In Professor Sendov's mind it seemed likely that the American scientist of Bulgarian ancestry had a reasonably solid claim to being the inventor of the first electronic digital computer – one of the great inventions of the century and perhaps one of the greatest inventions in the history of the world. To Sendov, it was worth some special attention. Professor Sendov wasted no time in doing further research to confirm the information in the book by Richards, and he followed up with some inquiry on the litigation brought against Sperry Rand with regard to the ENIAC and EDVAC patents. To Sendov the outcome of the patent litigation in the U.S. courts was secondary. One point was clear to him: An American of Bulgarian ancestry had a substantial claim to one of the greatest inventions of the century.

Sendov wrote directly to Atanasoff at his Maryland farm home with the assumption that his name was of Bulgarian origin and requested a reply containing as much precise information as possible on his Bulgarian ancestors. His letter delighted JV and Alice with the discovery that someone besides the Honeywell and Control Data lawyers was giving some attention to the Atanasoff Berry Computer. Atanasoff had some recollection of the stories his father had told about his youth and his relatives in Bulgaria. Fortunately, Atanasoff's mother was visiting them at the time Sendov's letter arrived, and he immediately asked his mother to put together a comprehensive memorandum, with Alice's help, of all she could remember that her Bulgarian husband had told her about the circumstances surrounding his birth, his youth, and his family connections in Bulgaria. That memorandum was not sent to Professor Sendov, but much detailed information from it was relayed by letter to Sendov including the names of Atanasoff's relatives and his father's home community in Bulgaria.[1]

---

1. After Atanasoff's mother was widowed at seventy-five, she opted to give up her home and live successively with each of her eight children. They encouraged her to write her memoirs for her children and grandchildren, and as her eyesight failed, she taught herself to use a typewriter. One of her most successful writings was a collection of stories she remembered her husband telling of his early days in Bulgaria before he emigrated at thirteen. This material was taken to Bulgaria in 1970 and given to Sendov. By the time Atanasoff and Alice traveled to his father's village a week later, this material had been widely read and evaluated. Many of the villagers were still there and remembered the same stories. Only three small errors were discovered: the boy's mother's name was Anya, not Anna; he was forced to drink rakia, not whiskey, and by a minor Turkish official, not a Sultan.

Atanasoff's letter confirming that his father had been a Bulgarian immigrant was all Sendov needed, for he had already satisfied himself and the Bulgarian Academy of Sciences that the Atanasoff Berry Computer was probably the first electronic digital computer. In the fall of 1970 he wrote to Atanasoff inviting the Atanasoffs to Bulgaria as guests of the Bulgarian Academy of Sciences. Atanasoff contacted lawyers for Honeywell and Control Data to make sure they would not need to consult with him for several weeks, before making arrangements to accept the invitation of Professor Sendov.

At the time he made those arrangements, JV did not know that the Bulgarian Academy of Sciences would honor him as the inventor of the first electronic digital computer. However, he and Alice were excited and interested in making what would be his first visit to the country where his father was born and where it had been reported that his paternal grandfather was a patriot. According to family legend JV's father was a small baby in his father's arms when Turkish invaders of the small Bulgarian village shot JV's grandfather. (This was later confirmed.)

Atanasoff had often thought of that village and the country his father had left at thirteen years of age, but this was the first time it had been practical to think of returning and trying to look up some of the Atanasoff family members. In mid-November 1970 JV and Alice flew to Germany, bought a large Volkswagen in Wolfsburg, and drove southeast across Germany, then across Yugoslavia, and into Bulgaria. Atanasoff had not informed Sendov and the Bulgarian Academy of Sciences when or how he was arriving. He drove into Sofia in midafternoon in the last week of November.

Through Professor Sendov's letter he had learned the address of the only Bulgarian student he had known at Iowa State College. Boris Iliev had been a student majoring in agriculture at Iowa State, but JV had lost track of him through the war years and the years that followed. In Sofia he made inquiries on the streets and found his way to Boris Iliev's home. That afternoon and evening JV and Alice visited with Iliev and did some catching up on what had happened in their lives since Iliev left Iowa State. He and Alice spent that night at a nearby hotel.

When they contacted Professor Sendov at the Bulgarian Academy of Sciences, he arranged to have them moved to one of Sofia's finest hotels "as guests of the Academy" and arranged to have lunch with them. Sendov at that time did not communicate fluently in English, and JV knew only a few words of Bulgarian; so it was arranged that Professor Boyan I. Penkov, another mathematician who was fluent in English, would accompany Atanasoff on this odyssey across his ancestral homeland. Sendov and others at the Bulgarian Academy of Sciences had been busy after receiving Atanasoff's first letter and had visited his father's home town, Boyadjik, in the Yambol district. It was in a rural district, and JV was told that eighty years had not dulled memories of his father or of the family.

Atanasoff spent a week in Sofia during which he gave a lecture on computers in a hall that was filled to overflowing, with others listening on loudspeakers in the cold outside. The next week he and Alice were given a tour of Bulgaria, which included a visit to his father's home village. There he met his father's younger cousin who remembered when his father had left for America. In another town he met his father's half-sister who was born after his father left Bulgaria.

During this visit to his father's village JV was given a letter written in Bulgarian which he was told had been written to Bulgarian relatives by his father in 1954. Because his father was a notoriously poor letter writer, Atanasoff was at first skeptical, but when he examined the envelope he saw that it was addressed in his mother's handwriting. After more celebration on the tour, JV and Alice returned to Sofia tired but exuberant. They wanted to have some peace and quiet, but they also wanted to stay.

On the day before their departure from Bulgaria, Atanasoff received a call from the secretary of the Academy of Sciences asking if they could delay their departure for one day. The Bulgarian Academy of Sciences had asked the Parliament to honor him with an award. The Bulgarian Parliament had approved honoring him with the Order of Cyril and Methodius, First Class, for work "of great merit and scientific contribution" as the inventor of the first electronic digital computer.

The Order of Cyril and Methodius, First Class, was presented to John V. Atanasoff with great ceremony. The U.S. ambassador and members of his staff were present. It was an exciting and morale-boosting experience to be so grandly feted in this manner in the land of one's ancestors, and it was with a warm feeling that JV and Alice drove from Bulgaria to Greece on Christmas day in 1970.

The Bulgarian experience, where he was already proclaimed to be the co-inventor of the electronic digital computer, was a confidence builder. But, as he returned to the United States, he and Alice knew that there were still many battles ahead in the U.S. courts before he could expect to be honored in his home country.

Sperry Rand had hundreds of millions of dollars riding on their claim that Mauchly had not derived his ENIAC computer concepts from Atanasoff. This Sperry Rand legal posture demanded they spare no expense in digging up every bit of evidence that might in any manner corroborate Mauchly's claim of having done research of any kind on the electronic digital computer concepts before meeting Atanasoff. It also meant that Sperry Rand lawyers would go to any extreme to develop evidence that would tend to discredit Atanasoff's claim that he taught Mauchly the computer concepts that were the basis of ENIAC's electronic digital computer operation. Atanasoff was confident that the truth was so well documented that it would eventually prevail against any odds.

CHAPTER 17

Dr. Atanasoff: Key Witness

J OHN VINCENT ATANASOFF was a well-prepared witness by the time U.S. District Judge Earl R. Larson started the trial on 1 June 1971. It had been more than four years since Atanasoff had his first conversations with the Control Data Corporation attorneys when he had given the Honeywell lawyers their first access to his files on the Atanasoff Berry Computer. But several days more would pass before Honeywell lawyers put him in the witness chair.

Henry Halladay, the Minneapolis trial attorney, and D. Dennis Allegretti and Charles G. Call had informed him there would be several days of testimony by Sam Legvold and others as well as the introduction of depositions and documents to set the stage for his testimony. Atanasoff enjoyed the prospect of watching the court process until that prospect was destroyed by a motion by Sperry Rand lawyers to exclude all potential witnesses from the court until after they had completed their testimony. It was a common practice to remove potential witnesses from the court to prevent them from being moved to consciously or unconsciously tailor their testimony to that of other witnesses.

While Sperry Rand lawyers were aware that Atanasoff had access to the depositions of other witnesses who would corroborate his testimony and had reviewed all or most of the relevant letters, reports, and other documents, there remained the chance that Atanasoff might give testimony that could be contradicted by some other witness on a significant point. From the outset it was recognized that Atanasoff was a key witness, and that any contradictions or seeming contradictions could be important to his credibility.

155

Although there were many other issues in the case, Honeywell lawyers Allegretti, Call, and Halladay understood the importance of protecting the credibility of their star witness on the central issue dealing with how Mauchly had obtained the basic electronic digital computer concepts he claimed were his own. The issues of "prior art" and "prior use" and antitrust law violations were for the most part unrelated to the issue of whether Mauchly had pirated his electronic digital computer ideas from Atanasoff.

It was Charles Call's job to bolster Atanasoff's confidence, to assure him that he had been a good witness in depositions, and to provide the charts, mechanisms, and documents necessary to remind him of vital details in reconstructing more than thirty years of history. While JV had a remarkable memory on most of the events involving his planning and construction of his computer, occasionally there were times when he tended to wander or go into details that were more confusing than clarifying to the public and to the court. Atanasoff's explanations were usually stated with precision and accuracy, but there were some occasions when his phrases and general terminology were such that only a student of mathematics or physics could get the full meaning of his testimony.

Honeywell Attorney Halladay guided JV through the chronological story of his life with emphasis on his early experiences—his interests in electricity, his precocious early development as a mathematical genius, and his early interest in the Dietzgen slide rule. He portrayed the picture of a boyhood where the access to the new Dietzgen slide rule and its instruction booklet had blotted out an early interest in baseball and had led him to his father's library full of books on electrical engineering and his mother's algebra text.

It was apparent that Judge Larson was impressed with the early life of the budding genius, his record of scholarly excellence at various schools in Florida, and his remarkable record at the University of Florida despite his heavy work load. It was not unlike Judge Larson's record when he was working his way through the University of Minnesota Law School.

By the time Honeywell Attorney Halladay had taken JV through his work as a teaching assistant, assistant professor, and associate professor at Iowa State, and his Ph.D. thesis at the University of Wisconsin, there was no doubt about his qualifications as a mathematician, electrical engineer, and theoretic physicist. The titles of the theses written by his students under Atanasoff's guidance and the papers he himself had written left no doubt about his long-time interest in developing a method of computing that would improve upon the best calculators being produced in the 1920s and the 1930s.

Atanasoff's efforts to develop an analog-type computer were well documented in the published papers he had done with his students and with Dr. A. E. Brandt. With those efforts to develop an analog machine frustrated, Atanasoff told the court of turning his attention to developing a computer that would perform the mathematical computations through electronic impulses.

It was late in the afternoon on his first day on the witness stand that Atanasoff spelled out for Judge Larson the story of the winter night in 1937 when he pulled it all together.

"I remember that the winter of 1937 was a desperate one for me because I had this problem and I had outlined my objective but nothing was happening," Atanasoff testified. "As the winter deepened, my despair grew. . . . I went out to the office intending to spend the evening trying to resolve some of these questions and I was in such a mental state that no resolution was possible."

"I was just unhappy to an extreme, and at that time I did something that I had done on such occasions," Atanasoff continued. "I went out to my automobile, got in, and started driving over the good highways of Iowa . . . at a high rate of speed. I remember the pavement was clean and dry, and I was forced to give attention to my driving, and as a consequence of that I was less nervous, and I drove that way for several hours.

"Then I sort of became aware of my surroundings. . . . I had reached the Mississippi River and was crossing . . . into Illinois at a place where there are three cities . . . one of which is Rock Island. I drove into Illinois and turned off the highway into a little road, and went into a roadhouse there which had bright lights.

"It was extremely cold and . . . I had a very heavy coat, and I hung it up, and sat down and ordered a drink. . . . As the delivery of the drink was made, I realized that I was no longer so nervous and my thoughts turned again to computing machines," Atanasoff told the court.

"Now, I don't know why my mind worked then – it had not worked previously – but things seemed to be good and cool and quiet. There were not many people in the tavern, and the waitress didn't bother me particularly with repetitious offers of drinks. I would suspect that I drank two drinks perhaps, and then I realized that thoughts were coming good and I had some positive results.

"During this evening in the tavern, I generated within my mind the possibility of the regenerative memory. I called it 'jogging' at that time. I'm thinking about the condensers for memory units and the fact that the condensers would regenerate their own state so their state would not change with time," Atanasoff said and stopped to explain to Judge Larson his meaning about their state not changing. "If they were in a plus state, for instance, they would stay in a plus state; or, if they were in the negative state, they would stay in the negative state. They would not blink off to zero. Or if you used two positive charges, they would retain their individual identity and would not leak across to each other."

Atanasoff continued his testimony. "During that same evening, I gained an initial concept of what is called 'logic circuits.' That is the non-racheting approach to the interaction between two memory units, or as I called them in those days, 'Abaci' workings. There would be a black box, and a state of Abaci 1 would pass into the box, the state of Abaci 2 would pass into the box, and the box would then yield the correct results on output terminals. And somewhere late in the evening I got in my car and drove home at a slower rate."

In answer to questions by Halladay, Atanasoff explained his black box as a "box of unknown contents." "I did not envision the contents of the box that night. I just envisioned that it might be possible to construct such a box . . . it's used in science when we have an input-output question before us, we are likely to use a black box with input terminals and output terminals."

In answer to Halladay's question as to whether he did "envision generally" any concept on "the innards" of the black box, Atanasoff responded: "Well, you see, since I was going to use condensers, why then I supposed the innards would be electrical in character, and I was well aware that the electrical entities which would be as suitable for such a purpose were vacuum tubes. I was not sure that nothing but vacuum tubes would be in the black box. I was not sure that there might not be other kinds of elements in the black box at that time."

Halladay asked about his use of the term "condenser" and to explain whether capacitors, as used by other witnesses, and condensers were the same.

"They are synonymous for the same object, and the modern parlance is probably more likely to be capacitor than condenser. I believe the word 'condenser' is still in good standing, however," Atanasoff responded.

As Halladay asked him about establishing a precise date for the drive to Illinois, Atanasoff replied he had no direct memory of the date except that it was in the winter of 1937–1938. He only remembered that it was extremely cold–subzero weather–and that the road was clear.

Atanasoff reported that within a few weeks of the drive he started to design circuits and attempted to realize the two concepts he had envisioned. "The regenerative condensers system was solved first," Atanasoff testified. "It seemed very simple. One had to generate a pulse circuit, which would generate a pulse of the type you desired when triggered by the pulse which remained in the condenser system. This isn't a very hard job. I think that any elementary student in electronics would soon master this task.

"The generation of a device suitable for putting in the black box was a more difficult problem, and occupied me literally for months. None of the modern metallic and logic theory was, of course, available, and we were attempting to devise it," Atanasoff stated.

"At the end of some months, I commenced to be able to write circuits which would solve this problem, first for the scale (base) of 'two,' and later I attempted, as an exercise, to accomplish the same purpose, with a scale of ten numbers," Atanasoff told the court. "When I attempted this the black box, with its internal workings, became complicated and unwieldy, and I have confirmation that the scale of 'two' was the direction in which to turn."

Atanasoff testified that by 24 March 1939 he had his concepts for an electronic digital computer worked out on paper and approved by the Physics Department of Iowa State College for submission to Iowa State College Research Council with a request for research funds.

Honeywell Lawyer Halladay submitted the 24 March 1939 letter of two pages of the Department of Physics for identification. Atanasoff said he had written the letter and that it was signed as approved by Dr. Jay W. Woodrow, head of the Physics Department.

According to Atanasoff, that research project would provide "for the mathematical treatment of many practical problems, [in which] one requires the solution of systems of linear simultaneous algebraic equations."

The "three examples" of such problems that were of continual interest to researchers on the Iowa State College campus, Atanasoff had enumerated in the letter: (1) electrical circuit analysis, (2) approximate solution of the differential equations of mathematical physics with special emphasis on their technological application, and (3) multiple correlation in statistics.

This letter stated that the theory and method of solutions of such systems was well known, and that when the numbers of unknowns were small, solution presents no great difficulty. "However, the satisfactory treatment of many problems, the three problems mentioned above for instance, frequently requires the use of many unknowns," Atanasoff explained.

In his letter Atanasoff stated that for six years he had been thinking about the possibility of mechanizing the solutions and had finally "succeeded in forming a rough outline of the process necessary."

Atanasoff spelled out his frustrations with earlier efforts to mechanize the solution of systems in linear algebraic equations, and noted in the 1939 letter: "About two years ago, I came to the realization that computing machines can be much simplified by changing from use of numbers to the base-ten to the use of numbers to the base-two.

"Further study has reinforced this point of view and it now seems possible to build into a small machine of perhaps the size and intricacy of a Monroe computational capacity over twice that of the eight-bank punched card tabulation. This would be, as far as I am aware, the most powerful computing machine in existence and would furnish a direct and satisfactory method of solving simultaneous linear equations."

In concluding the 1939 request for research funds, Atanasoff stated: "While the basic idea of this machine is original, I have made careful calculations and believe it will work." He requested $450 for a research fellow and $200 for material and mechanical assistance. Atanasoff was then asked to identify an 18 May 1939 letter from Professor E. W. Lindstrom notifying Atanasoff of the $650 research grant and Atanasoff's 23 May 1939 reply thanking Professor Lindstrom.

During Atanasoff's first day on the witness stand, Honeywell Lawyer Halladay established with written records and full corroboration that Atanasoff had conceptualized the major elements of an electronic digital computer with a base-two operational mode, with regenerative memory, and with logic circuits as early as 1939.

Before the recess at 4:40 P.M. of that first long day, Halladay had also laid the foundation for examining JV on the hiring of Clifford E. Berry, their work on the prototype, and the construction of the Atanasoff Berry Computer.

When JV resumed testimony on 16 June 1971, Halladay wasted no time in getting him to identify notes that he and Cliff Berry had written and hand-drawn sketches they had made as work progressed on the prototype computer. These papers included sketches made by JV that he had used in explaining the electronic digital computer project to Cliff Berry in their first meeting in May 1939 as well as hand-drawn sketches of the circuitry that were completed in November 1939, after the prototype was completed and when they were preparing a request for more research funds for the Atanasoff Berry Computer.

Despite the fact that he had the electronic theory worked out on paper, Atanasoff said he continued to worry throughout construction. "I knew the electronic theory, but I just couldn't convince myself that an electron tube would act like a gear tooth and form an adding machine, and I had to see it," he testified.

Through correspondence with suppliers of condensers and a wide range of other correspondence involving JV and Cliff Berry, Halladay was able to establish that the "prototype" or "breadboard model" was completed before Christmas in 1939.

Most of 16 June was spent on identifying thousands of exhibits involved in the trial, on Atanasoff's testimony on technical aspects of the "prototype," and on identifying pictures and drawings of the prototype. Exhibits included a letter Atanasoff had written on 10 July 1940 to President Howard A. Poillon, Research Corporation of New York City, asking for a $5,000 grant to supplement a $700 grant received from Iowa State on 1 July 1940 to complete work on the computer project.

In his letter Atanasoff stressed again the importance of getting a mechanism for the solution of systems of linear simultaneous algebraic equations. This time he set out nine types of problems that such a machine could solve and noted that "this list could be expanded considerably."

He declared that conventional computing machines did not have the capacity to perform the functions, and that three years earlier he had "a succession of ideas which enable me to design a computing mechanism along entirely new lines which is at the same time much simpler and much faster than any other mechanism."

"It is almost entirely electrical in nature; mechanical motions are only used to synchronize the cycles of the machines and there are no mechanical motions at the higher calculating frequencies," Atanasoff explained.

That letter disclosed how Atanasoff in 1939 explained what he had been able to prove with the $650 prototype about the feasibility of his new computing ideas. "With surprisingly little trouble [we] had it in actual operation by the end of the year," JV wrote. "We knew then that the fundamental principle was workable, simple and surprisingly cheap. With this encouraging result, we started work on the design and later the actual construction of various units of a complete machine having a computing capacity of 30 fifteen place numbers, i.e., of such size that it will solve a system of 29 equations in 29 unknowns with a high degree of accuracy."

That correspondence also established that Atanasoff had discussed the machine with Warren Weaver of the Rockefeller Foundation, and that Dr. Weaver would make himself available for discussions with Mr. Poillon or anyone else from the Research Corporation.

That July 1940 letter was used by Halladay to refresh Atanasoff's recollection that he had already received an additional $700 from the Iowa State College Research Foundation on 1 July and that he and Cliff Berry were far advanced in the task of constructing the component parts of the large Atanasoff Berry Computer.

Atanasoff said that Dr. Weaver had favored financing the computer construction with Rockefeller Foundation funds but had been informed that some technicalities with regard to the use of those funds barred financing of the computer. However Dr. Weaver had volunteered to try to be helpful in getting financing from some other sources.

Halladay also handed JV the copy of a news story that had appeared in the *Des Moines Tribune* in January 1941 showing Cliff Berry with one of the parts of the computer. Atanasoff identified the photocopy of the story that had appeared in the *Des Moines Tribune* on 15 January 1941 with the caption "Machine Remembers." The accompanying picture showed Cliff Berry, a machine with vacuum tubes, and a cutline that read: "The giant computing machine under construction at Iowa State College has a 'memory' consisting of 45 vacuum tubes."

Atanasoff said the cutline was incorrect, and he was sure that neither he nor Cliff Berry had made the statement that was quoted in the cutline. Atanasoff told the court the machine pictured in the newspaper "is a device for regenerating the memory, (and is) not the memory itself."

While quarreling with the picture cutline, the very precise Atanasoff did not argue, however, with the accuracy of the news story that read: "An electrical computing machine said here to operate more like the human brain than any other such machine known to exist is being built by Dr. John V. Atanasoff, Iowa State College, Physics Professor.

"The machine will contain more than 300 vacuum tubes and

will be used to compute complicated algebraic equations. The instrument will be entirely electrical and will be used in research experiments."

That news story in the *Des Moines Tribune* and the accompanying picture were full and total corroboration for Atanasoff's testimony as to the state of progress on the Atanasoff Berry Computer at the time Atanasoff had his first conversation with Mauchly in Philadelphia. That article described in general terms what Atanasoff and Cliff Berry had achieved at least six months before Mauchly's visit to Iowa State College in June 1941.

During his third full day of testimony in the huge courtroom with high ceilings and walnut panels, Atanasoff was wondering whether it would ever end. Halladay systematically presented all of the correspondence Atanasoff had during 1939 and 1940 with Dr. R. E. Buchanan and Dr. Jay W. Woodrow in getting his computer project approved, and all of the correspondence with Dr. Samuel H. Caldwell of the Massachusetts Institute of Technology (MIT), Dr. Warren Weaver of the Rockefeller Foundation, and Howard A. Poillon, president of The Research Corporation. These men had knowledge of the planning, financing, and development of the Atanasoff Berry Computer through their official positions in analyzing and approving the research grants.

On the one hand, JV was pleased to see the record being made for computer history, but the whole court process seemed ponderous and slow. That boring routine of identification of letters and documents continued throughout the afternoon and Friday, with much of the time taken up with the objections by Sperry Rand Lawyer Ferrill who was intent upon blocking Honeywell correspondence between Mauchly and H. Helms Clayton from the record.

In a letter to Clayton on 28 June 1941 Mauchly had told of his trip to Iowa State and had expressed enthusiasm over the computing machine he had observed. Ferrill argued that it was hearsay and irrelevant communication to a person not involved in the litigation.

Honeywell Attorney Halladay argued that Mauchly's letter to Clayton was "a contemporary recordation by Dr. Mauchly about his trip to Ames, Iowa, out of which the witness [Atanasoff] is going to testify."

"I want to be in the position to read it into the record as of the time frame of which it is important," Halladay told Judge Larson. He argued that Sperry Rand lawyers had rejected his request to produce Mauchly and he was laying the proper foundation for introduction of the letter into the record.

Halladay argued that Mauchly had identified the letter he had written to Clayton in deposition, and there was no doubt about the authenticity of the letter which he explained was important because it was "Dr. Mauchly's first recordation of his trip to Ames, Iowa, in June of 1941."

Judge Larson recessed court at 11:20 A.M. on that Friday without making a ruling on the admissability of Mauchly's letter, but did hear Atanasoff identify a model of his prototype computer that had been constructed at the request of Control Data Lawyer Allen Kirkpatrick.

Atanasoff testified that the model of the prototype computer was made from general instructions in his 1939 manuscript. "We tried to duplicate everything as exactly as possible, putting in resistors according to the general direction from the manuscript, and wiring in exactly the same way.

"There is one small difference. I knew I was going to use these add-subtract mechanisms in connection with a test set like this," he said pointing to the diagram, "and I didn't want to have the inconvenience of an extra lead, so instead of putting the ten-prong plug, which the original units contained, you will find in this unit a twelve-point plug."

On Monday, 21 June, Judge Larson called the court to order at 9:30 A.M., and in short order Lawyer Halladay moved Atanasoff through testimony on his first meeting with Mauchly at the AAAS meeting in late December 1940, and through identification of his correspondence with Mauchly in January, February, March, April, and May of 1941 as a prelude to Mauchly's visit.

This was the testimony that Atanasoff was anxious to give to let the court and the world hear his sworn testimony of what Mauchly had been told and had seen at Iowa State. The testimony of Sam Legvold and Ike Coleman, and the deposition of Lura Atanasoff were already a part of the record.

"I was in the front yard and he drove into my drive at 3439 Woodland and he had with him his son," Atanasoff told the court. He said it was toward the end of the week, and he believed Mauchly arrived on Friday, 13 June 1941.

"During the weekend, accompanied by Dr. Mauchly and the children, we went over and we entered the computing room . . . and the computing machine was shown to him in some detail and there were discussions during the week-end of the theory of the machine and the method of its operation," Atanasoff testified.

"When I found he was coming, I asked Clifford Berry what

state the machine was in and he said it was all torn up but he would take the pains to get it ready for Dr. Mauchly's visit. . . . He assembled all the units that were complete . . . so the machine was in complete form when Dr. Mauchly was there."

"Now, I remember Monday morning, I took Dr. Mauchly and we went over the first thing in the morning and went in to see the machine," Atanasoff testified. "Clifford Berry was there and there may have been one or two other people in the room at the same time, and Clifford Berry and Mauchly immediately went into discussion of the various details of the machine.

"During the morning, I took pains to show him . . . a copy of a document I have here before me," Atanasoff said and identified a 35-page booklet with a green cover describing the Atanasoff Berry Computer construction and concepts with hand-sketched drawings he had completed in August 1940.

"He [Mauchly] had a copy of this document while he was visiting me but at the end of the visit, he asked me if he could take it back to the east with him and I told him I preferred that he did not and he did not take it back, to the best of my knowledge and belief."

Atanasoff told the court that aside from a short lecture that Mauchly gave on meteorological studies, that his Pennsylvania visitor spent all of the time discussing or examining the Atanasoff Berry Computer or examining the green booklet dealing with its operation and design.

"He [Mauchly] was around the machine on frequent occasions . . . and on frequent occasions with me and on frequent occasions with Clifford Berry in various discussions and even manipulation of the parts of the machine. During this period the machine was demonstrated to him in detail," Atanasoff told the court. "He seemed to follow in detail our explanations and expressed joy at the results, at the fact that these vacuum tubes would actually compute. He was shown addition and subtraction and multiplication and he was also shown the process of punching cards but we only had one unit in operation during his visit and we weren't prepared to punch all of the thirty 'Abaci' simultaneously and no effort was made to fill the entire machine. He was shown the operation of converting base-ten cards to base-two numbers on the system and then the rest of the controls which we planned for the machine to make it operable in regard to the solutions of simultaneous linear equations. . . . We discussed the logic elements in considerable length with Dr. Mauchly."

Atanasoff told the court he had observed Mauchly reading his manuscript at length, although he could not state what parts of the green booklet Mauchly had read. "I remember an occasion in my home – he had the copy in his possession, he . . . read it evenings, and I remember us in my own study . . . in my home, reading and discussing the manuscript. I remember that one subject discussed at that time was the carry mechanism."

Atanasoff testified that he "explained the meaning of this, and I told him he could follow through for himself how the thing worked, and I don't know that he followed it through in complete detail and understood every step but he certainly understood the general features of the device."

"I remember him expressing his surprise that the base-two number system was advantageous for computing," Atanasoff said and added: "I am not sure that he was entirely convinced as to this." Atanasoff said it was necessary to show Mauchly how binary addition and subtraction was accomplished. "I did so show him," Atanasoff stated. "As a matter of fact, he seemed – I believe from my memory that he was not proficient in base-two calculations at the time he came to visit me."

A short time later, Lawyer Halladay introduced into the record Mauchly's typed manuscript entitled "Notes on Electrical Calculating Devices." It was written by Mauchly in August 1941, only a few weeks after he was tutored by Atanasoff and Cliff Berry on the operation and construction of the Atanasoff Berry Computer.

Halladay then introduced a letter that Mauchly had written to Atanasoff on 22 June 1941 in which he revealed that the visit to Iowa State had stimulated his thinking on computers. "On the way back east a lot of ideas came barging into my consciousness, but I haven't had time to sift them or organize them. They were on the subject of computing devices, of course. If any look promising, you may hear more later."

While Mauchly did not reveal in that letter to Atanasoff the specific ideas that were generated from the Iowa State visit, he was more detailed a few days later on 28 June 1941 in a letter to his friend H. Helms Clayton. Halladay read that letter into the record to demonstrate Mauchly's contemporaneous actions that were inconsistent with his later claim that he had learned nothing of value from the Iowa State visit with Atanasoff. It was with pleasure and satisfaction that Atanasoff listened to Lawyer Halladay read the following third paragraph of that letter: "Immediately after commencement here, I went out to Iowa State University to see the computing device which a friend of mine is constructing there. His machine, now nearing completion, is electronic in operation, and will solve within a very few minutes any system of linear equations involving no more than thirty variables. It can be adapted to do the job of the Bush differential analyzer more rapidly than the Bush machine does, and it costs a lot less."

"My own computing devices use a different principle, more likely to fit small computing jobs," Mauchly wrote of his harmonic analyzer, which operated on the "analog" principle rather than the electronic digital "pulse" principle of the machine he had studied at Iowa State.

With Mauchly's 15 August memorandum, "Notes on Electrical Calculating Devices" already in the record to demonstrate how Atanasoff's concepts had been incorporated, giving him some vague measure of credit, Lawyer Halladay introduced another letter by Mauchly to establish even more of his views on the Atanasoff Berry Computer.

While Halladay read the whole letter as relevant to the credibility of Mauchly and the theft of Atanasoff's concepts, Atanasoff took particular pleasure as he listened to the fourth paragraph: "A number of different ideas have come to me recently anent computing circuits—some of which are more or less hybrids, combining your methods with other things, and some of which are nothing like your machine," Halladay read and Atanasoff noted that Mauchly at the time made no claim to any original computer ideas.

Halladay continued reading about a request by Mauchly for use of some of Atanasoff's ideas: "The question in my mind is this: Is there any objection, from your point of view, to my building some sort of computer which incorporates some of the features of your machine? For the time being, of course, I shall be lucky to find time and material to do more than merely make exploratory tests of some of my different ideas, with the hope of getting something very speedy, not too costly, etc."

Mauchly, while asking for permission to use Atanasoff's ideas, had not revealed what he might bring to this cooperative venture, and the next paragraph was little more enlightening on that subject. Halladay read the revealing lopsided proposal Mauchly had made to Atanasoff in that 30 September 1941 letter. "Ultimately a second question might come up, of course, and that is, in the event that your present design were to hold the field against all challengers, and I got the Moore School interested in having something of the sort, would the way be open for us to build an 'Atanasoff Calculator' (a la Bush analyzer) here?"

Already in the record was Atanasoff's reply to Mauchly rejecting the offer of a partnership in the electronic digital computing project he and Cliff Berry had constructed to its final stages at Iowa State. In that letter Atanasoff had warned Mauchly in a polite manner that Mauchly's access to the Atanasoff Berry machine and the concepts had been on a confidential basis.

As he heard Mauchly's proposal read by Honeywell Attorney Halladay, Atanasoff reflected that he probably should have been sharper and more direct in his warnings to Mauchly not to attempt to steal his ideas in the Atanasoff Berry Computer. But hindsight is always better than foresight, and at the time he viewed Mauchly as a friend and colleague who was also an enthusiastic admirer of his and Cliff's accomplishments.

Even as he heard Mauchly's letters read into the court record by Halladay, he could not believe that at the time Mauchly had intended to engage in the theft of the electronic digital computer concepts.

Then Lawyer Halladay guided Atanasoff through his frustrations in getting perfection in the operation of the Atanasoff Berry Computer in late 1941 and 1942. Although all of the systems had been tested and were in functioning order at the time of Mauchly's visit, Atanasoff acknowledged that the machine had never actually gone through the total process of solving a large set or system of linear algebraic equations. Atanasoff stated the reason: "The data-in and data-out devices were not sufficiently satisfactory. I mean the scale of [base-] two card system. We found one piece of material [paper for the cards] that was satisfactory and gave good ratios of voltages so it looked as if it would be dependable, and then we commenced to looking for the source of that material and we couldn't locate it."

Months were lost while he and Cliff Berry searched for a source for the material for cards that would be consistently dependable during World War II "when the industrial supply situation was getting more and more difficult continuously."

Also, this was the period when young men were being drafted unless they were in war-related work. Atanasoff testified that Sam Legvold and the other graduate students he had at work on "Project X" for the navy had no problem with deferments, but that he was unable to get a deferment for Cliff Berry, who was indispensable to efficient progress in the perfection of the mechanisms to convert base-two cards to base ten.

Although Atanasoff believed then, and still believes, that the perfection of the Atanasoff Berry Computer could have been more important to the national defense effort than Project X, it was not financed and endorsed by the army or the navy so did not qualify for the deferment of either Atanasoff or Cliff Berry.

Cliff Berry was to receive his Master's degree in June, and he was spending a good deal of his time in the last months making the contacts for employment with a defense contractor, Atanasoff told the court.

During the spring and summer of 1942 Atanasoff was supervising Project X for the navy, consulting on defense contracts in Washington, and fighting a losing battle with navy officials who wanted him to head a research division at the Naval Ordnance Laboratory in Washington.

Atanasoff testified that on 7 April 1942 the *Des Moines Tribune* published another article on the computer machine that he and Clifford Berry were building at Iowa State. There was also a radio program on the Iowa State station WOI on which he was interviewed on the merits of his computer machine.

Atanasoff told the court that Clifford Berry, upon graduation, married Atanasoff's pretty, young, and vivacious secretary, Jean Reed. The young couple left for California and a job in the engineering department of a defense-oriented firm. He also testified that Harry F. Frissel, the young man who took Clifford's place, was a fine student who had been working on the project but lacked the genius intellect and practical mechanical ability to convert his ideas into effective mechanisms in a short space of time.

From the study he had done of patents and on the basis of research he and Cliff Berry had done at the Washington patent office in 1941, Atanasoff was sure that the information he had supplied to Iowa State's patent lawyer would be sufficient to file patent applications. Atanasoff stated that when he took a position with the Naval Ordnance Laboratory in September 1942, he was still certain that he had done all that was required to file patent applications for the inventions of new concepts of the electronic digital computer.

During that long Monday on the witness stand, Atanasoff testified that Mauchly came to see him at the Naval Ordnance Laboratory in Washington at some time in 1943, and after several meetings revealed that he was working on a computer project for the army at the Moore School of Electrical Engineering.

He also testified that Mauchly refused to discuss the details of the army computer project on grounds that it was "a classified project" and that the details were "confidential information." Atanasoff said he had met Dr. J. Presper Eckert on only one occasion in August 1944, when Mauchly and Eckert came to the Naval Ordnance Laboratory to ask him about "the possibility of building a mercury delay line with quartz transducers. The emphasis was on the technical aspects of the line. . . . They asked me if my staff could engineer such a device. I told them they could. There was talk of having such a project put in the Naval Ordnance Laboratory through the army and the navy, but no such project ever developed."

"That's the only time in my life I ever saw Mr. Eckert," Atanasoff testified. He also testified that he saw Mauchly on a couple of occasions at Naval Ordnance Laboratories after that 1944 date, but saw neither Mauchly nor Eckert at a time in 1946 when he was in a group invited to examine ENIAC.

When he visited ENIAC in 1946, Atanasoff told the court that he saw only the general publicity type of documents and received no confidential information as to the machine's internal concepts and operations, so had no knowledge at that time that his electronic digital computer concepts had been incorporated in the huge machine then billed as "the first electronic digital computer."

Atanasoff stated that a man from Remington Rand, whose name he had forgotten, arranged to meet him for dinner at the Cosmos Club in Washington, D.C. "We went into dinner and I was asked if I would turn over my written material to Remington Rand. I demurred, and that was the end of the conference."

Honeywell Lawyer Halladay then took Atanasoff through testimony of his meetings with lawyers for IBM, General Electric, and Burroughs during the 1950s and early 1960s to establish that IBM lawyers and lawyers for the predecessor organization to Sperry Rand had been on notice for some years of the role of Atanasoff and the possibility that Mauchly had pirated his ideas.

Lawyer Halladay asked him specifically about a meeting in the early summer of 1967 with lawyers for General Electric who were concerned that Sperry Rand would sue General Electric for patent violations. The lawyers were identified as Norman Fulmer, an electrical engineering graduate of Iowa State College who had worked on the Atanasoff Berry Computer as a student, George Eltgroth, and Howard Mial Dustin, counsel for the Computer Division of General Electric.

Atanasoff testified that Eltgroth, who had worked on the patent applications for Mauchly and Eckert, expressed surprise to learn that Mauchly had visited Atanasoff at Iowa State and had examined the Atanasoff Berry Computer. Atanasoff quoted Eltgroth as exclaiming: "My God, I have never heard of this. If I had known, I could have protected them."

"After that, Mr. Eltgroth said nothing more," Atanasoff said.

Atanasoff told the court that after the meeting with the General Electric lawyers, Norman Fulmer and Eltgroth, he received calls and had meetings with lawyers for Control Data and later with the Honeywell lawyers in connection with contemplated litigation against Sperry Rand.

Halladay asked Atanasoff if he had been questioned by Sperry Rand lawyers at any time after he was retained by Control Data and Honeywell, and he testified about the visit by Sperry Rand Lawyer Laurence Dodds and Mauchly in December 1967. He did not go into the substance of that day-long meeting at the Atanasoff farm during which Mauchly had confided that Sperry Rand lawyers had advised him that the less he remembered of his Iowa State trip the better off he would be.

The next day, Tuesday, 22 June, was Atanasoff's last day on the stand on direct examination, and the first day of three days of cross-examination by Sperry Rand Lawyer Thomas M. Ferrill, Jr. Most of the morning was taken up with routine identification of documents and arguments on the question of whether a proper foundation had been made for admission into evidence.

The Sperry Rand lawyer spent considerable time on the custody of the records Atanasoff had turned over to Control Data lawyers and Honeywell lawyers in August 1967 and what records had come into his possession later as a result of the work of Honeywell lawyers.

Ferrill asked Atanasoff about his motivation for cooperation with Honeywell lawyers. "Is it your purpose to attempt to obtain a judicial holding of the invalidity of the Eckert and Mauchly patents involved in this action or in the Control Data action?" Ferrill asked.

Atanasoff answered: "It is my present purpose that in one way or another the present patent holdings by Sperry Rand, derived from Eckert and Mauchly, will come apart at the seams and be held . . . in a different way than they are now held."

Ferrill's three days of cross-examination consisted of taking Atanasoff back through much of the correspondence and grilling him on details of mathematical formulas and technical questions related to the construction of the Atanasoff Berry Computer in hopes of tripping him up on detailed technical explanations in a manner that might reflect on Atanasoff's competence, memory, or credibility.

This pattern of questioning droned on from the time Atanasoff was seated in the witness chair shortly after 9:30 A.M. until court was recessed by Judge Larson shortly after 4:30 P.M. on Wednesday, 23 June and Thursday, 24 June.

On Friday, 25 June, Ferrill launched his last big effort to make a dent in Atanasoff's testimony. He sought to establish that in 1944, 1945, and 1946, Atanasoff had recommended Mauchly for a job in the Naval Ordnance Laboratory and had commented favorably upon the computer expertise of Mauchly and Eckert.

Atanasoff acknowledged that he had a role in the recommendation of Mauchly for a post in the statistics division at the Naval Ordnance Laboratory. He said Mauchly did not work for him but worked under another division chief who later informed him that Mauchly had not been useful.

Atanasoff denied commenting favorably upon Eckert as "a high-powered electronics expert" needed for the Naval Ordnance Laboratory computer development. He reaffirmed under oath that he had met Eckert on only one occasion and had no knowledge of his competence or expertise.

When Ferrill questioned him as to why he had not been successful in building a computer for the Naval Ordnance Laboratory in 1946, Dr. Atanasoff explained that lack of personnel and the pressure of several other projects requiring travel in the United States and Europe made it impossible for him to make progress before the project was cancelled. He testified he had taken on the project on the promise that he would be relieved of other duties but said that promise was not kept by his navy superiors.

Atanasoff flatly denied being present at a lunch with Mauchly and another scientist where he had asked Mauchly to give him help on the navy computer project. He declared that he had never asked Mauchly for assistance or advice of any kind relative to the navy computer project.

Honeywell attorneys were so pleased with the way Atanasoff had withstood the cross-examination that Halladay spent only a short time on redirect to clarify a few points that might have been obscured by the cross-examination.

"Was there a time, Dr. Atanasoff, by which the prototype of the ABC was completed so as to permit it to be demonstrated?" Halladay asked and Atanasoff responded: "There was."

"Was there a time at which it was completed with some kind of converter?" Halladay asked and Atanasoff answered: "There was."

Then, to clear the air with regard to a large drawing of one of the exhibits, Halladay asked: "Does . . . the large drawing we have here, does that show a converter?" Atanasoff replied: "It does not." Atanasoff said that the prototype of the Atanasoff Berry Computer could be demonstrated in the condition shown in the drawing, and "it was." He placed the date of those demonstrations as 1940.

"A test setup of an abacus add-subtract mechanism and converter was made in January 1940. This arrangement performed perfectly and allowed actual tests under working conditions to be given to various components," Atanasoff stated.

Halladay also established on redirect that the date on the green-covered booklet on that Atanasoff Berry Computer was 14 August 1940, and there was no doubt in Atanasoff's mind that "the date of the conception, the roadhouse event" was the winter of 1937–1938 rather than the winter of 1938–1939.

"When Dr. Mauchly was there in Ames, Iowa, Dr. Atanasoff, did you or did you not go through any one or more of the steps of that (computing machine) program with him?" Halladay asked.

"As far as I can tell, I went through every one of these steps. I didn't go through them in exactly this form, of course. The method of discourse between Dr. Mauchly and I and between the Court and I are somewhat different, but Dr. Mauchly was shown every detail of how the process of elimination takes place, and that would consist of this same set of directions."

Then to pin it down firmly, Halladay obtained specific confirmation from Atanasoff under oath that he had explained to Mauchly the base-two number system, the process of solving linear simultaneous equations, the timing mechanisms and synchronization of the ABC, the capacitor memories and readers, a one-cycle switch, the circuits and devices for automatic operation, and the subject of ring counter and racheting and the logic circuits.

Atanasoff said he had precise recollections of discussions on most of those factors with Mauchly, and that he remembered that others were discussed by implication. "I tried at various times to test Mauchly's knowledge of the conversations which we were having and this is a device that all teachers engage in and Dr. Mauchly is an apt pupil," Atanasoff told the court.

Through the correspondence of Capt. H. H. Goldstine, Ballistic Missile Research, Aberdeen Proving Ground, Maryland, Halladay established that 30 August 1944 was the date Mauchly and Eckert had called upon Atanasoff at the Naval Ordnance Laboratory to request his assistance in the construction of a delay-line register or storage device related to discussions with the army legal department concerning patents for ENIAC.

On the recross examination, Ferrill made reference to Atanasoff's testimony about going through all of the aspects of the Atanasoff Berry Computer with Mauchly. "You weren't suggesting, were you, from the witness stand that you actually carried out a demonstration of, or performance of those steps?"

"No," Atanasoff replied, "the machine was in no condition to carry out a full demonstration of these steps, and it only means discussions of various kinds which show the methods all to be employed in solving systems of equations."

"You said the machine was in no condition," Ferrill preceded his question. "The fact of the matter is that quite a number of things necessary for these steps hadn't even been worked out, isn't that correct?"

"Yes," Dr. Atanasoff acknowledged and continued, "and in such cases where they hadn't been worked out, only the function was described to Mauchly, the function to be fulfilled but not the details of the structure."

"In other words, what you hoped something would do if it was worked out for him?" Ferrill asked in Perry Mason fashion.

"Yes, exactly," Atanasoff replied quietly and the long cross-examination ordeal was over. When he left the U.S. District Court at about 5:00 P.M. on Friday, 25 June 1971, it was with a sense of accomplishment. He had given the court the truth under oath, and with full documentation for every step of the progress he and Cliff Berry had made in those long hours in the basement of the Physics Building at Iowa State.

Atanasoff knew it would be months before the trial was concluded and the decision rendered, but the record was made for computer historians. He wished that Cliff Berry was there to share the moment and to further corroborate his story. But Cliff Berry's letter to Dr. R. K. Richards in 1962 represented clear and precise testimony from his grave that forcefully contradicted Mauchly's deposition testimony on his Iowa State trip.

Honeywell lawyers Allegretti, Call, and Halladay breathed sighs of relief. Atanasoff's testimony was in the record and he had been an excellent witness all the way. Although Atanasoff was alert and vigorous, he did have some nagging health problems that could have resulted in his unavailability at any time.

Three days of cross-examination by Ferrill had failed to damage Atanasoff's credibility on any point. On a few minor points, Atanasoff had acknowledged that he had misspoken. In portraying confidence when he was sure he was right, and in quickly acknowledging a capacity for error, he had actually given strength to his overall credibility.

As JV and Alice left Minneapolis to return to their Maryland farm home, they were satisfied that the work done by the Honeywell and Control Data legal teams had put together a monumental documentation that established the Atanasoff Berry Computer's place in computer history. It was a record beyond the reach and resources of what any computer historian could compile at any later time.

While the court had yet to hear from Mauchly, Honeywell lawyers had skillfully used the deposition process in 1967, 1968, and 1969 to bind Mauchly into the position of acknowledging his faulty memory on detail in the crucial period of his meetings with Atanasoff.

Lawyers Allegretti and Call said later that their task was relatively simple involving Atanasoff's testimony. "Dr. Atanasoff had an excellent memory. He was telling the truth, and every additional document that turned up corroborated his testimony in some respect," Allegretti said. "I was glad I was not on the other side."

CHAPTER 18

Dr. Mauchly's Muddy Memory, 1971

I T was five long months between the time Atanasoff completed his testimony, and the 8 November 1971 date that Mauchly gave trial testimony on his version of his contacts with Atanasoff in the crucial period between 26 December 1940 and 18 June 1941. Much had happened in Judge Larson's walnut-paneled sixth-floor court as the Minneapolis weather changed from the scorching ninety-degree summer days of late June and July to the bitter cold days of November.

For a few brief days in late August, one of the Honeywell witnesses, Dr. Edward Teller, attracted considerable interest in the *Minneapolis Star and Tribune* and the *St. Paul Pioneer Press.* The appearance of Teller, the Father of the Hydrogen Bomb, gave the trial in Judge Larson's court the kind of celebrity status that so often catches the attention of the newspapers and television reporters who find it dull and even boring to deal with the more important basic issues of a case requiring more than a few hours of study.

While Judge Larson's huge sixth-floor courtroom was often only sparsely filled with patent lawyers and executives from the computer industry, it was filled to near capacity with television, radio, and newspaper reporters on Monday, 30 August 1971, when the shaggy-browed celebrity took the stand as a witness for Honeywell.

Honeywell lawyers produced Edward Teller and a group of other nuclear scientists to establish that ENIAC had been in use on important research on the Hydrogen Bomb project more than a year prior to the date in 1947 when Mauchly and Eckert had filed their application for the ENIAC patents. It was contended by Honeywell lawyers that because ENIAC was "put to an important public use" more than a year before the application for patent was filed, the patents were invalid.

Edward Teller, the Hungarian-born physicist, testified that his attention was called to ENIAC by Dr. John von Neumann, a brilliant mathematician at the Manhattan Engineering District's Los Alamos Laboratory, in 1945. John von Neumann had been called as a consultant by the Moore School of Electrical Engineering on the ENIAC project. It was suggested by von Neumann that the ENIAC machine might be useful in some H-Bomb feasibility calculations that were standing in the way of decisions on the H-Bomb project. In the spring of 1945 two Los Alamos Laboratory scientists, Dr. Stanley Frankel and Dr. Nicholas Metropolis, were sent to the Moore School to make the first examination of ENIAC and to analyze further its potential for the H-Bomb study. Through Teller's testimony it was established that the use of ENIAC had produced feasibility calculations that were of "decisive significance" in the Truman administration's decisions to discontinue and then resume research on the Hydrogen Bomb.

Frankel, Metropolis, and others were called to establish with documentation that the "Project A" studies were accomplished in the period between December 1945 and February 1946 – considerably ahead of the summer of 1947 when Mauchly and Eckert filed their first applications for patents on ENIAC.

Under cross-examination Teller said the ENIAC computations, which resulted in differing recommendations, were "insufficient and inaccurate" in some respects. But Teller declared that they were valuable because of that. "Without a complex exploration of your errors, you're not able to find the right way," Teller explained. He told Sperry Rand's lawyer, Francis DeLone, that a decision not to proceed with the H-Bomb in 1946 was reversed by President Truman in the 1949–1950 period because it was believed the Russians were also working on an H-Bomb.

The testimony of Edward Teller and other government scientists was only a part of the substantial evidence that Honeywell introduced on the issue of prior use. This evidence of prior use was not dealt with in the early litigation Sperry Rand brought against Bell Laboratories that had resulted in a verdict for Sperry Rand.

This was one of two major issues in the case when Mauchly took the witness stand. Judge Larson had ruled in favor of Sperry

Rand on a motion to dismiss the Honeywell charge that Sperry
Rand was involved in a violation of the Clayton Antitrust Act. Judge
Larson dismissed that aspect of the lawsuit subject to the provision
that he might reinstate it if the U.S. Supreme Court would make
some new ruling involving that issue.

Under questioning by Sperry Rand Lawyer DeLone, Mauchly
told about his education and career from his days at McKinley Technical High School where he was so precocious in science and mathematics that he was frequently left to teach the class. He testified
that he was named to the National Honor Society in high school and
that he was elected to Phi Beta Kappa as a result of his academic
record at the Johns Hopkins University where he was awarded a
Ph.D. in physics in 1932. He testified that he had started college as
a student of electrical engineering but had by-passed the Bachelor
and Master's degree programs and went directly to the Ph.D. in
physics. It was a distinguished academic record.

Under questioning by DeLone, Mauchly told the court of his
years of teaching at Ursinus College, Collegeville, Pennsylvania,
from 1933 to 1941, when he joined the Moore School of Electrical
Engineering at the University of Pennsylvania.

The major problem for DeLone and for Sperry Rand was to
establish a credible record of Mauchly's interest in and experimentation with electronic digital computing mechanisms prior to his meetings with Atanasoff in December 1940 and his visit to Iowa State
College in June 1941.

While Mauchly had informed Atanasoff in their December 1967
meeting that the Sperry Rand lawyers had advised him that the less
he remembered the better, his several sessions of depositions with
lawyers for Control Data and Honeywell had demonstrated the
grave error of that strategy.

In the initial discovery deposition, Mauchly indicated he had
spent a couple of days at Ames, and only "an hour and one-half
discussing the machine." That early deposition testimony by
Mauchly had been devastated by the testimony of Atanasoff, Lura
Atanasoff, Sam Legvold, and finally by his own later admissions
that he had arrived on a Friday night and left the next Wednesday
morning.

Mauchly's early deposition testimony was vague as to whether
he had seen the Atanasoff Berry Computer with the cover off, and as
to whether he had ever seen it in operation. That testimony proved
impossible to sustain even in later depositions. The same was true

relative to his initial deposition testimony that he had never examined the Atanasoff Berry machine in detail and had never had Atanasoff's 35-page green computer booklet in his possession.

Although Mauchly testified consistently through several discovery depositions that he had "been thinking" about electronic digital computer ideas prior to meeting Atanasoff, he had failed to name any specific living person to whom he had communicated any of those ideas.

In a deposition on 30 October 1968 Honeywell Attorney Halladay asked: "Did you while at Ursinus actually arrive at a concept then recognized by you as being of a general-purpose computer, electronic in character?"

When Mauchly replied "Yes," Halladay asked, "Did you describe that concept to anyone at Ursinus—and when I use the term 'while at Ursinus' I do not mean while you were physically there but while your association was there."

Mauchly replied "Yes" to the question of whether he had described his concepts to anyone, but when Halladay followed up with the question, "To whom?" Mauchly could give no named individual.

In that 1968 deposition Mauchly testified: "That is the rub. I don't know that I could recall now anyone to whom I could be sure that I said the right words, and still less could I be sure whether they understood what words I said."

In the depositions Mauchly consistently stated that he may have discussed his ideas before his classes at Ursinus but could not remember any student or other person he knew who had heard him give voice to his concepts of electronic digital computing or who had seen any of his experimentations with those concepts.

In the October 1968 deposition Mauchly volunteered that he could not remember if he had discussed his computer concepts with Atanasoff in either of their two meetings, but he did have a clear memory of discussing his electronic digital computer concepts with a number of people at the Moore School in the fall of 1941 and in 1942.

However, that was not the testimony Sperry Rand lawyers needed to hear and it was not testimony that Honeywell lawyers feared. Any conversation or papers dated after December 1940 and particularly after mid-June 1941 would carry the taint of possibly being derived from Atanasoff.

Attorney Laurence Dodds, who had been with Mauchly

through all of the early depositions, had been replaced by a new trial team. Mauchly's testimony in the earlier depositions was their cross to bear.

Attorney DeLone took Mauchly through his first experiences with calculating machines from his experimentation with a calculating machine in his father's office at the Department of Terrestrial Magnetism at the Carnegie Institution in Washington, D.C., through his purchase of a European-made calculator when he was the sole teacher in the Physics Department at Ursinus College.

Mauchly testified that he had been deeply interested in mechanical calculating devices from an early age, and DeLone stressed the importance of the electronics courses he had taken at Johns Hopkins and the auditing of another electronics course at the Moore School.

The construction of the harmonic analyzer—the subject of the lecture that had attracted Atanasoff—was believed to be one solid achievement Mauchly could claim with some considerable corroboration. However, that mechanical calculating mechanism, used in Mauchly's studies of the weather, was based on the analog principle as opposed to the electronic digital or electric pulse principle of the Atanasoff Berry Computer and the ENIAC machine built at the Moore School.

At the trial, DeLone asked him to identify a "cryptographic device" with "small neon diodes protruding from a raised panel." Mauchly testified that he constructed the "cryptographic device" at Ursinus in the mid-1930s, and he characterized it as "a digital device."

"So there are a lot of things here in the cryptographic device, we will say, which interact and (have) connection with applications to numerical devices and to digital computing devices as generally understood, although this itself did not work with numbers in any arithmetic way," Mauchly testified.

DeLone also had Mauchly identify another device that he explained was his early concept of a binary counter planned while he was at Ursinus College and in the months before he met Atanasoff.

In addition, DeLone asked Mauchly to identify papers containing rough sketches of circuits that were undated or dated in January 1941 and before June 1941. Mauchly identified these papers to demonstrate evidence that he was thinking in terms of an electronic digital calculating device and did not derive his ideas from his contacts with Atanasoff.

Mauchly's trial testimony regarding his meeting with Atanasoff had changed considerably from his previous recollection. He now acknowledged considerable discussions of the general concepts of Atanasoff's computing machine and his own interest in the details of how that machine operated. However, he testified that he was not so much interested in any of the ideas that Atanasoff discussed, which he indicated were not new to him, but in Atanasoff's claim that the desk model machine could be constructed in relatively inexpensive fashion, "at $2 per digit." Mauchly testified that Atanasoff said the machine was in operation at Iowa State College, but that he would not discuss it further unless Mauchly came out to Ames.

Mauchly acknowledged the correspondence with Atanasoff starting in January 1941 in which he set the stage for his trip to Iowa in June. He testified that he and his son, Jimmy, had arrived at the home of Atanasoff on or about 13 June 1941, a Friday, and did not leave until the following Wednesday morning.

At the trial Mauchly abandoned his early position that he had seen Atanasoff's machine only in a very poor light and with the cover on. "The clearest things I remember is that there was a large frame made out of angle iron and that within that there was some sort of bearing with axle and rotating drum which was studded with contacts, which presumably were connected to condensers inside the drum," he stated. "Although I never took it apart, I had every reason to believe there were condensers inside that drum."

Mauchly identified a picture of the external appearance of the machine taken in May 1941 as depicting the Atanasoff Berry Computer that he saw at Iowa State. Now Mauchly, who had testified he could not remember Clifford Berry, had a clear recollection that Cliff Berry was present at some demonstrations of the operation of the computer machine. But he continued to contend that he had learned nothing new about electronic digital computing after viewing the machine and emphasized that the major reason for the trip to Iowa State had been to learn about "a cost of $2 per digit" that Atanasoff had mentioned in their talk the prior December.

"I didn't learn a great deal about that," Mauchly testified. He said the trip was "a disappointment" because he had gained the impression from Atanasoff's comments at the University of Pennsylvania that it was "a fully electronic device." "This thing," Mauchly said in a disparaging comment about the Atanasoff Berry Computer, "is a mechanical gadget which uses some electronic tubes in operation, but it's still restricted in speed and was not what I was interested in from the point of view of electronic speed gadgets. . . . It became perfectly clear without much examination or talking that it wasn't electronic in whole and it was sacrificing too much of the electrical end."

In another disparaging comment, Mauchly declared that the Atanasoff Berry Computer was "a special class, not a general class. . . . His machine was specifically deliberately constructed with the idea that when finished it would solve simultaneous linear algebraic equations, which is a very special class of problems. . . . My interest was in trying for a versatile machine."

At the trial Mauchly remembered that Atanasoff had given him something to read but told the court: "I don't remember much about it. My main memory on this, you might say . . . is that what impressed itself on my memory was that I was not allowed or given anything that I could take home to read. I had to read it there."

"He [Dr. Atanasoff] did not want any information in written form to leave his laboratory office, and so he made it clear to me. . . . He was not bashful. . . . It was a clear understanding that 'We do not want this material circulated, and so, to prevent this from happening why we will not let any written material be taken away,' " Mauchly testified.

Mauchly acknowledged writing a letter to Atanasoff on 22 June 1941, after the visit to Iowa State in which he had expressed pleasure at what he had seen at Iowa State College and said it had stimulated his thinking.

In like manner, he acknowledged writing the 30 September 1941 letter to Atanasoff suggesting a cooperative venture on a computer and suggesting that they build "an Atanasoff Calculator" at the Moore School of Electrical Engineering where he had just joined the faculty.

While contending he had learned nothing from his visit to Iowa State, Mauchly testified he made the suggestion to Atanasoff because "my contact with him indicated he was a pretty intelligent fellow who had a lot of good ideas, and also he wasn't always saying everything he knew."

"So this was sort of an open proposition, you might say, that if you got something which you think might be useful to build, perhaps the Moore School could be interested in doing this," Mauchly told the court. "I was looking for any kind of project which would assist calculation."

Mauchly had no problem in demonstrating his interest in electronic digital computing and in corroborating his interest from August 1941, when he drew up his first comprehensive paper with concepts of electronic digital computing, logic circuits, and the base-two concepts, and with his projections of the future of electronic digital computers to the exclusion of analog devices.

Sperry Rand Lawyer DeLone guided him through his story of the electronic course he took at Moore School in the fall of 1941 when he met J. Presper Eckert, an electronic specialist, and through his contact with Dr. Carl Chambers, a faculty member at the Moore School who in 1942 first suggested that he put his proposal for an electronic digital computer "in writing, and not just talk about it."

In August 1942 he wrote the memorandum on the project that became ENIAC. Still later, it was the comment of army Lieutenant H. H. Goldstine, of the Ballistic Research Laboratory, that prompted him to dictate a "five or six page memorandum" to Dorothy Shisler, a secretary at the Moore School, that was completed on 2 April 1943.

In identifying those documents and testifying on the progress, Mauchly said there was a lack of enthusiasm that greeted his first suggestions in the fall of 1942. It was not until Lieutenant Goldstine had sold the idea to the Ballistic Research Laboratory at the Aberdeen Proving Ground that higher officials at the Moore School exhibited any great interest, Mauchly also testified.

On 8 April 1943 John Mauchly told the court that he and Presper Eckert, Dr. J. G. Brainerd, and Lieutenant Goldstine drove from the Moore School in Philadelphia to the Aberdeen Proving Ground in Maryland to present the final proposal to Col. L. E. Simon, Director of the Ballistic Research Laboratory.

When the plan was approved, it set the stage for the financing of $100,000 for the engineering, testing, mechanical design, and production of an electronic digital computer for the army. Eventually, the cost exceeded $500,000 before it was formally dedicated in 1946.

While the initial concepts were from Mauchly's memorandums as drawn in August 1942 and refined in later drafts, he was not placed in charge of any of the three divisions that worked on the project. J. Presper Eckert was put in charge of the Engineering and Testing Division, where he was to be aided by Mauchly. The Mechanical Design and Drafting Division operated separately as did the Production Division.

Dr. Harold Pender, assistant professor of electrical engineering at the Moore School and assistant supervisor of laboratory research for the army, was given the responsibility to obtain Selective Service Occupational Certification for those working on what was officially called "Project PX."

The engineering, testing, mechanical design, and production moved swiftly in 1943 and 1944, and by the summer of 1944 Eckert and Mauchly were exploring ways in which they could obtain commercial patent rights for the ENIAC's electronic digital computer concepts. At that time ENIAC was only a few months away from use by Edward Teller and the science team from Los Alamos Laboratory for the first feasibility calculations on the Hydrogen Bomb.

Internal feuding started at the Moore School when it became apparent that Mauchly and Eckert were involved in a strategy to obtain broad patent rights to the electronic digital computing concepts in ENIAC, Mauchly confirmed. Some believed that since ENIAC was developed with government funds that it should not be used for the financial profit of anyone. Others believed that the moves by Mauchly and Eckert were designed to get other Moore School scientists to give up legitimate claims to important parts of the completed project.

Sperry Rand Lawyer DeLone guided Mauchly quickly and methodically through the tender of his resignation from the Moore School in March of 1946 and the subsequent establishment with Eckert of Electronic Control Company in the summer of 1946 for the purpose of filing an application for patent rights on ENIAC and on the regenerative memory computer concept that was incorporated in EDVAC.

Mauchly told the court that Electronic Control Company became Eckert-Mauchly Computer Corporation and that he and Eckert sold the Eckert-Mauchly Corporation together with their patent rights to Remington Rand Corporation in 1950. Mauchly said he remained with the UNIVAC Division through Remington Rand's merger with Sperry Rand in 1956 and until his resignation in 1959. He then organized a firm known as Mauchly Associates in 1959 and continued to operate under that name until 1968 when he formed a new company, Dynatrend.

Lawyer DeLone guided Mauchly through an impressive number of scientific societies he and Eckert had joined and awards the two men had received for their pioneer work with the electronic digital computer concepts in ENIAC and EDVAC. Mauchly said he and Eckert were awarded the Potts Medal and Life Membership in the Franklin Institute in 1949 for "The ENIAC Computer Development." Other honors they received included the Modern Pioneers Award of the National Association of Manufacturers and the Scott Medal award from the City of Philadelphia. He testified he was among the founders and had been a former president of the Association of Computing Machinery, and had been elected a Fellow of the Institute of Electrical and Electronic Engineers.

That distinguished record did not frighten Honeywell Attorney Halladay when he launched the cross-examination of Mauchly at 1:45 P.M. on Wednesday, 10 November 1971. However, Halladay feigned a deference to the scientist as he made reference to Mauchly's testimony in deposition and commented I "found myself foundering probably because of your superior intelligence."

Halladay routinely asked him how he had prepared for his testimony. Mauchly testified that he had read the depositions of Atanasoff, Sam Legvold, John G. Brainerd, Herman Goldstine, and Louis D. Wilson and Kenneth Rose – the latter two electronic experts from Auerbach Associates.

Then Halladay questioned him on the details of his knowledge of an amendment to the ENIAC patent application that he had signed on 20 May 1963. It was the contention of Honeywell lawyers that information on that amended application was false, so Halladay pushed hard for Mauchly's recollection of what he had sworn in connection with that amended patent application.

"You are trying to get from me, I gather, a positive statement where I feel that my memory is not sufficiently strong to justify a positive statement," Mauchly replied. "I do not recall what the paper work was or what the main purpose of the visit was, but that is just a fault of memory that I have to acknowledge."

Mauchly also testified that he had "no memory" relative to a 16 September 1963 affidavit filed in his name in connection with the amendment application for the ENIAC patent rights.

Then Halladay quizzed Mauchly on his recollection of the December 1940 meeting with Atanasoff and the [railroad flasher] device [Plaintiff Exhibit 21,374] that he testified he had built before that meeting.

"When, before that meeting in December 1940, was it that you built this [railroad flasher] device?" Halladay asked.

"I can't now remember whether it was a year before, or two years before . . . but it was considerably before," Mauchly replied.

"Before you built it, had you worked out the circuit on a document, scheme, a drawing, a sketch, or anything?" Halladay asked.

Mauchly replied "Yes," and Halladay followed with, "Have you produced here any of your writings that show and provide a date for that circuit which allowed this device to go on and off alternately, as you have told us it did?"

"I don't know what the dates are on some of the drawings and

which ones show this, but the one on an exhibit . . . [and] for which
you asked . . . the original, which was a drawing of notes made between Atanasoff and myself at the time of that December meeting,
show the circuit for this," Mauchly replied.

After bringing forth the admission that the sketch had "Atanasoff" written beside it, Halladay asked, "And you did in fact do that
before you ever met Atanasoff?"

"Yes," Mauchly replied, and Halladay moved to questions about
whether Mauchly considered this device to be "counting in a binary
sense."

"No," Mauchly replied and reaffirmed when Halladay asked him
if a gadget with a light that simply was "going on and off would not
be counting [in] a binary sense."

"Would it not be fair to say, Dr. Mauchly, that in order to call a
device a counter which counts in the binary mode that it had to do
more than show on or off alternately, as was the case with your
railroad flasher depicted in [Exhibit number] 21,374?"

Mauchly replied, "We have just got through, of course, with
questions and answers which show this device could operate in two
modes . . . [one] was called the railroad flasher mode."

"All right," Halladay continued. "Now, under what circumstances did you consider it to be a binary counter?"

"Under the circumstances . . . where there was sufficient potential in the battery to ignite one lamp but not to cause this sponta-
neous oscillation between the two," Mauchly replied and explained:
"Now, a two-state device which maintains one state until it receives
a signal which causes it to change state and always on perceiving
that signal changes from one state to the other is to my way of using
the word binary counter."

"You agree, do you not, that it would be impossible to use that
device in that condition with nothing added to count in a binary
mode, do you not?" Halladay asked. When Mauchly said "I do not
agree," Halladay asked what he would do to get the device "to get
over two."

"This device won't count over one," Mauchly finally conceded
and Halladay declared that if the device "won't count over one [it]
does not permit successive enumeration. Is that right?"

"I am not answering your question about successive enumeration," Mauchly snapped back. "I am answering your question about
whether it is a binary counter, as I understand it, and I say it is a
binary counter."

"Even though it won't count over one?" Halladay queried.

"That is right," Mauchly replied.

Halladay, having established Mauchly's interpretation of a gadget that would not count above one as a "binary counter," turned to inquiry of the first drawings or sketches that Mauchly had among his papers "that show a binary counter which you consider to be such?"

"Well, here is one here," Mauchly said pulling a paper from his file.

Halladay noted that the paper was dated 1 January 1941 and asked: "Is that a binary counter of the sort reflected on Plaintiff's Exhibit 21,374?" The lawyer made reference to the exhibit they had been discussing.

"Almost the same sort," Mauchly answered.

"And that device that you have depicted there [is] one that involved the use of vacuum tubes?" Halladay asked and Mauchly responded: "Yes."

"And is that device that you depicted on this note of 1 January 1941 of your own devising?" Halladay asked, pinpointing a date that was less than a week after Mauchly's first meeting with Atanasoff.

When Mauchly answered that the 1 January 1941 sketch was of his own devising, Halladay asked him if there was any sketch or drawing "that shows a binary counter as you have defined it at a date earlier than January 1941?"

"No, it won't be here, because these are all dated later," Mauchly replied. "You have to look elsewhere. This group of drawings here is later. So I can't say whether there are earlier ones on exhibit or not."

"Well, do you remember, Dr. Mauchly, ever finding any drawing or sketch showing a binary counter of your authorship at any date prior to January of 1941?" Halladay asked.

"I haven't actually looked to compare dates that way," Mauchly testified. "It didn't occur to me, because I know that this thing [his flashing railroad stop sign] is much earlier than that."

In his response to questions by Halladay, Mauchly said he had searched his files in answer to subpoenas and had been unable to find any drawings or sketches of a binary computer that was dated prior to his December 1940 meeting with Atanasoff.

Next, Halladay turned Mauchly's attention to the photograph of his harmonic analyzer, which Mauchly acknowledged was "an analog device" as opposed to being a pulse-activated electronic digital device [harmonic analyzer, Exhibit 21,378].

Halladay read from a letter Mauchly had written to General

Radio Company, Cambridge, Massachusetts, on 2 November 1940, in which he asked for "some advice in connection with a research project we are now undertaking—namely, the construction of a network for the purpose of performing Fourier analyses."

The letter continued: "The circuit is already worked out [a modification of one used at MIT some years ago] and a twelve-ordinate analyzer, or perhaps one and a half percent accuracy has been built, using G. R. voltage dividers."

When Halladay had finished reading that paragraph he asked Mauchly: "Does that not refresh your memory that the twenty-one-ordinate harmonic analyzer which is depicted, Plaintiff's Exhibits 21,379 and 21,378, stems from the work of somebody besides yourself?"

Mauchly quibbled: "It does not really refresh my memory as to what had been done earlier at MIT and how much of a modification there was from that. I just don't remember."

"Would you agree, however, that the harmonic analyzer which is depicted in the exhibits before you, 21,379 and 21,378, was not entirely your design, but in fact was a modification of one used at MIT some years prior to 1940 and which had come to your attention in one way or another?" Halladay pressed, but Mauchly refused to respond and repeated that he would "stand by what I said in my letter."

Finally, Judge Larson intervened to instruct. "The Question has been stated several times, Dr. Mauchly. Please answer it."

While Mauchly repeated the phrase "I stand by my letter," this time he continued: " . . . which says that I had received some kind of a suggestion from some prior work, which I do not now recall, but which is referred to in the letter and which apparently no one else can find right now."

Mauchly continued: "So that this [harmonic analyzer idea] was not a flash from heaven, a full-blown device without any prior suggestion as to how anybody could do anything, but neither was any other calculating machine, as far as I know, and neither were the mechanical type calculators and harmonic analyzers, so far as I know. Each one was building on somebody else's work."

Halladay interjected: "Then you do agree, Dr. Mauchly—"

"I agree I did not do this [create the harmonic analyzer] in a vacuum," Mauchly cut him off.

"You agree that you didn't do it in a vacuum, that it was not entirely your own design, and that it was in fact a modification of one used at MIT some years prior to 1940?" Halladay had him on the ropes. "Will you not agree that that is a suitable and correct statement?"

"I will agree if that's what my letter says," Mauchly responded petulantly and Halladay continued to read: "My circuit is . . . a modification of one used at MIT some years ago, and a twelve-ordinate analyzer of perhaps one and a half percent accuracy has been built, using G. R. voltage dividers."

"I don't know whether what I did adapt was a different kind of circuit which came for a different purpose to a harmonic analyzer or whether MIT had already published and I had read about a . . . harmonic analyzer," Dr. Mauchly said in acknowledging that his proudest work up to 1940 had been a product of many borrowed and published ideas.

But Halladay had more on Mauchly's harmonic analyzer, and asked Mauchly if he remembered reading a 1930 thesis by a Mr. Bower entitled "Periodogram Analysis."

"I don't remember that now," Mauchly answered. "It is the sort of thing that I would read, but I don't remember now."

"As a matter of fact, by the time you had built the harmonic analyzer there had been a substantial volume of literature on the subject, had there not?" Halladay asked and Mauchly answered quietly: "I would believe so."

"And you had done research in that literature to educate yourself on how to build such a device, had you not?" Halladay asked.

"I had read the literature," Mauchly responded and added: "I really hadn't done something I would dignify by calling research."

Halladay asked a much subdued Mauchly if his harmonic analyzer part which he had referred to as "potentiometers" was not "the same thing to a layman that he would regard as a rheostat."

"It's almost the same thing," Mauchly replied.

Having established the simplicity of the devices that made up Mauchly's harmonic analyzer, Halladay asked Mauchly if in his discussions with Atanasoff in December 1940 he had told him "of any plan or idea which you had to attack the question of harmonic analysis in a way different than by the use of your harmonic analyzer."

In these series of questions Halladay had damaged Mauchly's initial insistence that Atanasoff was vitally interested in learning about Mauchly's new ideas with regard to harmonic analysis.

Then Halladay turned to a swift series of questions relative to whether it was or was not a fact that Atanasoff had told him of his use of IBM punch cards for converting base-ten to base-two and the reverse. Mauchly said he didn't recall.

However, Halladay continued to quiz him on testimony in which Mauchly recalled that Atanasoff had told him the electronic pulse computer being constructed at Iowa State College utilized vacuum tubes.

"Do you recall Dr. Atanasoff describing to you how his vacuum tubes functioned?" Halladay asked.

Mauchly answered: "My recall is that he didn't describe anything of that nature. That was exactly the point where he was saying if I wanted to know anything more about this, I would have to go to Iowa."

Mauchly had given deposition testimony that his conversation in the school room at the University of Pennsylvania lasted from "20 to 30 minutes," and that he could not remember whether Atanasoff had told him the machine was designed to solve sets of simultaneous linear algebraic equations.

After Mauchly insisted that he could not remember when he had learned that Atanasoff's machine would give solutions of simultaneous linear algebraic equations, Halladay asked him if he would deny Atanasoff told him that in December 1940.

"No, I wouldn't deny that," said Mauchly.

"And you, of course, knew, did you not, Dr. Mauchly, that solution of large sets of simultaneous linear equations could be employed in an attack on nonlinear problems at that time, did you not?" Halladay asked.

"I knew that, as well as many other things," Mauchly replied.

Halladay followed up: "And in order to get arithmetic answers to nonlinear problems in the field of physics, linear algebra equations were of great utility? You knew that, did you not?"

"I not only knew that, but, as far as I know, every physicist who had a Ph.D. knew that," Mauchly responded.

"Well, in any event, Dr. Mauchly, you knew, did you not, in December 1940 before you ever went to Ames, Iowa, that a computer which could use vacuum tube techniques to solve . . . 29 linear algebraic equations and 29 unknowns . . . would represent a considerable advance in the computing arts?" Halladay asked.

Mauchly hedged saying "not necessarily" and Halladay followed up: "You didn't recognize that?"

"It depends on how efficiently and how easy it is to use, how much it costs, and so on. It's a matter of economics, too."

Mauchly haggled for several minutes, refusing to answer the question of whether in 1940 electronic computing with vacuum tubes would not have been a substantial advance in the computing art form. Mauchly rejected the idea of answering the question if not related to cost.

Then the Honeywell lawyer turned to a question to which he expected a simple admission from Mauchly that he had first heard of the distinction between analog and digital or pulse-computing machines from Atanasoff. There was a footnote containing that statement in a comprehensive memorandum on electronic digital computing that Mauchly had written in August 1941, two months after his trip to Iowa State College.

"Is it fair to say, Dr. Mauchly, that you learned of the difference between an analog device and an impulse device, in terms of computers, from Dr. Atanasoff?" Halladay asked.

"Heavens, no," Dr. Mauchly responded. "Where did you get that idea?"

"Well, probably from reading one of your letters, or a document composed by you," Halladay said. He handed Mauchly his August 1941 memorandum, commenting: "Plaintiff's Exhibit 847 is of your authorship, is it not?"

"Yes, sure," Mauchly responded and Halladay read the date of 15 August 1941 and the title: "Analog versus impulse types."

Halladay read a note from Mauchly's paper in which he stated that "computing machines may be conveniently classified as either 'analog' or 'impulse' types." Mauchly acknowledged that the statement was from his paper.

Then Halladay called attention to an asterisk next to that sentence that referenced a footnote stating: "I am indebted to Dr. J. V. Atanasoff of Iowa State College for the classification and terminology here explained." Again Mauchly acknowledged that statement was written by him in August 1941.

Halladay followed up quickly: "And you did, did you not, before you went to Ames, Iowa, write to Dr. Atanasoff and ask him to explain to you what was an analog device?"

"No, I don't believe so," Dr. Mauchly answered. "I have no recollection of writing to ask him what an analog device was, but I may have done so. I can't deny that I might have done that, but I don't understand it now. I have no recollection of it."

Halladay then asked him to identify a letter Mauchly had written to Atanasoff dated 24 February 1941 — about two months after his December 1940 conversation at the University of Pennsylvania.

After Mauchly had acknowledged it was his letter, Halladay read a paragraph of the letter that spoke about an "analogue machine" and a "differential analyzer." Halladay stressed the last sentence in which Mauchly had written, "Incidentally, do you consider the usual d. analyzer [differential analyzer] an 'analogue' machine? If so, how about a polar planimeter?"

"Were you not seeking advice from Dr. Atanasoff, Dr. Mauchly, as to the difference between an 'analogue' device and an impulse device?" Halladay asked.

"I don't think I was seeking advice," Mauchly responded. "I was asking him what he considered these devices to be. He was the one that was defining them."

Although Mauchly argued about whether he was seeking advice or simply asking a question, the letter did establish that he had some discussion of the distinction between analog and impulse devices prior to the June 1941 trip to Iowa State and that it was probably at the December 1940 meeting, which was the only time they had been together at the time that letter was written.

"So far as I know," a more cooperative Mauchly said, "I have given credit in some of these exhibits to Dr. Atanasoff for having applied the word 'analog' to a class of computers to distinguish them from another class of computers. He also applied the word 'impulse,' I believe, to a class of computers, digital, sometimes called discrete variable devices."

Even after that admission, Mauchly balked at acknowledging he had "learned the term" from Atanasoff, but Halladay gave it one more try.

"Would you not say that you learned the term 'analog device' from Dr. Atanasoff as applied to such devices as the harmonic analyzer which you had built . . . [and to] the differential analyzer which you at some point saw at the University of Pennsylvania?" Halladay asked and this time Mauchly responded: "This is a possible way of stating things, yes."

Halladay then turned to the trip to Iowa State College, and drew the testimony from Mauchly that he had made the trip to Ames to see an electronic device that operated on some pulse or impulse base.

Halladay then asked Mauchly if he could now recall in his conversation with Atanasoff in December 1940 that Atanasoff had spoken to him "of his machine's regenerative memory."

When Mauchly responded that he had no recollection of Atanasoff mentioning his machine's "regenerative memory," Halladay asked, "Did he not tell you in the discussions in . . . December of 1940 that in order to do arithmetic automatically, you had to have a memory?"

Mauchly said it would have been unnecessary for Atanasoff to have made mention of a storage or memory device because anyone familiar with mathematical calculations would know that such a storage or memory was essential.

Halladay returned to questioning Mauchly about the various sketches and circuits he had drawn in January 1941, a few weeks after the December meeting with Atanasoff.

In emphasizing his interest in computing in the period just before and after the December 1940 meeting with Atanasoff, Mauchly made himself a target for Halladay's next line of questions.

"And then when Dr. Atanasoff spoke to you in December 1940 of a computer which would provide a discrete variable attack on these vast problems of physics and such, it excited your imagination, did it not?" Halladay asked and Mauchly answered, "Yes, yes, it did."

"And then you went out to Ames, Iowa, with that measure of excitement, did you not?" Halladay asked and again Mauchly answered: "Yes, I did."

"Now, do you want the Court to believe when you got there and you saw what Dr. Atanasoff had constructed by that time, that you felt a real sense of disappointment?" Halladay asked with skepticism.

"Well, I did feel a sense of disappointment," Mauchly said. "I think that what I wanted the Court to believe is the truth."

"And, do I understand that the disappointment which you say you felt at the time was because of the fact that the Atanasoff device was not all electronic?" Halladay asked.

When Mauchly said that at least a large part of his disappointment was because Atanasoff's device was not all electronic, Halladay handed him a copy of Atanasoff's manuscript on "Computing Machines for the Solution of Large Systems of Linear Algebraic Equations" and asked him if he remembered reading such a manuscript at Iowa State College.

"My memory is that I did read some kind of manuscript which he allowed me to read while I was there," Mauchly said. "At this time in history I can't recall the details of that manuscript or say whether this was the thing I read or not. It seems to be in general what I had access to. Whether it had the same completeness or not, I don't know."

Halladay asked Mauchly if in preparation for his role as a witness for Sperry Rand he had read this Atanasoff manuscript, and Mauchly replied: "Not a great deal. I scanned it. . . . Actually, I did have an opportunity, but I didn't read it."

"However, in Ames, Iowa, you didn't just scan it, did you?" Halladay asked.

"Well, it depends on which 'it' you're talking about. I probably read the one I saw at Ames, Iowa," Mauchly said, making his greatest admission on his complete scrutiny of this detailed report about the Atanasoff Berry Computer that was given him by Atanasoff in June 1941.

However, Mauchly continued to quibble as to whether the report he had in Ames in 1941 was the same report, and as to the care and attention he had given to reading the report he had at that time.

"Do you want the Court to understand, Dr. Mauchly, that you spent from Friday evening, June 13, 1941, until Wednesday morning the following week and did not read the Atanasoff manuscript with professional care?" Halladay honed in on the crucial point.

"It's the phrase 'with professional care,' I guess, that is the hooker here," Mauchly responded. "I read whatever I read then with sufficient care to satisfy myself as to what it was that seemed to be described there, but not—I wasn't interested in all the details of what was described there, so why should I read details?"

"Now, if you didn't use your usual standard of professional care in reading the Atanasoff manuscript, then tell us that you didn't," Halladay insisted and the objection by Sperry Rand Attorney DeLone was overruled by Judge Larson's instruction to Mauchly: "You may answer."

That opened a torrential explanation from Mauchly: "It may be a little hard for anyone to understand at this late date just what my attitude was and why I did what I did in those days, but I was searching for ideas which might be useful to help me in computing," Mauchly said. "I wasn't even thinking about inventing computing machines. . . . But I was looking in various places for better ways of implementing computational jobs, many of which I had in front of me if I wanted to do the research work, on weather, and such things.

"I came to Iowa with much the same attitude that I went to the World's Fair and other places. Is there something here which would be useful to aid my computations or anyone else's computations?" Mauchly continued.

"Once there I found out rather quickly the general nature of what Dr. Atanasoff's machine was intended to do and how he was intending to go about this. I no longer became interested in the details, but there I was and I talked with him about other methods of doing things, wondering why he didn't do it a different way, why he didn't make use of the vacuum tube speeds and things of that sort," Mauchly explained.

"We talked about ferromagnetics – or whatever they called them then – magnetic devices for storing, and so on. We talked about a range of topics which he and I were both interested in, familiar with, some of them not having to do with computers at all, I suspect, such as my weather work or his work on something," Mauchly continued.

"But there wasn't any great reward for me at that point to try to memorize the details of this book," he told the court. "There was no sense to me in doing that, and that apparently is the difficult thing to get across, that why should I use my professional time in reading a description of a device which I wasn't particularly interested in thereafter when I could be talking to Atanasoff about things which he and I were both interested in. I would much prefer personal contact with the man than reading something here which was about an idea which wasn't, apparently, coming to fruition in the direction that I was interested in."

When Mauchly had concluded his explanation, Halladay commented that it was "not an answer to the question" and said he would try again.

Halladay again pressed Mauchly on the "professional care" he had used with regard to details in the Atanasoff manuscript, and Mauchly said, "In this case the coarse things (rough general examinations) were enough."

"I can't say I wasn't interested in the way he described the various applications that this machine might be good for," Mauchly testified. "It's always interesting to see how somebody puts in words things that you already know and you want to see how they treated them, but when it comes down to what today we would call the nitty gritty details of how he implemented or intended to implement something, this was not something that I was particularly interested in."

"Well, is there any doubt in your mind, Dr. Mauchly, that you asked Dr. Atanasoff to allow you to take a copy of the manuscript home with you?" Halladay asked.

"I would have liked to have taken a copy home, and in general wherever I go, whether I am going to sales – take sales literature from a store, or something – I like to take home with me things I can refer to later," Mauchly commented.

"Is the short answer to my question, Dr. Mauchly, that you did ask Dr. Atanasoff for permission to take back with you to

Collegeville, Pennsylvania, a copy of his manuscript?" Halladay asked, still trying to get a direct answer.

"The short answer is, I don't know," Dr. Mauchly replied.

As Halladay followed up, Mauchly said he could neither affirm nor deny testimony by Atanasoff that he had asked to take a copy of the manuscript and that Atanasoff declined to allow him to take it with him to Pennsylvania.

On still another attempt, Halladay was successful in extracting from Mauchly the admission that Atanasoff "made it plain to me that I could not" take the manuscript.

For nearly three days they fenced, with Halladay making progress using a slow and patient style that finally brought out grudging admissions from Mauchly, who was sharply resentful of questions that indicated that he "had learned" anything of substance from Atanasoff. But in the end, the monumental documentation that Call had organized was established in the court record on most key points.

Halladay drew from Mauchly the testimony that he had been searching for employment as a teacher or as an employee of an agency or institution of learning in the weeks just prior to his visit to Iowa in June 1941.

Mauchly acknowledged that he had changed his plans abruptly after the visit with Atanasoff and had enrolled in an emergency defense training course in electronics at the University of Pennsylvania before 28 June of that year.

Halladay asked Mauchly to identify the 15 August 1941 memorandum that he had typed which argued enthusiastically for pulse or digital computers over the analog calculators he had been more familiar with up to that point. In connection with that paper, and accompanying sketches drawn by Mauchly, Halladay requested and received confirmation that they contained "electronic digital computing or counting circuits" and "triode vacuum tubes."

Halladay next questioned Mauchly about the letters that he acknowledged writing to Atanasoff and to his meteorological friend, Helms Clayton. Sentence by sentence, Halladay read the letters filled with enthusiasm over the Atanasoff Berry Computer that sharply contradicted Mauchly's testimony that he had "learned nothing" from Atanasoff and had been "disappointed" with the Atanasoff Berry Computer.

Halladay called attention to the testimony of Sam Legvold that in June 1941 he had seen Mauchly with his coat off and his sleeves rolled up working on the Atanasoff Berry Computer with Cliff Berry.

Mauchly avoided a direct answer by testifying that it was possible that he might have been "hot" and "might have taken off my coat" and that it was "perfectly possible" that Cliff Berry had asked him to help hold one end of something.

"I wouldn't deny that," Mauchly told the court.

Then step by step, Halladay drew from Mauchly his acknowledgement of observing and understanding the vacuum tubes, the add-subtract mechanism that operated in the binary mode, the logic circuits, and the regeneration process.

Mauchly grudgingly said he viewed a demonstration in which the add-subtract mechanism was operating in the binary mode, and finally in response to Halladay's last question on that subject the physicist answered: "I was perfectly convinced that what Dr. Atanasoff said and what I saw at that time was this add-subtract mechanism that did in fact work."

Before he left the witness chair, Mauchly had confirmed the following points on the December 1940 meeting with Atanasoff:

1. The meeting lasted between twenty and thirty minutes and had in a general way touched upon the general operation of the Atanasoff Berry Computer that was under construction at Iowa State College.

2. The discussions dealt with Atanasoff's "pulse" principle (electronic digital computing) as opposed to the "analog" or mechanical principles of the Bush differential analyzer that had been built by Vannevar Bush at MIT. Atanasoff had refused to discuss more details of the computer but promised to explain his theories in detail if Mauchly would visit Iowa State.

3. Mauchly was "excited" about the prospect of the visit to Iowa State and the possibility of seeing what he believed was an electronic computer that would perform faster than the Bush differential analyzer and could be constructed for "$2 per digit unit."

Even more important, Halladay, after nearly three days of quibbling over semantics, had finally persuaded Mauchly to confirm the following points:

1. He spent from 13 June 1941 to the morning of 18 June 1941 as a guest in Atanasoff's home in Ames.

2. During this period as Atanasoff's guest he spent uncounted hours in discussions of the Atanasoff Berry Computer and computer theory with John Atanasoff and Clifford Berry.

3. On three or four days he accompanied Atanasoff to his office in the Physics Building and observed the Atanasoff Berry Computer in the company of Atanasoff and Clifford Berry.

4. He had seen demonstrations of the operations or some phases of the functions of the Atanasoff Berry Computer and might have engaged in manipulation of some parts of the machine with Clifford Berry.

5. He was permitted to read Atanasoff's 35-page manuscript on the construction and operation of the Atanasoff Berry Computer from cover to cover and probably did read it. Atanasoff and Berry had willingly answered questions and entered into discussions with him about the machine and the booklet, but Atanasoff had refused to let him take a copy to Pennsylvania.

6. Immediately after his visit to Iowa State in June, Mauchly had written letters to Atanasoff and to his meteorologist friend, Helms Clayton, expressing enthusiasm about the Atanasoff Berry Computer and had taken a crash course in electronics at the University of Pennsylvania.

7. On 15 August 1941 he wrote a comprehensive memorandum on the difference between analog calculators and pulse devices that incorporated some ideas that were almost identical with those in Atanasoff's 35-page manuscript on the Atanasoff Berry Computer.

8. On 30 September 1941 he had written to Atanasoff suggesting a cooperative effort to develop an Atanasoff computer and had asked if Atanasoff had any objection to him using some of the Atanasoff concepts in a computer machine that he was considering building.

Significantly, Mauchly testified that he probably did not mention his trip to Iowa and his conversations with Atanasoff to his colleague, J. Presper Eckert, Jr., in 1941, 1942, or 1943 when they were engaged in their first discussions and planning for the electronic digital computer that was constructed as ENIAC. This trial testimony by Mauchly was consistent with Eckert's testimony that he had no recollection of hearing Atanasoff's name until a few months before meeting Atanasoff on one occasion in August 1944.

It had been a lengthy ordeal for Halladay and for Mauchly, but Allegretti and Call were satisfied that the cross-examination was more productive than they had imagined it would be in the light of Mauchly's testimony in early depositions.

There were several more months of trial testimony from technical witnesses dealing with the soundness of Atanasoff's concepts, as well as on the issues of "prior art" and "prior use" of the ENIAC patents, but the testimony that was most vital to Atanasoff and to computer history was now in the record. Honeywell Attorneys Allegretti and Call had stored the information in their computerized filing system and were in a position to file computerized briefs within a few hours.

Call gave Atanasoff an optimistic report on the result of the cross-examination of Mauchly and on his belief that the evidence now showed that Atanasoff was the inventor of the first electronic digital computer and that Mauchly had derived the major new ENIAC concepts from him. But he cautioned Atanasoff against any premature celebrations, because it was a complicated case with many issues pending upon which the testimony of tutorial witnesses would be important.

CHAPTER 19

Charges of Patent Fraud
and Dissembling, 1972

WHEN U.S. District Judge Earl R. Larson rolled down the curtain on the Honeywell–Sperry Rand litigation on 13 March 1972, there were no oral arguments and thus no dramatic speeches that are so often associated with the conclusion of an important trial. This was not a jury trial, and neither Judge Larson nor the lawyers believed that anything would be gained through dramatic orations.

And so one of the longest and most important trials in the history of the federal courts ended with the shuffling of papers and the checking and rechecking of the exhibits. It had been nearly five years since the 26 May 1967 date when the Honeywell and Sperry Rand lawyers made the "race to the courthouse" that was so close it had taken nearly a year to get the jurisdiction firmly set in Minneapolis with Honeywell in the plaintiff role.

The trial that started on 1 June 1971 consumed over 135 days or parts of days. A total of seventy-seven witnesses had given oral testimony, and an additional eighty witnesses were presented through deposition transcripts. Honeywell had introduced 25,686 exhibits to be marked by the court, and lawyers for Sperry Rand and its subsidiary, Illinois Scientific Development (ISD), had directed the court's attention to another 6,968 exhibits.

Size of those exhibits had ranged from 1-page letters to a 496-page book by Charles Babbage dealing with his theories and projections on high speed mechanical computation devices. Honeywell exhibits were labeled "PX" for Plaintiff's Exhibits, and Sperry Rand exhibits were labeled "DX" for Defendant's Exhibits.

One of the defendant's exhibits labeled DX-2 was a collection of documents relating to the ENIAC patent application that occupied a four-drawer legal filing cabinet. The highly complicated trial transcripts stretched to over 20,667 pages, and Judge Larson was put on notice that unless his decision was flawless in law and fact it was likely to be appealed.

The trial had been one of the most complicated in the history of the federal courts because of the technical nature of the subject, the number of witnesses, and the number of exhibits. It would have been virtually impossible to digest and organize the Honeywell case if it had not been for the Electronic Legal File (ELF) used by the Honeywell attorneys.

During the early stages of the litigation and the trial the Sperry Rand lawyers did some good natured joking about the Honeywell lawyers' ELF, but by the time the litigation was over, they were envious of the manner in which Honeywell lawyers could obtain detailed answers within a relatively short period of time.

While it was true that the trial lawyers in the courtroom still had to have an almost instantaneous grasp of all aspects of the complicated litigation and could not count on stopping in the midst of questioning to push buttons on a computer, the ELF made it possible to screen vast amounts of copy for specific information during recess periods.

More important perhaps was the ability of the Honeywell lawyers to put together a 500-page brief within a month with confidence that it was virtually free of the errors that inevitably creep into copy in the process of having it typed and retyped many times. The final brief was filed 30 September 1972.

The most often repeated charge in the 500-page computerized brief filed by Honeywell lawyers was the allegation that Sperry Rand witnesses and lawyers were "dissembling" about crucial facts with relation to the "public use" or "prior art" or antitrust issues in the case. (The word "dissemble" means to knowingly give a false impression about something or to conceal one's real motives.)

The Honeywell brief charged Mauchly and Eckert "dissembled" on the "derivation from Atanasoff" in actions that "patented the unpatentable."

"The Patent Statute makes it clear that patents can be granted only to those who are truly inventors," the Honeywell brief argued and cited the following sections of the law:

Whoever invents or discovers any new and useful . . . machine . . . or any new and useful improvement thereof, may obtain a patent therefore, subject to the conditions and requirements of this title. (35 U.S.C. Section 101)

A person shall be entitled to a patent unless . . . inter alia [among other things] he did not himself invent the subject matter sought to be patented. . . .

The applicant shall make oath that he believes himself to be the original and first inventor. . . .

After quoting those portions of the law, the Honeywell brief argued:

It is essential to the validity of a patent that it be issued only upon the application of the original inventor. A patent issued upon the application of one who is not the original inventor is unauthorized by law, and does not confer any right or title upon the patentee.

Patent applicants frequently have special knowledge of the prior work of others in the fields to which their alleged inventions relate. This was certainly true in the case of Eckert and Mauchly. Before the ENIAC machine was designed, they were fully informed of the prior electronic digital computer work at Iowa State College. . . .

The brief then cited the case of *Norton v. Curtis* (433 F.2d 779) relative to the duty of patent applicants, such as Mauchly and Eckert, to adhere to the highest standards of honesty and candor in their representations to the Patent Office.

With the seemingly ever-increasing number of patent applications before it, the Patent Office has a tremendous burden. While being a fact-finding as well as an adjudicatory agency, it is necessarily limited in the time permitted to ascertain the facts necessary to adjudge the patentable merits of each application. In addition, it has no testing facilities of its own. Clearly, it must rely on applicants for many of the facts upon which its decisions are based. The highest standards of honesty and candor on the part of the applicants in presenting such facts to the Office are thus necessary elements in a working patent system.

The Honeywell brief went on to state:

The duty of disclosure in this case (along with any suggested "claim by claim" argument) should be judged in light of defendant's contention that Eckert and Mauchly, and they alone, are the first true inventors of the "automatic electronic digital computer."

The fact that the defendants define the scope of their claim patent dominance in such broad language, accordingly, makes all prior work on electronic digital computers relevant which was (1) known to Eckert and Mauchly and (2) not disclosed to the patent office.

The Honeywell lawyers charged that Mauchly and Eckert "dissembled" with regard to a series of specific concepts that were "derivations from Atanasoff."

Eckert and Mauchly filed patent applications on the entire ENIAC machine, the EDVAC regenerative memory, and the ASM (add-subtract mechanism) serial binary delay adder, knowing that subject matter claimed in those applications had not been invented solely by them, but had been derived from the prior work of John V. Atanasoff at Iowa State College.

Then Honeywell lawyers argued in the brief that Sperry Rand and other defendants

have attempted to create the impression that, in order for Honeywell to defeat their claimed patent monopoly over all electronic digital computation, Honeywell must show that the entire ENIAC machine was derived from Atanasoff.

That, of course, is not the issue. Honeywell has never suggested that the design of the ENIAC machines was appropriated, in toto, from Atanasoff or from any other single source.

Honeywell lawyers declared:

In short, the ENIAC machine and the Atanasoff Berry Computer (ABC) are different, but there is no difference between what Mauchly learned from Atanasoff in June, 1941, and what Eckert and Mauchly were later to claim to have invented alone. As the record shows, Eckert and Mauchly made these false claims, not just in the ENIAC patent application, but in the EDVAC regenerative memory patent and in the ASM serial binary delay adder patent.

Honeywell lawyers noted the Sperry Rand argument that even assuming the similarity of the Atanasoff Berry Computer and ENIAC as far as regenerative memory and the ASM (add-subtract mechanism), the Atanasoff machine was inoperative, never completed, never solved equations, and was thus rendered incapable of any claim against the ENIAC patents.

While Honeywell argued that the Atanasoff Berry Computer was an operable device, Honeywell lawyers declared that even if it had been proven an inoperable device the Sperry Rand contention would be "irrelevant to the statutory prerequisite for originality."

"To argue, as defendants (*Sperry Rand et al.*) do, that the knowledge of one man's design cannot be conveyed to another until the first designer actually builds a practical, useful device, is contrary to law and opposed to common sense," Honeywell lawyers stated and then explained further: "One cannot claim a conception derived from another as his 'original' invention even though he may have built the first device based upon that conception."

Honeywell lawyers then turned their attention to the arguments of Sperry Rand and the testimony of Mauchly that derided the Atanasoff Berry Computer by comparing it with the sophisticated and expensive army-financed ENIAC. "By criticizing the ABC machine and comparing it to the ENIAC machine, defendants (*Sperry Rand et al.*) cannot hide the fact that Eckert and Mauchly did not, free of derivation from Atanasoff, invent regenerative memory or the series binary adder or the automatic electronic digital computer as they swore they had in the applications in files EM-1, EM-25 and EM-6 (ENIAC) patents," Honeywell lawyers explained.

Then the Honeywell lawyers declared that Sperry Rand and its representatives had "dissembled on the burden of proof of derivation" in citing cases that were not comparable to the relationship that existed between Atanasoff and Mauchly. In the case of *Drumm v. Turner* (219 F. 188, 196, 197 in the 8th Circuit in 1941) "there was no evidence . . . that the patentee derived his conception of his invention directly or indirectly from Turner," Honeywell lawyers stated.

Here [in the case of Dr. Atanasoff and Dr. Mauchly], the opportunistic pupil takes the master's concept from the true originator and claim as their joint invention, and theirs alone, concepts actually derived from, among others, John V. Atanasoff and Clifford E. Berry of Iowa State College.

The record clearly shows that, in June of 1941, John Mauchly spent nearly a week at Iowa State College as the houseguest of the Atanasoff family, at which time the entire depth of the design of the ABC was fully disclosed to him; no questions were left unanswered.

Later, Mauchly and Eckert claimed, in at least three different patent applications, that they were the "original and first inventors" of concepts which Mauchly was taught by Atanasoff.

Honeywell lawyers turned their attention to the Sperry Rand argument that when Mauchly visited Iowa State College in June 1941, Atanasoff's ideas and his computer "were only in the embryonic stage." They pointed out that this argument was not one of controlling significance, but that it was "surely relevant" to the credibility of Mauchly's uncorroborated testimony, because the heavily documented evidence demonstrated that "the design of the ABC had been completed, except for a few details, prior to Mauchly's visit."

They quoted from a memorandum that Atanasoff had written on 10 June 1940 in which he had summarized the status of the Atanasoff Berry Computer in his search for additional funds. This was written "nearly a year before" the visit of Mauchly, the Honeywell lawyers' brief pointed out to Judge Larson.

Honeywell lawyers followed this up by calling the attention of the court to Atanasoff's comprehensive manuscript on the Atanasoff Berry Computer, written in August 1940, which was reviewed at the time by Professor Caldwell of MIT and Thornton C. Fry, Mathematical Research Director of Bell Telephone Laboratories and "both recommended that Research Corporation support the project."

Honeywell's brief noted that expert witness, Paul Winsor, had examined Atanasoff's August 1940 manuscript on the Atanasoff Berry Computer and had testified that "the manuscript by itself provided adequate teaching to enable one to build the ABC, using ordinary and straightforward engineering skills and techniques available in 1941."

According to Winsor's testimony "the subject matter of ENIAC, claimed by Eckert and Mauchly, was described in Atanasoff's 1940 manuscript," the Honeywell lawyers told the court. "It is equally clear that John Mauchly was given an opportunity to read, and did read, that Atanasoff manuscript during his visit to Iowa State College in June 1941; he discerned a new principle as described by Atanasoff."

Honeywell lawyers argued then that if Mauchly had only read the manuscript, as he admitted doing, and had not seen the Atanasoff Berry Computer or had it explained to him by John Atanasoff and Cliff Berry, he would have been in possession of "full derived knowledge of the subject matter later claimed by himself and Eckert as originated by them alone."

Honeywell lawyers stated that it followed that Mauchly gained a full and complete understanding "of the conceptual and operational details of the ABC and the logic and electronic philosophy of its design."

"Mauchly could not have forgotten this fact by 1947 when he and Eckert claimed to have invented the automatic electronic digital computer (ENIAC) or the regenerative memory or still later ASMs," stated the Honeywell lawyers in the brief.

The Honeywell lawyers then called attention to the Sperry Rand argument that Mauchly had testified he "was disappointed" when he saw the Atanasoff Berry Computer, which he said was "inoperative." "How different this argument is than Mauchly's true attitude as he revealed in his correspondence with his friend, H. Helm Clayton, on June 29, 1941."

Honeywell lawyers followed this with a quotation from Mauchly's letter to Clayton in which he told of viewing the Atanasoff Berry Computer at Iowa State College, and described it in these terms: "His machine, now nearing completion, is electronic in operation, and will solve within a very few minutes any system of linear equations involving no more than thirty variables. It can be adapted to do the job of the Bush differential analyzer more rapidly than the Bush machine does, and it costs a lot less."

Honeywell lawyers then explained the steps that Mauchly took to utilize the ideas he had learned from Atanasoff. "After his trip to Iowa State College, Mauchly took a crash course in electronics and joined the Moore School of Engineering in Philadelphia, where he began to consider applying his understanding of new impulse or digital principles he had been taught by Atanasoff to do the job of the Bush differential analyzer," Honeywell lawyers stated in their brief.

Then Honeywell lawyers noted that Mauchly in a memorandum on the ideas he had learned from Atanasoff had given brief credit to Atanasoff "for teaching him the distinction between analog or continuous variable computers and discrete impulse types, now known as digital."

Furthermore, the Honeywell lawyers commented that Mauchly "was expressing no disappointment" with what he had learned from Atanasoff when he wrote to him on 30 September 1941, asking if there was "any objection, from your point of view, to my building some sort of computer which incorporates some of the features of your machine?"

Honeywell lawyers told the court that Mauchly and Eckert, in filing their patent applications for ENIAC in 1947, had a legal duty to make a full disclosure of the information they had derived from Atanasoff, but instead, had "dissembled" by not disclosing the information and by signing papers and swearing that the ideas were their original concepts.

"Full disclosure could and should have been made to the Patent Office but was not," Honeywell lawyers stated. "Invalid patent matter could and should then have been disclaimed or cancelled. But the Patent Office was never given an opportunity to consider any of this vital information bearing on originality, and defendants (*Sperry Rand et al.*) still persist in their attempt to enforce their derivative and inclusive claims to subject matter Mauchly was taught by Atanasoff."

Then Honeywell lawyers called attention in their brief to what they viewed as misquotations of the record by Sperry Rand lawyers. "Atanasoff had a vacuum tube device which added and subtracted, and contrary to defendant's repeated misquotation of his testimony was capable of division (if not suitable) by being arranged to count the number of subtractions; the Atanasoff modular ASM's were triggered by pulses and worked at electronic speed except while resting in wait for the next pulse instructions from the abaci drums."

"Eckert and Mauchly both knew they had no right to describe an arrangement substantially identical to Atanasoff's, and then claim a cyclically moving carrier bearing electrostatic charges as if they were the first inventors of such a drum or disc," Honeywell lawyers stated and followed up with the assertion that Mauchly and Eckert had no more right to claim Atanasoff's series binary add-subtract mechanism, or to make the broad patent claims to "automatic electronic digital computers."

"Such activities were fraudulent whether Atanasoff or Berry had never turned a screw, soldered a single connection or pulsed a single vacuum tube," Honeywell lawyers contended, concluding their arguments on that issue. "The conceptions were Atanasoff's and not Eckert's and not Mauchly's."

The rest of the lengthy brief was spent in arguing that the ideas that Mauchly and Eckert did not "derive" from the work of John Atanasoff and Clifford Berry were borrowed from the work of Radio Corporation of America, Bell Telephone Laboratories, International Business Machines, National Cash Register, Massachusetts Institute of Technology, or from the members of the team at the Moore School of Electrical Engineering at the University of Pennsylvania.

It was a powerful, well-documented and well-argued brief. It was opposed by the Sperry Rand brief that leaned heavily upon the arguments that there was a legal presumption that the patents granted by the Patent Office to Mauchly and Eckert were valid, and that Honeywell had the burden of proving that Mauchly obtained the ideas for the ENIAC design from Atanasoff.

They also argued that Mauchly had thought about electronic digital computing in the months and years prior to meeting Atanasoff, and that he had done some experiments by himself that demonstrated prior knowledge of some of the concepts of electronic digital computing.

Sperry Rand lawyers argued forcefully that the patent sharing agreements that they had with IBM and Bell Telephone Laboratories did not constitute violations of the federal antitrust laws or an unlawful restraint of trade.

When the Sperry Rand brief was filed in August 1972, it was the beginning of Judge Larson's ordeal—putting together a decision that would stand against any appeals from either of the well-financed litigants. He knew it would be an opinion of importance to the whole computer industry, and it would also be one that would be combed over for years by computer historians. It was his burden now as he settled down for months of work in the court that had become known as the Sperry Rand–Honeywell room in the U.S. District Court House in downtown Minneapolis.

CHAPTER 20

Judge Larson: Mauchly "Derived" Ideas from Atanasoff, 1973

THE first public indication of Judge Larson's decision came in April 1973, after he provided lawyers for Honeywell and Sperry Rand copies of a proposed decision and asked for their comments on that decision. Since it was a long and complicated case, Judge Larson wanted to avoid any technical errors that might result in a reversal of his decision, and he wanted both sides to have one last opportunity to point out any conceivable error of fact or of law for his consideration.

That tentative decision was leaked to the *Minneapolis Tribune and Star* and staff writer Bob Lundegaard wrote an exclusive story for the 12 April 1973 newspaper stating that Judge Larson had ruled that the basic ENIAC patents held by Sperry Rand were invalid. It was not revealed how Lundegaard received the information, or whether the unauthorized leak had been a delivery of all or part of the text of Judge Larson's tentative decision.

That story did not mention whether Judge Larson had ruled on the question: Did Dr. Mauchly derive his electronic digital computer concepts from the Atanasoff Berry Computer? In fact, that news story made no reference to either Atanasoff or Mauchly but had concentrated on the "public use" issue.

Reporter Lundegaard noted only the name of "Dr. Edward Teller, father of the H-Bomb," as among "the hundreds of witnesses at the trial." His story stated briefly that Teller testified that ENIAC was used in calculations that were of "decisive significance" in decisions on the Hydrogen Bomb and that these calculations were made in 1945 and 1946.

That page-1 copyrighted story was headlined:

Computer patent ruled invalid: Honeywell owes no royalties

Lundegaard explained that Sperry Rand was seeking $20 million in past royalties from Honeywell alone, but that Sperry Rand had contemplated litigation to collect more millions from other major computer firms with the totals running into hundreds of millions of dollars.

Atanasoff learned of that news story through Honeywell lawyers. Although they were generally optimistic in their comments about Judge Larson's views that the evidence supported their contention on Mauchly's theft of major electronic digital computer concepts from Atanasoff, they stressed that the circulated opinion was not final.

Honeywell lawyers did tell Atanasoff that the tentative decision indicated that Judge Larson believed Atanasoff had been a credible witness and that Mauchly had an extremely poor memory or was engaged in falsification.

Atanasoff now felt more confident than ever that the court would rule that Mauchly had stolen his ideas, and he was alternately patient and impatient waiting and hoping for the time that the formal public decision of Judge Larson would proclaim to the world that the Atanasoff Berry Computer, constructed at Iowa State College, was the first electronic digital computer.

While the decision was coming too late for John Atanasoff or Clifford Berry's heirs to receive any direct financial benefits, it would be of immense personal satisfaction to have formal recognition as the father of one of the most significant inventions of the century.

When Judge Larson distributed the formal opinion on 19 October 1973, it was everything that Atanasoff had hoped it would be. It was a clear and unequivocal finding that Mauchly's basic ENIAC ideas were "derived from Atanasoff, and the invention claimed in ENIAC was derived from Atanasoff."

In extensive findings, Judge Larson declared: "Eckert and Mauchly did not themselves first invent the automatic electronic digital computer, but instead derived that subject matter from one Dr. John Vincent Atanasoff."

In further statements on the evidence relative to the Atanasoff

Berry Computer, Judge Larson declared: "Honeywell has proved that the claimed subject matter of the ENIAC patent relied on in support of the counterclaim herein is not patentable over the subject matter derived by Mauchly from Atanasoff. As a representative example, Honeywell has shown that the subject matter of detailed claims 88 and 89 of the ENIAC patent corresponds to the work of Atanasoff which was known to Mauchly before any effort pertinent to ENIAC machine or patent began."

"The Court has heard the testimony at trial of both Atanasoff and Mauchly, and finds the testimony of Atanasoff with respect to the knowledge and information derived by Mauchly to be credible," stated Judge Larson in rejecting Mauchly's vague, contrived, contradictory, and uncorroborated contention that he had learned nothing of consequence from the Atanasoff Berry Computer.

Judge Larson was kind to Mauchly in not castigating him as a willful liar and falsifier and in accepting the possibility that his incredible and uncorroborated testimony might have been a result of a bad memory and confusion.

To Judge Larson, there was no conceivable doubt about the work and achievement of John Atanasoff and Clifford Berry at Iowa State College in the period prior to December 1940, when Atanasoff met Mauchly for the first time.

"Between 1937 and 1942, Atanasoff, then a professor of physics and mathematics at Iowa State College, Ames, Iowa, developed and built an automatic electronic digital computer for solving large systems of simultaneous linear algebraic equations," Judge Larson stated in his opinion.

Then Judge Larson went through a recitation of the chronology of events that established, with corroboration, the progress Atanasoff and Berry had made on the electronic digital computer prior to December 1940.

"In December, 1939, Atanasoff completed and reduced to practice his basic conception in the form of an operating breadboard model of a computing machine," Judge Larson stated. "This breadboard model machine constructed with the assistance of a graduate student, Clifford Berry, permitted the various components of the machine to be tested under actual operating conditions. The breadboard model established the soundness of the basic principles of design, and Atanasoff and Berry began construction of a prototype, or pilot model, capable of solving with a high degree of accuracy a system of as many as 29 simultaneous equations having 29 unknowns."

Judge Larson called attention to the state of progress in August

1940, which was more than four months before Atanasoff met Mauchly at the AAAS convention in Philadelphia.

"By August, 1940, in connection with efforts at further funding, Atanasoff prepared a comprehensive manuscript which fully described the principles of his machine, including detail design features. By the time the manuscript was prepared in August, 1940, construction of the machine, destined to be termed in this litigation the Atanasoff Berry computer or "ABC," was already far advanced. The description contained in the manuscript was adequate to enable one of ordinary skill in electronics at that time to make and use an ABC computer."

Judge Larson noted that the advanced state of the Atanasoff Berry Computer was not just the hindsight view of Atanasoff or of Iowa State officials, but was the opinion of outside experts who viewed and examined the machine as well as Atanasoff's plans in the 1939 to 1941 period of time.

"The manuscript was studied by experts in the art of aids to mathematical computation, who recommended its financial support, and these recommendations resulted in a grant of funds by Research Corporation for the ABC's continued construction," Judge Larson stated before going into his analysis and conclusions on what Mauchly learned from his contacts with Atanasoff.

Judge Larson reviewed the first meeting of Mauchly and Atanasoff at the AAAS meeting in Philadelphia where Atanasoff "generally informed Mauchly about the computing machine under construction at Iowa State College."

"Because of Mauchly's expressions of interest in the machine and its principles, Atanasoff invited Mauchly to come to Ames, Iowa, to learn more about the computer," Judge Larson stated and continued: "After correspondence on the subject with Atanasoff, Mauchly went to Ames, Iowa, as a houseguest of Atanasoff for several days, where he discussed the ABC as well as other ideas of Atanasoff's relating to the computing art."

Judge Larson then described the opportunities Mauchly had for unrestricted access to the secrets of the Atanasoff Berry Computer:

> Mauchly was given an opportunity to read, and did read, but was not permitted to take with him, a copy of the comprehensive manuscript which Atanasoff had prepared in August, 1940.
>
> At the time of Mauchly's visit, although the ABC was not entirely complete, its construction was well advanced so that the principles of its operation, including detail design features, was explained and demonstrated to Mauchly.

The discussions Mauchly had with both Atanasoff and Berry while at Ames were free and open and no significant information concerning the machine's theory, design, construction, use or operation was withheld.

Judge Larson's decision then dealt with Mauchly's contention that he was deeply knowledgeable and interested in developing an electronic digital computer before meeting Atanasoff or going to Iowa State in June 1941.

"Prior to his visit to Ames, Iowa, Mauchly had been broadly interested in electrical analog calculating devices, but had not conceived an automatic electronic digital computer."

Then in more stately legal terms, Judge Larson reported his conclusion that Mauchly had pirated or stolen Atanasoff's electronic digital concepts. Judge Larson used the legal term "derived" to leave the way open for the possible interpretation that Mauchly may have inadvertently or unknowingly misappropriated Atanasoff's computer concepts.

As a result of this visit, the discussions of Mauchly with Atanasoff and Berry, the demonstrations, and the review of the manuscript, Mauchly derived from ABC "the invention of the automatic electronic digital computer" claimed in the ENIAC patent.

Having ruled that Mauchly derived his basic electronic digital computer concepts from the Atanasoff Berry Computer, Judge Larson turned to Honeywell's claim that Mauchly and Eckert had wrongfully claimed credit for the work of others who had helped develop ENIAC at the Moore School of Electrical Engineering in the 1943 to 1946 period.

Judge Larson reviewed the chronology of work on the ENIAC machine, and the fact that Mauchly and Eckert had filed for patents on 27 June 1947, after he on 19 June 1947 had "executed an oath as the sole co-inventors in support of the ENIAC patent application."

"I am inclined to the point of view that the work on the ENIAC was a group or team effort and that inventive contributions were made by [T. K.] Sharpless, [Arthur W.] Burks, [Robert F.] Shaw, and others," Judge Larson stated.

Judge Larson then proceeded to list the names and specific contributions made to ENIAC development by Sharpless, Burks, Shaw, John H. Davis, Frank Mural, Chuan Chu, S. B. Williams, Joseph Chedaker, James Cummings, Harry Gail, and Robert Michael.

However, Judge Larson ruled that Honeywell had failed to

prove that Mauchly and Eckert had wrongfully claimed patent rights because those individuals had not asserted their claims in proper fashion and in time to call those claims to the attention of the U.S. Patent Office.

Atanasoff was thoroughly pleased with Judge Larson's opinion, but he was just as thoroughly disappointed with the news stories on that decision. The news stories were brief in announcing Honeywell's triumph over Sperry Rand, the invalidation of the ENIAC patents, and in reporting the failure of Honeywell to establish the multimillion dollars in damages they sought from Sperry Rand for violation of the federal antitrust laws.

The timing of the publication of the decision on 19 October 1973 brought it into competition with the explosive "Saturday Night Massacre" in the continuing Watergate scandal of the Richard Nixon presidency.

That particularly explosive story on the firing of Special Watergate Prosecutor Archibald Cox dominated the news holes on most national newspapers and would have reduced the display on any other story that night. However, that does not adequately explain the ignoring of a story that was of great significance to the world of science—mathematics, physics, and the rest of the world influenced by and vitally interested in computer science.

Judge Larson had ruled that John Vincent Atanasoff and Clifford Berry had constructed the first electronic digital computer at Iowa State College in the 1939–1942 period.

He had also ruled that John Mauchly and J. Presper Eckert, who had for more than twenty-five years been feted, trumpeted, and honored as the co-inventors of the first electronic digital computer, were not entitled to the patent upon which that honor was based.

Furthermore, Judge Larson had ruled that Mauchly had pirated Atanasoff's ideas, and for more than thirty years had palmed those ideas off on the world as the product of his own genius.

The length of Judge Larson's decision, the many complicated issues involved in the case, and the length of the trial were all factors that would have had some influence on the total ignoring of a significant decision on the history of the development of the electronic digital computer in the initial news stories.

John and Alice Atanasoff were disappointed in the news stories that failed to mention that a U.S. district judge had proclaimed Atanasoff the inventor of the first electronic digital computer. The lack of press coverage of the Atanasoff-Mauchly story was even more difficult to understand when one took into account the dramatic personal story of Atanasoff's triumph in federal court over the man who thirty years earlier had appropriated his ideas.

Atanasoff and Alice waited patiently for weeks passing the word quietly to family members and intimate friends of Judge Larson's decision but avoiding overt actions that would seem immodest or might be characterized as "pushy." They heard nothing from anyone but the Honeywell lawyers who sent them a copy of the 246-page opinion.

They had believed that someone from Iowa State University, where the first electronic digital computer was built, would call with congratulations and with an eagerness to do something of significance to call attention to the fact that one of the great inventions of the century was conceived and constructed on their campus. Atanasoff and Alice had expected that the University of Florida, where JV received his B.S. degree in electrical engineering, or the University of Wisconsin, where he received his Ph.D. in theoretic physics, would have had more than casual interest in the decision involving one who had studied in those institutions. The problem was simply that no one at those institutions was aware of the momentous decision involving Atanasoff because there had been no news stories that had focused on that historically significant decision.

More frustrating and infuriating than the lack of attention on JV's achievement were reports that Mauchly had given speeches and had a "fireside chat" with computer scientists in Italy in which he had repeated his own discredited story about the invention of the electronic digital computer and made no mention of Judge Larson's decision that had rejected his claim.

After two months of frustration and private irritation, Alice decided they should quietly explore what they might do to get some public attention on Judge Larson's decision as it related to the invention of the electronic digital computer.

It was mid-December 1973 when Alice placed her call to me, as the Washington bureau chief for the *Des Moines Register*. She knew me from high school days in Webster City, Iowa, where she was a grade or two behind me in school. I knew her as Alice Crosby, the younger sister of a classmate, Victor Crosby. I remembered her clearly, even after more than thirty years. She had been in biology class with me. She introduced herself, said she was not asking me to do a story, but wanted advice with regard to her husband, John Atanasoff.

When she stated that he was "the inventor of the computer" and that he was having difficulty getting proper public credit for his invention, I was not immediately impressed. However, she was a friend from high school days, and it would not be too much trouble to lend a sympathetic ear to her problem.

John Atanasoff was her husband and she probably had an exaggerated view of his achievements and was unduly upset that her spouse had not been accorded the honor she believed was due him. When she mentioned that he had been a professor of mathematics and physics at Iowa State College, I believed it plausible that he might have some legitimate computer invention claim that would be worth exploring for a story in the *Des Moines Register*.

It was not until Alice made mention of a U.S. District Court decision that established he was the legal father of the electrical digital computer that I became deeply interested, but still with some caution. I asked her several questions about the contents of the decision, and after she read me several paragraphs from that decision, I was convinced. It could be a great story for Iowa and Iowa State University, as well as for the Atanasoffs.

CHAPTER 21

Dr. Mauchly's Fireside Chat and Other Deceptions

JUDGE LARSON'S long and detailed ruling on 19 October 1973 did not end Mauchly's continuing assertions that he was the originator and inventor of the first electronic computer. The lack of newspaper attention to Judge Larson's ruling made Mauchly bold and arrogant. He believed that he could continue to claim that he was the inventor and did not derive or steal any of the basic electronic digital concepts from Atanasoff. Few newspaper reporters had the patience to plow through the complicated 200-page opinion, much less comb through the thousands of pages of depositions and trial transcripts upon which Judge Larson's opinion was based.

On 13 November 1973 – only about three weeks after Judge Larson's ruling – Mauchly gave an after-dinner talk at the plush "Les Aigles" Villa near Rome, Italy. He was billed as "the co-inventor of the first electronic digital computer" at a seminar for senior managers from government, industry, and academia at the International Executive Centre at the Villa maintained by Sperry Rand at that time.

In the elegant drawing room complete with Persian carpets and Roman artifacts and a huge Italian Majolika fireplace mantle, John Mauchly held forth on "The History of the Computer." It was an interesting fireside tale, according to Mauchly's friend Carl Hammer. Mauchly told the story with "changing moods, relaxed contemplation, and dramatic flair" in his history reportage.

Hammer reported on Mauchly's fireside chat with enthusiasm

and color in the July 1982 issue of *Annals of the History of Computing*. "We all became witnesses through the eyes of this great inventor and innovator whose role in relation to technological advances would be remembered for centuries," Hammer wrote in recounting how Mauchly had mesmerized his audience for the better part of a half-hour. The speech was a repetition of the story he had told in Judge Larson's court with some embellishments, but with no reference to John Atanasoff, Clifford Berry, his 1941 trip to Iowa State College, or to the fact that his claim as the inventor was under any challenge. The presentation was misleading at best.

Mauchly was vague on dates but long on colorful discussions of the manner in which his original proposal for an electronic digital computer was rejected and temporarily lost by the Dean of the Moore School and the professor to whom he said he sent it. But Mauchly did pay tribute to J. Presper Eckert, whose electronic expertise he leaned upon heavily after they started their first discussion in 1942 on the computer project that became ENIAC. He made no reference to the seven years of litigation over the ENIAC patents or to Judge Larson's opinion.

When Alice Atanasoff called me over the Christmas season in December 1973, she and JV were unaware that Mauchly was ignoring the federal court ruling and generally trashing Judge Larson's decision. Her deep concern then was the total lack of any stories in newspapers or magazines on what to them was the big and significant story: A federal court had rendered a decision that John V. Atanasoff was the father of the electronic digital computer, one of the great inventions of the century.

When Alice first stated that a court decision was being ignored, I was certain that there must be some mistake in the way the Atanasoffs were interpreting the legal opinion. Her brief recital of the fact that Atanasoff's computer ideas were stolen more than thirty years earlier and that a court had recently judged him to be the inventor was so astounding that it seemed unbelievable.

However, when Alice read only two paragraphs from Judge Larson's decision, I was convinced that the Atanasoff story was worth pursuing in depth at the first break in my very full schedule. It was more than a week before I was able to find the time to drive to Atanasoff's Maryland farm home to examine Judge Larson's opinion and to study the key documents (see Appendix A). I was particularly anxious to read Mauchly's letters that were written to Atanasoff in the summer and fall of 1941, immediately after his visit to Iowa State.

Everything in Judge Larson's opinion was as Atanasoff and Alice reported. Mauchly's letters were, on their face, expressions of enthusiasm for the Atanasoff Berry Computer, coupled with a desire to work out some way to persuade Atanasoff to enter into a cooperative development of an electronic digital computer.

The September letter carried only a typed name and did not have Mauchly's signature, but Alice assured me that Mauchly at the trial had acknowledged he was the author of the letter and that the letter was a part of the trial record.

While I believed the assurances of John and Alice Atanasoff, I recognized that they were parties with a great interest in the matter and that they might have been mistaken with regard to whether Mauchly's letter was, in fact, made a part of the trial record. Even though Judge Larson's opinion was thoroughly supportive that Mauchly's letters were in the trial record, I wanted to talk to Mauchly himself, to hear what he had to say. It was always possible that Mauchly would deny having written the 30 September 1941 letter that was so damaging to his contention that he had learned nothing from his visit with Atanasoff at Iowa State.

During the period I was trying to reach Mauchly by telephone, the *Washington Post* on Sunday, 13 January 1974, published a story by W. David Gardner, industry editor of the monthly magazine *Datamation*, that dealt with Mauchly, Eckert, and the Atanasoff Berry Computer. The Gardner story spelled out with relevant detail the story of how Judge Larson's decision had invalidated the ENIAC patents held by Sperry Rand through Mauchly and Eckert. He used colorful characterizations picturing Mauchly and Eckert as being to the computer industry what Henry Ford was to the Model T and the automotive industry and what Orville and Wilbur Wright were to Kitty Hawk and the airplane industry.

It was an excellent story and I feared it would be read and published by the editors of the *Des Moines Register* and would kill the Iowa impact for the story I was still working on at that time. Certainly some editor for the Associated Press or some other wire service syndicate would see the story in the Outlook section of one of the largest newspapers in the nation.

It was a relief to me to discover a few days later that the *Des Moines Register* editors had not seen the Gardner story, and also had seen nothing about a former Iowa State College professor being declared the inventor of the first electronic digital computer. I went ahead with my efforts to contact Mauchly by placing telephone calls to his home.

When I finally got a response, Mauchly himself answered the telephone, and briefly identified himself before I identified myself as a reporter and related my interest in asking him a few questions about the origins of the electronic digital computer concepts in ENIAC. I told him that I had read Judge Larson's opinion and that I wanted to ask him a few questions to get his side of the case.

Even as he said he did not want to discuss the case, Mauchly launched an attack on Judge Larson's opinion, stating that Judge Larson simply did not understand some technical aspects of the case and that the decision "was wrong."

Why hadn't Sperry Rand appealed the case? I asked. Mauchly said he believed that Sperry Rand should have appealed, but the lawyers had never explained to his satisfaction why they did not appeal.

Mauchly acknowledged two points:

1. He had visited Atanasoff at Iowa State College for several days in June 1941.
2. He had seen the Atanasoff Berry Computer and had some discussion of the operations of the machine with Atanasoff.

Mauchly's comments about Atanasoff and the Atanasoff Berry Computer were thoroughly derogatory. He characterized the machine as "just a little piece of junk" and contrasted it to ENIAC, which he said was a "highly sophisticated and operational machine."

I asked Mauchly how he could characterize the Atanasoff Berry Computer as "a crude little machine that wouldn't do anything" and at the same time insist that he had not examined it closely or observed its performance.

Mauchly grew irritated and said he was not going to answer a lot of specific questions but that "Judge Larson's decision was wrong." He declared that Judge Larson "didn't take into account some very important technical evidence." Then Mauchly declined to identify or explain the nature of the "technical evidence" he claimed Judge Larson had not taken into account.

After Mauchly rejected my repeated efforts to gain an explanation of this technical evidence, I asked him if he had read Atanasoff's manuscript and taken notes from it.

"I don't think I learned anything from his (Atanasoff's) papers, and I was merely trying to help the guy in case Iowa State didn't finance him," Mauchly replied without making a direct response to whether he had or had not taken notes from Atanasoff's computer manuscript.

I raised questions related to letters he was purported to have written to Atanasoff in 1941 after his visit to Iowa State College in which he had expressed his admiration for the Atanasoff Berry Computer and seemed to be seeking to get Atanasoff to cooperate with him in a joint computer project.

Mauchly acknowledged writing the 30 September 1941 letter that was a part of the court record but refused to discuss the implications that he had learned a great deal of computer information from the Iowa State visit and was seeking a partnership in the development of Atanasoff's new concepts.

"I was just trying to do the guy a favor in getting financing for his machine," Mauchly repeated.

I raised again the question of why Sperry Rand had not appealed Judge Larson's decision if it was as flawed as he contended. Mauchly replied he had suggested to Sperry Rand that they appeal the decision, but Sperry Rand had not followed his suggestion. He said he did not know why.

I remembered that Atanasoff had told me he had given testimony relative to Mauchly's visit to his Maryland farm home to try to get him "not to remember some details" of the conversations at Iowa State. I asked Mauchly if he could give me an explanation of his reason for that visit to Atanasoff's home in December 1967.

Mauchly said he did not want to discuss the meeting, would not answer any more questions, and hung up the telephone to end the conversation.

My story on the front page of the *Des Moines Sunday Register* on 27 January 1974 was the first information the Iowa State University public affairs office had that a federal court had ruled that the first electronic digital computer had been invented at Iowa State. I had avoided any calls to Iowa State before my story appeared to reduce the possibility that somehow it might be leaked to Iowa newspapers before I was fully prepared to publish.

Carl Hamilton, then vice-president of Iowa State University in charge of public affairs, was elated. Within days, he set the wheels in motion to honor Atanasoff by making him Grand Marshall of the Veishea Day Parade. It was the first of a series of events Iowa State University staged over a period of years to honor John Atanasoff and Clifford Berry, who as professor and graduate student had constructed the first electronic digital computer at Iowa State.

However, the myth persisted that John Mauchly was the originator and inventor of the computer concepts he "derived" from Atanasoff. It created a continuing confusion and unjustified suspicion about the soundness of Judge Larson's opinion. Mauchly and his friends and supporters contributed also to the confusion with specious arguments that avoided the hard fact that Mauchly's testimony simply was not credible.

Some of Mauchly's defenders explained that they did not believe he was a willful liar in his ever-changing testimony about his visit with Atanasoff, but rather believed he was a man with a very poor memory who was not properly prepared by the Sperry Rand lawyers for the depositions and the trial. They argue that Sperry Rand lawyers did not analyze the nature of the issues that would emerge in the Honeywell litigation, and were caught off guard by the emergence of Mauchly's letters to Atanasoff and to Helms.

Until his death in 1980 Mauchly never made a public concession stating that he had "derived" the basic concepts of his initial electronic digital computer plan from Atanasoff, but he did modify his claim. Instead of saying he was the inventor of the first electronic digital computer he claimed he was "the co-inventor of the first general purpose electronic digital computer, ENIAC."

In his last years, he acknowledged the Atanasoff Berry machine as a "special purpose" electronic digital computer, and stated that its use was limited to doing systems of algebraic equations. He claimed that it was ENIAC, EDVAC, and UNIVAC that had opened the eyes of the world to the potential of the electronic digital computer's uses.

The debate over Judge Larson's decision was continued in the pages of the *Annals of the History of Computing* where Bernard A. Galler, editor-in-chief, found merit in keeping the controversy going. He professed to keeping an open mind about Judge Larson's decision.

In the October 1981 volume of the *Annals of the History of Computing,* Arthur W. and Alice R. Burks examined the history of ENIAC and the record of the Honeywell–Sperry Rand trial. Arthur Burks was one of the half dozen scientists and mathematicians at the Moore School of Electrical Engineering who had worked with Mauchly and Eckert on ENIAC and was in the group that had made significant contributions to the development of ENIAC.

The Burkses wrote that "two major advances in computer technology mark this pioneering period" and identified them in these terms: "The first, culminating in the ENIAC, was the introduction of vacuum tubes for fast, reliable digital computation. It began with John V. Atanasoff's digital electronic, special-purpose computer conceived and built at Iowa State College between 1935 and 1942."

The Burkses stated firmly that "it led to the ENIAC through an idea Atanasoff conveyed by letter to John W. Mauchly in 1941." Even as the Burkses gave credit to Atanasoff for the invention of the first electronic digital computer, they characterized ENIAC as "the first general-purpose electronic computer, capable of solving a wide variety of problems in science, engineering, and number theory at a high rate of speed."

The Burks article stated that ENIAC "was roughly 1000 times faster than its closest competitor, the electromechanical Harvard Mark I." "It was only about 100 times faster than the differential analyzer, but, being digital, it achieved much greater accuracy than the analog differential analyzer and could solve a much wider range of problems."

"As a consequence of its speed and power, it [the electronic digital computer] solved computational problems previously beyond the reach of man, thereby establishing the feasibility and value of electronic digital computation," the Burkses wrote.

The Burkses reviewed the history of efforts to develop a computing machine from the time of Charles Babbage's "analytical engine" a century before Vannevar Bush invented the differential analyzer at the Massachusetts Institute of Technology in 1930.

"Differential analyzers were, by the combined criteria of computing power and generality, the best computing instruments available from about 1930 until the appearance of the large digital machine," the Burkses wrote. "They [differential analyzers] constituted the crown of analog computation, now completely outmoded: slide rule, planimeter, harmonic analyzer, electric network analyzer, etc."

It was against this background of analog computation that Atanasoff conceived the concepts of electronic digital computing in the late 1930s, and with Clifford Berry "finished a successful prototype in late 1939, and worked over the next several years to construct the complete machine," the Burkses stated.

"Thus John Vincent Atanasoff was the inventor of the first electronic computer. It was an automatic digital machine, and it was special-purpose in that it solved only linear algebraic equations," the Burkses wrote and made reference to it as "this landmark in the history of computers." The Burkses spelled out in scientific detail the manner in which Atanasoff and Berry had pioneered the development of the major concepts used in ENIAC and now common to all computers.

The Burkses explained that by May 1942 the Atanasoff Berry Computer attained its final state. "All of the parts had been completed, and the machine had been assembled and tested. Everything worked well, with the exception of the electric-spark method of punching holes in the binary cards. This had succeeded in preliminary tests in 1939, but now failed, though only rarely. Because the rate of failure was so low—perhaps once in 100,000 times—the computer could solve small sets of equations correctly; it could not solve large sets however, on account of the great number of binary digits to be recorded and read in these."

The Burkses concluded that it was unfortunate that this minor difficulty had not been overcome by the fall of 1942 when Dr. Atanasoff and Cliff Berry left Iowa State College for war-related employment during World War II. "Nevertheless, Atanasoff had succeeded in designing and building an electronic computer whose computing system worked; the fact that its electromechanical input-output system was not perfected does not detract from the success of the invention in terms of electronic computation. Moreover, a functional input-output system was already in existence, but not available to Atanasoff, and was, as we shall see, used in ENIAC."

"So, clearly, Atanasoff had achieved a great deal in his pioneering effort," the Burkses wrote and concluded to the utter disgust of Mauchly and Eckert: "Atanasoff's principles for electronic computation played a crucial role in the circuitry of ENIAC and all its successors."

One could have believed that the careful and well-documented technical article by the Burkses might have ended the efforts by Mauchly and Eckert and their supporters to discredit and scoff at Atanasoff's achievement as the inventor of the first electronic digital computer. However, that was not the case.

Mrs. Kathleen R. Mauchly, long after John Mauchly's death, continued to espouse the thesis that her husband had learned little or nothing from Atanasoff and certainly had not "derived" the basic concepts of ENIAC from the Atanasoff Berry Computer.

Kathleen Mauchly, the second wife, did not know John Mauchly in the period prior to his 1941 visit to Iowa State, and did not marry him until after 1948. What she knew about the state of his knowledge on electronic digital computing prior to 1941 was only what he communicated to her years after the fact.

Annals of the History of Computing for October 1981, included the "comment by J. P. Eckert and Kathleen R. Mauchly" that was critical of the Burkses for their conclusion on "events which occurred prior to his [Arthur Burks's] arrival on the ENIAC project scene."

In the "comment" Eckert and Kathleen Mauchly did not specify the "many inaccuracies of fact, supposition and conclusions," which they contended the Burkses made except on one point they wrote:

> By way of example, since John W. Mauchly is deceased, Burks could, at least, have interviewed J. Presper Eckert (co inventor of the ENIAC) before he concluded that John Mauchly derived anything from Atanasoff with respect to ENIAC. Burks never took the time to interview Eckert on this matter but instead proceeded to concoct the story about Atanasoff's influence on the ENIAC project through Mauchly.

Eckert and Kathleen Mauchly also contended that the Burkses had taken "excerpts from Mauchly's letter out of context to bolster their argument while ignoring the full text." Judge Larson's interpretation of Mauchly's 1941 letter to Atanasoff and others was essentially the same as that of the Burkses. (Appendix A contains the full text of Mauchly's letter so the reader can make the judgement on that point.)

Since Eckert's testimony on his relationship with Mauchly is available in the court record, it is understandable why the Burkses would not believe it would be useful or necessary to conduct an interview with Eckert that would not be under oath. However, in an effort to forestall that particular criticism, I planned to contact Eckert to determine if there was any new information that he might have to offer, or if he changed his mind about John Atanasoff or on Judge Larson's opinion.

J. Presper Eckert had engaged in a persistent and continuing effort to discredit Judge Larson's opinion. It is understandable why Eckert would be bitter about the federal court's decision that invalidated the patent rights he and Mauchly had been granted on ENIAC and that up until the time of that decision had been universally lauded and applauded as the first electronic digital computer.

J. Presper Eckert, until that opinion, was honored and feted as the co-inventor of the first electronic digital computer. After being in that enviable position of honor, where he was acclaimed as the man responsible for one of the great inventions of the century, Eckert was not content to be known as one of the team that used Atanasoff's concepts in constructing ENIAC.

While at work on the last chapters of this book, I did call Eckert to determine if he had undergone a change of heart about Atanasoff's contribution to electronic digital computing and specifically to ENIAC. The record seemed to indicate that Eckert had no direct knowledge of what Mauchly may have learned through his contacts with John Atanasoff and Clifford Berry in the period from December 1940 through June 1941.

At the time of my conversation with Eckert in April 1987, he was a bitter man and still unwilling to accept Judge Larson's decision as the final word on JV's pioneering role in electronic digital computing concepts.

After introducing myself and telling him I was writing a book about Atanasoff, ENIAC, and Judge Larson's decision, Eckert launched into a tirade of harsh criticism. He trashed the Atanasoff Berry Computer, attacked Atanasoff's credibility, and criticized Judge Larson's decision. Eckert was equally caustic as he spoke of Sperry Rand's lawyers and their handling of the investigation and trial, and of the Sperry Rand management for the decision not to appeal Judge Larson's opinion.

"You don't call that an opinion do you?" he snapped before I had the opportunity to give any indication how I felt about Judge Larson's opinion.

"The trial was a farce," Eckert continued without giving me a chance to get in a question or comment. "It was before a nutty judge. He didn't know what he was doing, and was so egotistical that he rejected suggestions that he appoint a technical expert to help him."

"Atanasoff's machine was a joke," Eckert continued. "It was simply a mathematical device of very limited ability. It had defective circuits, and it wasn't even patentable."

"Atanasoff was a liar about what he said Mauchly saw, and he was paid a lot of money for the testimony he gave at the trial," Eckert charged.

Eckert did not bother to respond to my question about how he knew what Mauchly had or had not learned at Iowa State College but rambled on: "The only reason that Mauchly spent four days at Iowa State was to accommodate the people he was picking up for the return trip to Pennsylvania."

"What was wrong with the trial?" I asked. "Didn't Dr. Mauchly get a chance to tell what he knew at that time?"

Eckert declared that Sperry Rand lawyers did not go into all the evidence at the trial, and characterized the Sperry Rand lawyers as "incompetent" or "not knowing what they were doing."

"From the time this thing with Honeywell started, Sperry Rand changed lawyers four times," Eckert said. "None of them seemed to know what they were doing. They didn't pay any attention to our suggestions."

"I have a lot of material, material that was not used at the trial, and the Mauchly family has a lot of material that will prove what a farce the trial was," Eckert stated.

Eckert would not comment on the nature of the material that he and the Mauchly family had accumulated, but said "we will bring it out at the right time – after everyone else has had his say about this matter."

The irate scientist said he and Mauchly were particularly angered at Sperry Rand's decision not to appeal. "We felt certain the decision would be overturned on appeal," Eckert said. "I was told the reason they didn't appeal was because the judge almost threatened them with some antitrust action that they didn't want to get into."

He noted that Sperry Rand had successfully defended the ENIAC patents against legal challenges by IBM and Bell Telephone "before Dr. Atanasoff was brought into the case."

"They were sure they could win again, but they ended up not using all of the information they had," Eckert snapped. Eckert also commented that Sperry Rand was at a disadvantage in trying the case in the U.S. District Court in Minneapolis "because that circuit had only one case that upheld a patent in history."

"The courts out there in that country have no experience in patent law because all they have are cases involving farming and business," Eckert declared. "Sperry tried to get the case tried in another circuit, but I don't think they tried hard enough to get a change of venue," Eckert commented. "We should have tried it some place besides Honeywell's backyard."

I asked Eckert if he would make his undisclosed material available for examination for possible use in my book, but Eckert declined. He said he isn't yet "ready to zap the critics" who are relying upon the court decision stating that Mauchly "derived" many of the basic concepts of ENIAC from Atanasoff.

I asked Eckert how he knew that Mauchly did not derive some of the basic ENIAC concepts from Atanasoff since he did not meet Mauchly until after Mauchly's visit to Iowa State College in June 1941.

Eckert declared that he worked with Mauchly in the development of the ENIAC, and that the idea of a regenerative memory was his development in 1943. He said he invented it without any assistance from Mauchly.

Eckert emphasized that he had never heard Mauchly speak of Atanasoff or of his trip to Iowa State College "until after we were well into ENIAC" in late 1943. He said Mauchly did not mention Atanasoff's ideas on regenerative memory "until long after I had developed it [the regenerative memory concept] on my own."

Eckert stated that in conversations with Mauchly, long after he had independently developed the idea of regenerative memory, it was mentioned by Mauchly that Atanasoff had developed a comparable concept at Iowa State. Eckert explained that this was the reason he had given credit to Atanasoff for regenerative memory in the footnote of his 1953 article.

Eckert declared that he and Mauchly were "like the Wright Brothers" and the airplane. "The Wright Brothers did not invent all of the parts of the first airplane, but they put it together in a complete system for the first time including parts that had been developed by others."

"We [Eckert and Mauchly] did the same thing Thomas Edison did in developing the light bulb that was effective," Eckert claimed. "Many people had constructed light bulbs earlier, and less effective light bulbs were actually sold in England years earlier. Thomas Edison put together an effective system. That is what we did with ENIAC."

Eckert said that the claims of Atanasoff that he taught Mauchly the concepts of the first electronic digital computer "are phoney." He also branded as "phoney" the claims that John von Neumann had invented some concepts in ENIAC, and that some of ENIAC's ideas "were copied from (Charles) Babbage and Lady Lovelace."

"We had never heard of Babbage or Lady Lovelace, and the record will show the stage of development of ENIAC before von Neumann ever saw the project," Eckert declared.

If Mauchly was not interested in learning from Atanasoff, why did he spend at least four days at Iowa State examining the Atanasoff Berry Computer? I queried.

"Dr. Mauchly told me the only reason he stayed four days in Ames was because he was waiting so he could pick up some people who were going to ride back [to Pennsylvania] with him," Eckert explained. "He [Mauchly] said he didn't learn anything from that visit that he didn't already know."

Even as Kathleen Mauchly and Presper Eckert and their supporters continued an assault on Judge Larson's decision, more and more people were examining the massive court record and were agreeing with the Burkses that Mauchly had indeed "derived" important new electronic digital concepts from Atanasoff.

One of the most significant comprehensive articles in support of Judge Larson and in accord with the conclusions of the Burkses was published in *Physics Today* in March 1987. The article was written by Allan R. Mackintosh, professor of physics at the H. C. Oersted Institute of the University of Copenhagen and director of the Nordic Institute for Theoretical Physics in Copenhagen. Professor Mackintosh, a distinguished physicist and scholar, was totally supportive of the conclusion that Atanasoff was the inventor of the first electronic digital computer, and he expressed some surprise that general recognition for Atanasoff was so long in coming.

I believe that anyone who impartially studied the evidence–as contained, for example, in the record of the Honeywell-Sperry case–would be led to the same conclusion.

Atanasoff's contribution is becoming increasingly recognized in the computer literature–he is acknowledged as the inventor of the computer in several recent books–but physicists are still surprisingly ignorant of the fact that this supremely important machine was invented not by an engineer, nor indeed by an experimental physicist, but by a theorist.

The Mackintosh article entitled, "The First Electronic Computer," carried the subhead: "John Vincent Atanasoff, a theoretical physicist, faced with tedious quantum mechanical computations, built an electronic device that featured binary logic, regenerative memory and vector processing in 1939."

Professor Mackintosh noted that until recently "most Europeans interested in computing would have claimed that the first electronic computer was the Colossus, designed and constructed in Bletchley, England, by the mathematician Alan Turing and his colleagues, and operational in December 1943 and used to decipher the German Enigma code, with a decisive effect on the course of World War II."

He noted that most Americans at that time "would have given the honor to the Electronic Numerical Integrator Calculator (ENIAC), built by John W. Mauchly and J. Presper Eckert at the Moore School of Electrical Engineering . . . and operational in late 1945."

Professor Mackintosh related that he spent six years working in the Physics Department at Iowa State in the early 1960s and heard nothing of the Atanasoff Berry Computer that had been constructed on the outside of a basement room where he had coffee on an almost daily basis.

The Danish scholar characterized the Bush Differential Analyzer, a mechanical analog computer, as the most advanced machine for doing mathematic calculations until Atanasoff came along with a "diametrically opposite" approach.

Professor Mackintosh explained how Dr. Atanasoff's approach was entirely different and new:

1. A method of computation that was digital (for the sake of precision) and based upon the logical manipulation of binary numbers.

2. A means of computing by electronics (for the sake of speed) for control, logic and arithmetic operations.

3. The preliminary concept of a computing machine, with an architecture in which the computational function and the regenerative binary memory are separated.

"These three approaches are among the fundamental principles on which modern electronic computing is based," Professor Mackintosh wrote.

Acknowledging that the Atanasoff Berry Computer had flaws in the binary card system, Professor Mackintosh commented: "Considering the remarkable speed with which this project was carried out, it is reasonable to assume that the problem with the binary card system would have been solved within a few months."

Professor Mackintosh analyzed in scientific detail the achievements of John Atanasoff and Cliff Berry, and concurred with the conclusion of the Burkses that "Atanasoff's principles for electronic computation played a crucial role in the circuitry of ENIAC and all its successors," and that "John V. Atanasoff even contributed the original idea that resulted in the ENIAC, the idea that the machine he had developed could be 'converted into an integraph,' or differential analyzer."

The Danish physicist and scholar also gave his view as to "the reasons for the extraordinary delay of over forty years before the significance of Atanasoff's achievement was appreciated."

He first noted that World War II terminated Atanasoff's work on the Atanasoff Berry Computer "when he was just on the verge of triumphant success."

"The confusion of the early war years was also largely responsible for Iowa State's failure to file for the patent that would have established his priority," Professor Mackintosh wrote. He then noted that "there was no organization or person" with an interest in pushing recognition of Atanasoff's achievement prior to the Honeywell–Sperry Rand trial.

He also commented: "It is surprising that Mauchly, who was received in so friendly and open a manner in Ames, and who was initially so enthusiastic about ABC (the Atanasoff Berry Computer), was unable in later life to acknowledge having learned anything of significance from Atanasoff."

Professor Mackintosh said that to some degree Atanasoff had "the character of the true inventor" and that this tendency to be "fully engrossed with the problem of the moment" and then to move on to other ideas meant that he did not do all he could have done to explore the significance of his contribution.

That Iowa State was not close to the major centers of academic influence was, in Professor Mackintosh's view, an important factor in the lack of earlier recognition of the Atanasoff Berry Computer. "I believe that if Atanasoff had carried out his work at Berkeley or Harvard, or indeed Cambridge or Copenhagen, he would have been recognized as the inventor of the electronic computer long ago," Professor Mackintosh said, adding that Atanasoff's contribution has "now become widely recognized" and honored.

CHAPTER 22

Honors Awarded and Honors Delayed

N May 1974, JV returned to Iowa State University in triumph. He was the guest of honor and parade marshall for the traditional three-day extravaganza that Iowa State called "Veishea"—an acronym of the first letters of study at the Iowa land-grant institution: Veterinary Medicine, Engineering, Industrial Science, Home Economics, and Agriculture. To central Iowans, Veishea was their Mardi Gras, the largest student-run festival in the nation, attracting more than 250,000 people annually.

As JV and Alice Atanasoff rode across the rolling green hills of the campus in a maroon Cadillac convertible, JV reflected back to forty-nine years earlier when he first arrived on the campus as a twenty-one-year-old graduate assistant. As he and Alice took their places on the reviewing stand with Iowa State University President William Robert Parks, his eyes traveled to the familiar sight of the Campanile, and his mind wandered to Beardshear Hall where he had been welcomed to Iowa State by Dr. E. R. Smith and met Dr. A. E. Brandt, who later became a close friend.

Musing on Beardshear Hall recalled happy memories. It was there Atanasoff had his first office as a graduate assistant, as an instructor, and as an assistant professor before moving to the Physics Building. Reflecting on his first floor office in the Physics Building reminded him of his first meeting with Clifford Berry in May 1939. That was thirty-five years ago, and Atanasoff wished that Cliff Berry could be there to share this exhilarating moment of triumph at his alma mater.

Atanasoff recalled the tragedy of Cliff Berry's death, and momentarily wondered again if his untimely and mysterious death was in any way related to Berry's renewed interest in 1962 in digging into the links between the Atanasoff Berry Computer and ENIAC.

The large signs on the review platform proclaimed Iowa State to be the birthplace of "the first electronic digital computer in the world" and that an Iowa State College professor and graduate student were the inventors. Atanasoff thought Cliff Berry would have been as pleased as he was at that sign and other signs around the campus quoting Judge Larson's decision that the Atanasoff-Berry team had constructed that first electronic digital computer.

Atanasoff felt a warm self-satisfied glow. He was surrounded by friends from Iowa State – some of whom had known him from his first years in Ames – and by two of his three children and their families. His oldest daughter, Elsie, was in Indonesia with her husband, Richard Whistler and their three children and had been unable to attend the Veishea celebration. But John was there with his wife and three children, and so was Joanne, now Mrs. Charles E. Gathers, with her husband and three children.

Atanasoff had noted that *News of Iowa State,* an Iowa State University publication, had devoted a large portion of copy to quotations from Judge Larson's opinion concerning his decision that Iowa State was the site of the construction of the first electronic digital computer and that the basic concepts of ENIAC had been "derived" from the Atanasoff Berry Computer.

Atanasoff was accustomed to academic recognition and honors for his scientific inventions as well as government citations, including the Distinguished Service Award from the U.S. Navy, but he was not accustomed to this kind of regal treatment for such an extended period of time. It was tiring, but he enjoyed this first formal recognition in the United States as the inventor of the computer. It was doubly nostalgic because it was sponsored by Iowa State where he and Cliff Berry had constructed the pioneer electronic computer.

In August 1974 the University of Florida awarded Atanasoff an honorary Doctor of Science degree. Dr. Marshall Criser presented the citation noting with pride that Atanasoff had received a Bachelor of Science degree in electrical engineering from the University of Florida in 1925 and had more recently been on the University of Florida campus to receive a Presidential Medallion and to speak at an electrical engineering honors banquet.

That citation quoted from Judge Larson's decision confirming that Atanasoff was the inventor of the electronic digital computer, and stated: "Much of the computer world today leans on the work of Dr. Atanasoff, and there is even a court edict to prove it." The citation made no direct reference to either Mauchly or Eckert.

The turmoil of the Veishea ceremonies had barely subsided when Carl Hamilton, vice president and director of information and public affairs for Iowa State University, took the first steps to arrange for the production of a film story on the construction of the Atanasoff Berry Computer.

After several months, Hamilton and his assistant, Ned Disque, concluded that such a film was possible and contacted O. S. Knudsen, who was in charge of actual research and writing of such documentary films for Iowa State University. While sure in their own minds that JV and Cliff Berry had constructed the first electronic digital computer at Iowa State, they were aware that there was a continuing dispute engendered by Mauchly and Eckert and their supporters as to whether Mauchly had "derived" his electronic computer ideas from Atanasoff.

Discussion of various ways to approach the documentary film continued over months and then years before it was decided to skirt the controversy by simply letting Atanasoff tell his own story relating how he developed the initial concepts of electronic digital computing, and how he and Cliff Berry constructed the prototype and then the Atanasoff Berry Computer in the basement of the Physics Building.

Carl Hamilton and others associated with the film project realized that wide recognition of Iowa State as the site of the construction of the first electronic digital computer was important to the university, its student body, and its faculty. But since the film involved establishing credit for one of the great inventions of the century, they were aware that the film should be well researched and sound and not vulnerable to charges of superficial research or technically unjustified conclusions.

This effort to make certain that Iowa State would not be embarrassed by seeming to claim more for John Vincent Atanasoff and Clifford Berry than was justified slowed the progress on the documentary for several years. In the meantime, Iowa State University took the initiative to nominate John Atanasoff into the Iowa Inventors Hall of Fame. The ceremony took place on 6 June 1978.

On 31 May 1981, Moravian College, Bethlehem, Pennsylvania, awarded Atanasoff the honorary degree of Doctor of Science for his work as a "scientist, inventor, businessman and teacher."

"Few individuals have had as profound an impact on science, industry, and the whole fabric of life within our society as has Dr. Atanasoff, for he is the inventor of the modern digital computer," said Computer Science Professor Walter E. Brown in presenting John Atanasoff to President Herman E. Collier.

Professor Brown summarized Dr. Atanasoff's achievements in originating "the concept of regenerative memory, logic circuits, and digital encoding of information" that are "principles now routinely found in contemporary computers."

Noting Judge Larson's decision, Professor Brown stated: "In 1974, after several years of legal proceedings relating to corporate patent rights, Dr. Atanasoff was recognized as the inventor of the digital computer and placed by his colleagues in the ranks of Edison, Bell, and Whitney."

The Iowa State film "From One John Vincent Atanasoff" was completed in 1981, but it was decided to hold its release until October 1983, when Iowa State would celebrate the tenth anniversary of Judge Larson's historic decision. On 21 October 1983, this celebration was held on the Iowa State campus and JV was given a Distinguished Achievement Citation by the Iowa State University Alumni Association. Cliff Berry's widow, Jean Reed Berry, and his mother, Mrs. Grace Berry, were in attendance and were recognized as relatives of the co-inventor of the Atanasoff Berry Computer.

That Iowa State University gala featured O. S. Knudsen's twenty-eight-minute film, "From One John Vincent Atanasoff." There were speeches of tribute to Atanasoff and Berry by Charles G. Call, one of the Honeywell lawyers, and by Bernard Galler, professor of computing and communication science and associate director of the Computing Center at the University of Michigan. Galler was also editor-in-chief of *Annals of the History of Computing*.

Iowa State University's tenth anniversary celebration set the stage for more study of the in-depth analysis that Arthur and Alice Burks had done on the technical aspects of the relationship between Atanasoff's electronic digital computer concepts and ENIAC. That detailed analysis concentrated on the lack of any credible evidence showing that Mauchly had any record of interest in, or development of, electronic digital computer principles prior to his visit to Iowa State in June 1941.

The Burks analysis carried substantial quotations from Mauchly's letters to Atanasoff and to Helms H. Clayton demonstrating his enthusiasm for the performance of the Atanasoff Berry Computer he had seen at Iowa State, which contradicted his sworn testimony that he had learned nothing new about electronic digital computing from Atanasoff.

But even more persuasive than the Burks study was the extensive article that Atanasoff wrote for the *Annals of the History of Computing* for July 1984. That issue of *Annals* also carried a letter from Robert M. Stewart, Department of Computer Science at Iowa State University, explaining that it was he who "dismantled" the original Atanasoff Berry Computer in 1948 on the orders of Professor G. W. Fox, then the head of the Physics Department at Iowa State.

Professor Fox, who had been named as head of the Physics Department after Atanasoff had turned down the post, told Stewart, then a graduate student, that they needed the basement space in the Physics Building and that Atanasoff would not be returning.

"I had no idea what the equipment might be used for and whether or not it might be functional," Stewart wrote. He said "Atanasoff's machine was dismantled," and "the usable parts were returned to stock; the balance of the machine went to the loading dock to be hauled off with other trash."

"The only identifiable remnant of the system are the two studded drums that were the internal storage 'calculator,'" Stewart wrote. It was one of those drums that Sam Legvold had salvaged.

The Burks study and Atanasoff's article, drawn largely from Judge Larson's federal court record, were persuasive and even devastating answers to the critics.

In May 1984 Western Maryland College, Westminster, Maryland, conferred an honorary Doctor of Letters degree upon John V. Atanasoff with this commendation:

> The one in whose mind in 1937 four basic concepts fell together to serve in combination as the theoretical basis for the modern computer: (1) a binary numerical system, (2) the use of condensers for memory, (3) the use of "regeneration" to avoid lapse and (4) the employment of direct logical action instead of mathematical enumeration; a scholar recognized legally and in academic circles as the inventor of the modern computer. . . .

The Institute of Electrical and Electronic Engineers on 18 September 1984 recognized Atanasoff as a "Computer Pioneer" for having "Designed [the] First Electronic Computer With Serial Memory." It was ironic that he was given the Computer Pioneer Medal in 1984, years after John Mauchly and J. Presper Eckert were made "charter recipients" of the Computer Pioneer Awards for development of the "First All-electronic Computer – ENIAC."

In October 1984 Atanasoff was the guest of honor in Omaha, Nebraska, at a celebration of the eleventh anniversary of Judge Larson's decision. The Omaha celebration was the brainchild of Cecil A. Johnson, a wealthy retired lawyer-businessman who had taken the initiative to nominate Atanasoff for a Nobel Prize and to utilize his contacts in Swedish-American organizations to promote the project through a luncheon before the large Omaha Rotary Club.

The energetic Johnson's list of speakers included W. H. F. Wachtmeister, the Swedish ambassador to the United States, and John McCredie, president of Educational Communications (EDUCOM), a consortium of more than 500 colleges and universities created to keep those institutions up to the minute on advances and application of computing. But at least as important for JV was the presence on the speakers list of Allan R. Mackintosh. He was then a professor of physics from the University of Copenhagen in Denmark.

Although JV had read Allan Mackintosh's writing, including a letter to the editor of *Physics Today* in praise of Atanasoff's pioneer work in electronic computing, he had only previously met him briefly at the 1983 celebration. The meeting in Omaha inspired Mackintosh to further research and writing on the Atanasoff Berry Computer, which resulted in his major article in *Physics Today*, published in March 1987.

On 8 January 1985 Atanasoff was awarded the Governor's Science Medal by Iowa Governor Terry E. Branstad with the laudatory commendation:

> Sweeping technological advancement; monumental change; a restructuring of the work force and the work place – the computer revolution – all of this can be traced to John V. Atanasoff, inventor of the first electronic digital computer.

Governor Branstad reviewed the details of the contribution of Atanasoff and Berry to science and concluded:

> While the historic record detailing the contribution of Dr. Atanasoff was becoming clearer, the world was simultaneously experiencing explosive growth in the number of computers and their capacities. It is now easy to foresee a time when access to a computer will be as essential to modern life as access to a telephone or to transportation. Indeed, Dr. Atanasoff's accomplishments at Iowa State University were revolutionary and heralded the technological age in which we live today.

That was the first of four awards in 1985. On 17 May 1985 Atanasoff was awarded the Order of Bulgaria, First Class. On 1 November Atanasoff was given the Computing Appreciation Award, by EDUCOM, and on 20 November he was awarded the Holley Medal by the American Society of Mechanical Engineers.

The Holley Medal was "for pioneering research, invention and construction of the first electronic digital computer, providing the basic concepts of the use of electric and electronic means, the use of binary numbers, the use of direct logic for calculation without enumeration, and the use of regenerative memory, all used in modern computers."

The citations on the awards by these distinguished institutions and professional societies were written after in-depth research and with an understanding of the controversy that was still kept stirring by the supporters of Mauchly and Eckert.

On 15 September 1986 Atanasoff was guest of honor at the Colorado Association of Commerce and Industry Awards Luncheon. Atanasoff received the first Coors American Ingenuity Award in recognition of the "substantial impact on the national business community" through "his invention of the automatic electronic digital computer in 1939."

It was noted Atanasoff "has received little recognition for developing this revolutionary instrument despite the 1973 U.S. District Court decision which declared him the official inventor."

"When you consider the effect that Dr. Atanasoff's invention has had on American business and industry, there are few people more deserving of the first Coors American Ingenuity Award," Jeff Coors, president of Adolph Coors Company said in presenting the award symbol – a 16-inch-tall bronze "Bugling Elk" sculpted by Alonzo Clemens, a well-known Colorado artist.

Colorado Governor Richard D. Lamm signed a proclamation making it "Dr. John Vincent Atanasoff Day" in Colorado. The Adolph Coors Company established an Atanasoff scholarship at the University of Colorado in Boulder, Colorado, for a computer science student.

Early in 1987 Atanasoff was notified that he was to receive an honorary degree from the University of Wisconsin on 16 May 1987 in Madison, Wisconsin. This was particularly pleasing since he had received his Ph.D. in theoretic physics from Wisconsin in 1931. Also, it was important from a standpoint of general recognition because of the prestige of the University of Wisconsin and the fact that the faculty committees from several departments had screened

Atanasoff's record and had approved the award. This approval was almost certain to do a great deal to overcome any lingering doubts that Atanasoff was the inventor of the first electronic digital computer.

The publication of Allan Mackintosh's scholarly article in *Physics Today* in early March 1987 was also significant. In addition to its impact on educators in the world of physics, it was noted by Gordon P. Eaton, the new president of Iowa State University. President Eaton, in his inaugural address as the twelfth president of Iowa State, reflected on "the fascinating story of John V. Atanasoff" as told by Professor Mackintosh.

President Eaton told his audience that the experience of John V. Atanasoff held some important lessons for the future of Iowa State University and all public universities.

"It [the Mackintosh article] speaks to some unmet responsibilities to research at our institutions in the past," President Eaton said. "It is a story with several interesting morals, not in the least of which relates directly to a lost opportunity for enormous economic growth in Iowa."

President Eaton reported that Professor Mackintosh had observed "Iowa State is an excellent university with one of the first and best material science centers anywhere in the world," but that in handling the Atanasoff Berry Computer, "those who should have been concerned with promoting these activities frequently left much to be desired." Eaton noted that Mackintosh had said, "Iowa State deserves credit for supporting his (Atanasoff's) project at its inception," but that "the officials concerned clearly had no concept of its significance, and their obtuseness cost the university dearly when they failed to apply for a patent."

President Eaton then called attention to Mackintosh's account of how IBM in 1940 had also passed by Atanasoff's offer trying to interest that huge corporation in his electronic computer idea. Atanasoff "could not convince them of the potential of electronic computation," Mackintosh had written in demonstrating that the lack of foresight on the potential for the electronic digital computer was duplicated in a major corporation. President Eaton cited Professor Mackintosh's analysis of the failure of Iowa State officials and IBM officials to recognize the potential of Atanasoff's ideas for electronic digital computing "as a classic example of the perfect vision that all of us have in hindsight, but it is a lesson for the future, both for us and for other land-grant institutions."

It was too late for Iowa State University or John V. Atanasoff to

benefit financially because of mistakes of judgment made by officials at Iowa State in the late 1930s and throughout the 1940s, but
President Eaton expressed the hope that the past failures will serve
as a warning that the genius of the John Atanasoffs and the Cliff
Berrys of the future would be recognized, encouraged, and given
administrative support.

Atanasoff found the awards and recognition by these many
American institutions to be pleasant, and perhaps even more stimulating as an octogenarian whose honors had been delayed for more
than forty years through the continuing deceptions by those men
who had taken his ideas and used them for their own financial benefit.

As Atanasoff often said during the years of litigation: "Why do
they go to these extremes to deny me my proper credit? There was
enough credit in the invention and development of the electronic
digital computer for everyone."

The University of Wisconsin conferred the honorary degree of
Doctor of Science upon John Vincent Atanasoff on 16 May 1987 for
solving the conceptual and technical problems that enabled him to
build the Atanasoff Berry Computer. That citation stated:

> This computer utilized four important ideas which are still present in
> modern computers: first, the use of electronics for control, logic and
> arithmetic operations; second, digital rather than analog computation;
> third, the use of binary numbers; and fourth, a regenerative memory. It is
> clear from the record that Atanasoff did indeed enunciate and implement
> ideas that are at the heart of modern computing.

The citation was accompanied by an unusual five-page summary of his biography, a summary of his honors, a condensed history
of the Atanasoff Berry Computer, a section entitled "Beyond The
ABC" with a summary of Dr. Atanasoff's inventions over the broad
range of agricultural implements, defense weapons and technology,
and even a binary alphabet. (See Appendix B.)

John Atanasoff's trip to Madison, Wisconsin, to receive an honorary degree of Doctor of Science was a wonderful homecoming
with old friends as well as significant recognition by one of the
nation's most prestigious research universities.

On the evening of 15 May, John Atanasoff and Alice were the
guests of honor at the home of Dr. Bernice Durand, an associate
professor of physics at the University of Wisconsin and the daughter
of Dr. Henry M. Black, a professor emeritus of mechanical engineering at Iowa State who knew Atanasoff in his years as a graduate
student and as a faculty member.

He met many old friends at dinner and the receptions and it was a broadly smiling Atanasoff who heard Edwin Black, Chairman of the Committee on Honorary Degrees, (no relation to Henry Black) read the words that so beautifully summarized the substance and the meaning of his life.

"John Vincent Atanasoff earned his Doctor of Philosophy degree from the University of Wisconsin-Madison in 1930," Edwin Black told the assembled 2,500 students who were receiving their graduate and professional degrees. "While yet a graduate student, he experienced intensifying intellectual frustration because of the cumbersome and inadequate computation machines available at the time.

"That benign perplexity—a condition that is not unknown to graduate students—haunted John Vincent Atanasoff during his post-doctoral years until, in one eventful evening in 1937, he had the central insight that led to one of the most momentous inventions of the century, the electronic digital computer," Dr. Black explained with clarity and emphasis to inspire the assembled graduate students with their own potential.

"His invention is transforming our world," Black declared. "It accelerates mathematical calculations beyond the dreams of our ancestors; it enhances our collective memory; it functions as a surrogate to human intelligence in applications so numerous that not even a computer can aggregate them all.

"Yet, this astonishing innovation did not exhaust John Vincent Atanasoff's ingenuity. He holds thirty-two patents for subsequent inventions in such diverse fields as agriculture, transportation, and information science. His contributions to technology have been protean and abundant."

The graduate students and friends and relatives, now aware that they were in the presence of one of the great inventors of the century, applauded and cheered as the bright yellow hood was put over John Atanasoff's head and draped between his shoulders. He shook hands with Chancellor Cohen in accepting his congratulations, waved to the applauding graduate students, and moved behind the microphone.

Atanasoff, an octogenarian with periodic health problems, drew a muffled chuckle with his comment: "I might say, I am glad to be here."

Then in a soft voice he explained that it was as a graduate student at Wisconsin that his frustrations with the monotony of mathematical calculation created his resolve to find a better way. He said he "turned my spare time and attention" to the problem and "within ten years the object had been accomplished." It was all he had to say after Edwin Black's beautiful introduction.

The exhilarating days in and around his old haunts at the University of Wisconsin were followed by an equally stimulating visit to Iowa State University in Ames, and the Iowa Historical Building in Des Moines.

JV and Alice drove from Madison, Wisconsin, to Ames on Monday morning, 18 May, to be guest of honor at The Knoll, the Iowa State University home of President and Mrs. Gordon Eaton. It was John Atanasoff's first opportunity to visit at length with the new Iowa State University president, and there was enthusiasm and rapport on both sides.

President Eaton had given more than sixty speeches since joining Iowa State a few months earlier, and he had mentioned John Atanasoff and the computer in nearly every one for he sensed that Atanasoff and the story of the Atanasoff Berry Computer could be an inspiration to all who visited the Iowa State campus. He was eager to create a significant memorial so the inspirational story would not be missed.

Atanasoff was also pleased to see many old friends at the luncheon and some newer friends who were important in his struggle for recognition. There was time to talk of the old days with Dr. Lester Earls, professor emeritus in physics who had been the department head during Atanasoff's teaching days. He and Alice had a chance to talk with Dr. R. K. Richards and again express their appreciation for his early research on the Atanasoff Berry Computer origins. The paragraphs in his 1966 book had called patent lawyers' attention to John Mauchly's examination of the Atanasoff Berry Computer before he planned ENIAC.

Grace Berry was seated at the table with John Atanasoff, and both he and Alice spoke about Clifford Berry's indispensable help in the construction of the Atanasoff Berry Computer. Atanasoff was also pleased to see that Dr. Allan Mackintosh had arrived from Denmark and would be on hand to join in the warm recognition he was to receive. The articles by Mackintosh in *Physics Today* and other technical publications were scientific endorsements of stature to Judge Larson's opinion.

It was stimulating to meet Becky Wemhoff, student winner of the J. V. Atanasoff Fellowship in Computer Science for the 1987–1988 year and to respond to the enthusiasm of Dr. Arthur Oldehoeft, Chairman of the Department of Computer Science, and George

Strawn, Director of the Computation Center.

After luncheon at The Knoll, Atanasoff was taken to the Department of Computer Science and to the Computation Center. In conversations with Professor Oldehoeft, JV was told of plans for a new building to be known as John Vincent Atanasoff Hall.

In the evening the Atanasoffs attended a picnic buffet at the home of the Oldehoefts where most of the nearly one hundred students present had the opportunity to speak with the pioneer of electronic digital computing. It was tiring, but it was stimulating to talk with students and to hope that some thought, some word, from his lips would be important in firing their creativity.

Fortunately Tuesday was relatively quiet and Atanasoff was able to rest in preparation for a visit to the new Iowa Historical Building and Museum in Des Moines. John and Alice Atanasoff first viewed the impressive new Iowa Historical Building and Museum from the Des Moines Club, high atop the Ruan Center in Des Moines, where they were guests of honor at a luncheon hosted by Iowa Historical Society Director David Cross. Later they visited the new Historical Building and were told of plans for a room that would house a part of his memorabilia and would be designed to tell the story of the invention and construction of the Atanasoff Berry Computer.

That evening the Atanasoffs were entertained at a small dinner hosted by the Iowa State University Physics Department where Dr. Atanasoff had the opportunity to renew his acquaintance with Mrs. Sam Legvold, the widow of one of his oldest friends at Iowa State and one of the talented crew he assembled for scientific research at the Naval Ordnance Laboratory. He also talked with O. S. (Steve) Knudsen, retired manager of the Iowa State University film production unit, and Bob Lindemeyer, the assistant director of Media Resources. Both Knudsen and Lindemeyer had been involved in the planning and production of the movie "From One John Vincent Atanasoff."

Atanasoff had hoped to see Robert Stewart, the professor of electrical engineering who as a student had been directed to dismantle the original Atanasoff Berry Computer. While the dismantling of the original computer had been a shock to JV and Cliff Berry, he had recognized that Stewart as a student was only following the orders of a faculty member. Stewart, who was in Russia and was unable to attend, left a note expressing his gratitude for his association with Atanasoff and for his example as a teacher and researcher.

As the Atanasoffs started their drive home from Iowa to Maryland, they were satisfied that the final bridge to general recognition of Atanasoff as the inventor of the first electronic digital computer had been crossed. The powerful forces that had been at work against the acceptance of Judge Larson's decision were finally in retreat in the face of the overwhelming evidence establishing that John W. Mauchly derived the basic concepts of ENIAC, EDVAC, and UNIVAC from John V. Atanasoff.

A Des Moines patent attorney, Bruce McKee, had asked for a list of Atanasoff's most important patents and had volunteered to nominate Atanasoff for the National Inventors Hall of Fame. McKee, an Iowa State graduate, explained that Atanasoff's invention of the electronic digital computer would not qualify him for inclusion in the Hall of Fame because he had not obtained a patent for it.

However, McKee advised that there probably was some other invention or combination of inventions for which Atanasoff held patents that could form the basis for nomination to the Hall of Fame.

There were also suggestions that the invention of the first automatic digital computer might merit a Nobel Prize as one of the greatest inventions of this century. A Nobel Prize might make the long wait worthwhile and might to some degree compensate for the long years John V. Atanasoff and Clifford Berry were denied proper recognition.

AFTERWORD

THE story of John Vincent Atanasoff's invention of the electronic digital computer, and its aftermath, is both dramatic and absorbing, and provides a remarkable illustration of the process of invention and the factors which foster creativity. It is therefore particularly fortunate that the distinguished Iowan, journalist Clark Mollenhoff, has written the history of the first electronic computer with the clarity, balance, and respect for the truth which characterize journalism at its best.

Mr. Mollenhoff has given an accurate description of the general technical features of Atanasoff's invention, quite adequate for the reader to comprehend the extraordinary originality and importance of his achievement, but has naturally chosen to concentrate on the historical, human, social, and legal aspects in his narrative. A rather complementary account, in which the technical details are described with exemplary clarity, has been given by Alice and Arthur Burks in their recently published book *The First Electronic Computer: The Atanasoff Story*. Building on the evidence presented at the Honeywell-Sperry patent trial, and utilizing Arthur Burks' unique insight into the history of electronic computing, they more than anyone have been responsible for establishing that Atanasoff was indeed the inventor of the electronic digital computer. His prototype of 1939, and the description of it and the Atanasoff Berry Computer contained in Atanasoff's great article of 1940, would in themselves have been adequate to substantiate this claim. Well before anyone else, Atanasoff proposed and demonstrated his novel principles for electronic computing; electronics for speed, digital computation for accuracy, and a computer architecture with an electronic logic, arithmetic control unit, and a refreshable memory unit. The prototype was of course a very primitive machine, but prototypes generally are. The first radio, the first airplane, the first transistor, the first laser were all primitive devices, but embodied in each case the principles which launched a technological revolution. Once Atanasoff's principles of electronic computing had been formulated and translated into practice, the path to the modern computer was open.

In hindsight we can share the frustration of Atanasoff and Clifford Berry as they struggled to correct the trivial problem that prevented the ABC from functioning without error. However, even in its fallible form, their computer was an amazing technical achievement. The electronic computation and memory units carried out their function of calculating the eliminant between two equations effectively and accurately; only in extracting and using the result did a very occasional mistake occur. Reading Atanasoff's description of the ABC today, it is difficult to believe that it was written nearly half a century ago. The ideas expounded in it are so modern, and the overall design is so perfectly conceived, that it is difficult even now to see how it could be improved upon with the resources that were available to him. Atanasoff's linear-equation problem may be solved on modern computers constructed especially for this purpose, and their overall design bears a close resemblance to that of the ABC. They are however prodigiously faster.

It is ironical that it was John Mauchly who was destined to do Atanasoff the great service of bearing his ideas into the mainstream of computing, and hence ultimately of establishing their importance. Without Mauchly, Atanasoff would still have been the inventor of the electronic computer, by any reasonable interpretation of the phrase, but his work would have had very little influence on subsequent developments, and his contribution would presumably never have been recognized. Mauchly's behavior and attitudes are in retrospect almost incomprehensible. The natural, sensible, and honorable course of action would surely have been to invite Atanasoff to join the ENIAC project, particularly since his inventive skills would have been of enormous benefit in its execution. With his help, the ENIAC might have been the first operating large-scale electronic computer. Instead the British Colossus enjoys this distinction, even though its importance and even existence was obscured for many years by the secrecy associated with the sensitive nature of its mission, the wartime breaking of the German ENIGMA code.

Mauchly and Eckert deserve great recognition for being the principal inventors of the world's first general-purpose electronic computer; unfortunately their actions and statements have left behind an indelible image of two men who attempted to claim credit for the achievement of a third, to whom they owed much of their fame and fortune. Their disparaging remarks about Atanasoff and the ABC make depressing reading indeed. It would be unfortunate if the readers of this book gained the impression that such meanness of spirit is common among scientists. On the contrary, it is my experience that the humility of a true scholar, and his willingness to honor and recognize the efforts of those who have made his own contribution possible, increases with his eminence. As Isaac Newton, perhaps the greatest of all scientists, put it, "If I have seen further than other men, it is because I have stood on the shoulders of giants."

Atanasoff's invention of the electronic digital computer has a place among the great feats of innovation in the history of mankind, and it is therefore important to understand the means by which he performed the formidable task which he had set himself. A successful inventor requires motivation, which inspires the necessary enthusiasm and persistence, knowledge and training, and imagination. Atanasoff's motivation did not stem primarily from an ambition to initiate a technical revolution, but rather from his desire to solve problems in basic physical research. His education as a theoretical physicist was also an unconventional background for an inventor but, when asked about the origin of his inventive skills, he replied, "I couldn't have had a better training. Theoretical physics is a uniquely effective discipline." Although his innovative genius was unquestionably nurtured by his training as an electrical engineer and physicist, his whole career, as described in this book, demonstrates that he was blessed from birth with an extraordinary creative originality.

The way in which Atanasoff conceived the basic principles for his computer is a perfect example of the process of creation, which is familiar to scientists, artists and indeed all whose work requires imagination, originality and insight. He started with the long and frequently frustrating process of immersing himself in all aspects of the problem, without making much obvious progress. But when he had absorbed all this information, and his mind had time to work on it, largely unconsciously, the perfect solution became apparent to him while he was engaged in a completely different activity. His 200-mile drive through the state of Iowa is rapidly entering into the mythology of computing. He embarked on it, attracted not by the lure of a distant drink, but because he appreciated that his conscious mind needed to concentrate on a simple problem, while his unconsciousness faced a much more difficult challenge.

Not the least of the pleasures of reading Clark Mollenhoff's stimulating account of Atanasoff's achievement is the illustration which it provides of many fundamental truths about research and innovation. Technological revolutions are generally driven by scientific research, and investment in basic research is an essential component of progress. Decisive advances seldom arise through improvements in existing technology, but rather depend on the invention of completely new technical solutions to old problems. The planning of research and development is an occupation fraught with difficulties, and those who are engaged in it often show a surprising lack of foresight. A training in basic research, which strains a student's personal resources of imagination and ingenuity to the utmost, is a very effective preparation for a career as an inventor. Motivation is the strongest driving force towards original thinking and accomplishments. In order to function effectively, the mind needs change and relaxation. Finally, and perhaps most importantly, the traditional scholarly values of integrity, openness, and humility are beneficial not only for promoting research but also, in the long run, for the reputation of the individual scientist. J. V. Atanasoff is finally receiving the recognition which he so richly deserves, and this book will make an important contribution to securing his place in history.

−A. R. MACKINTOSH

APPENDIX A

John V. Atanasoff Testimony,
vol. 15, pp. 2116–17.

Trial Exhibit PX-711, Letter from Dr. John V. Atanasoff to Dr. John W. Mauchly on 7 March 1941, renewing the invitation to Mauchly to visit Iowa State and commenting in general on progress on the computing machine.

Dear Dr. Mauchly:
By all means, pay us a visit if you can arrange it. Just drop me a line letting me know when you will get here so I will be sure to be on hand. At present, I am planning to attend the Washington meetings at the end of April. Several of the projects which I told you about are progressing satisfactorily. Pieces for the computing machine are coming off the production line and I have developed a theory of how graininess in photographic materials should be described and have also devised and constructed a machine which directly makes estimates of graininess according to these principals. We will try to have something here to interest you when you arrive if nothing more than a speech which you made.

Signed,
DR. JOHN V. ATANASOFF

John V. Atanasoff Testimony,
vol. 15, pp. 2125–26.

Letter from Mauchly to Atanasoff on 27 May 1941, dealing with his travel plans from Pennsylvania to Iowa and his interest in electronic computing methods. Honeywell lawyer Henry Halladay read the letter into the record. The letter follows:

It was a disappointment to me, too, not to get in touch with you while in Washington. After leaving the message at the desk, I haunted the groups out on the grass in front of the East Building. Then when I again inquired at the desk I found that you had just collected the message and gone. Apparently you left the Bureau at once, so I went out to Urry's hoping to hear from you before we left. I fear that the message as you received it may not have contained the "deadline" clause – that we were leaving about 8 o'clock.

Well, anyway, there is more than a little prospect of my making the trip, starting from here about the tenth of June. I have a passenger who will very likely pay for the gas, and that will help.

From your letters I have gathered that your national defense work is unconnected with the computing machine. This puzzles me, for as I understand it, rapid computation devices are involved in N.D. In a recent talk with Travis, of the E.E. School at U. of Pa. I asked him about this, and the matter seemed the same way to him. But if Caldwell has looked over your plans (I think you said that he was out there) and hasn't seen any N.D. possibilities, I suppose that means your computer is not considered adaptable to fire control devices, or that they have something even better. Travis (who goes into active duty with Navy this week) pointed out the advantages of lightness and mass-production for electronic computing methods, but said that when he was consulting with General Electronic over plans for the G. E. differential integraph they figured it would take about one-half million dollars to do the job electronically, and they would only spend $\frac{1}{5}$ of that, so they built the mechanical type with polaroid torque-amplifiers.

I note that there is a physics colloquium at U. of Iowa June 12–14, and Sutton from Haverford is to be there. I wonder how he's travelling – maybe I could pick up another passenger!

It's too bad you couldn't stop when you were east, but try again – no doubt you will have to come east more often.

Sincerely yours,
J. W. MAUCHLY

John W. Mauchly's Testimony, vol. 80, pp. 12, 186–87.

Plaintiff Exhibit PX-795, 31 May 1941, from J. V. Atanasoff to John W. Mauchly. This letter was the last letter Atanasoff wrote to Mauchly before Mauchly's visit to Iowa State College in June 1941.

Honeywell lawyer Henry Halladay read the letter into the record during the cross-examination of Dr. Mauchly to establish what Mauchly had been told by Atanasoff prior to the visit.

May 31, 1941

Mr. J. W. Mauchly
Ursinus College
Collegeville, Pennsylvania

Dear Doctor Mauchly:
I think that it is an excellent idea for you to come west during the month of June or any other time for that matter. You might visit the Physics Colloquium at the University of Iowa if you wish. I generally do not go because the discussions are mainly in the field of physics teaching. But you could either go back by Iowa City or stop on your way west. Or, if it proves more convenient, I could drive you over. We have plenty of room and will be delighted to have you stay with us while here.

As you may surmise, I am somewhat out of the beaten track of computing machine gossip, and so I am always interested in any details you can give me. The figures on the electronic differential integraph seem absolutely startling. During Dr. Caldwell's last visit here, I suddenly obtained an idea as to how the computing machine which we are building can be converted into an integraph. Its action would be analogous to numerical integration and not like that of the Bush Integraph which is, of course, an analogue machine, but it would be very rapid, and the steps in the numerical integration could be made arbitrarily small. It should therefore equal the Bush machine in speed and excel it in accuracy.

Progress on the construction of this machine is excellent in spite of the amount of time that defense work is taking, and I am still in a high state of enthusiasm about its ultimate success. I hope to see you within two or three weeks.

Very sincerely yours,

J. V. ATANASOFF
Associate Professor, Math. and Physics

JVA:vb

Atanasoff Testimony, vol. 15, pp. 2169-70.

Mauchly's letter written to Atanasoff, dated 22 June 1941, was read into the record by Honeywell lawyer Henry Halladay. It follows:

Dear J.V.,

The trip back here was uneventful, except for the fact that I was carrying on a mental debate with myself on the question of whether to teach at Hazleton, or to learn something of U. of Pa. My natural avarice for knowledge vied with that for money, and won out, so after obtaining assurance from Marsh White at State College that they could find someone else to take the Hazleton work, I dropped that and prepared to become a student again.

I drove to Southbridge, Mass., Friday evening, and looked through the American Optical plant on Saturday morning. They seem quite serious in their intentions toward me, but no decision is to be made for several weeks.

On the way back east a lot of ideas came barging into my consciousness, but I haven't had time to sift them or organize them. They were on the subject of computing devices, of course. If any look promising, you may hear more later.

I do hope that your amplifier problem has been licked by some adequate design. The tubes that I ordered two weeks ago aren't here yet, so I couldn't try anything here even if I had time.

I forgot to ask what happens to Cliff Berry after he gets a master's degree – does he stay on for Ph.D. work?

Please give the enclosed note to your wife. We enjoyed our trip very much, and hope you can stop here some time.

Sincerely,

J. W. Mauchly

Atanasoff Testimony, vol. 15, pp. 2170-71.

Letter from John W. Mauchly to H. Helms Clayton, a meteorologist friend, on 28 June 1941, recounting the experience of his visit to Iowa State College and examining the Atanasoff Berry Computer with John V. Atanasoff and Clifford E. Berry. That letter was read into the record by Honeywell lawyer Henry Halladay to demonstrate through Mauchly's own words his impression of the Atanasoff Berry Computer. The letter follows:

Dear Mr. Clayton,

Up to a few days ago I was in hope of making a trip to Massachusetts this June with the possibility of returning the Sundstrand machine which you so kindly lent us. Now it appears that I can't do that, and within the week I shall properly pack the machine and forward it by express.

I know this must have inconvenienced you already, and I feel that we owe you a great deal for your loan.

Immediately after commencement here, I went out to Iowa State University to see the computing device which a friend of mine is constructing there. His machine, now nearing completion, is electronic in operation, and will solve within a very few minutes any system of linear equations involving no more than thirty variables. It can be adapted to do the job of the Bush differential analyzer more rapidly than the Bush machine does, and it costs a lot less.

My own computing devices use a different principle, more likely to fit small computing jobs.

All my time since coming back from Iowa has been taken up with an Emergency Defense Training Course at the Univ. of Pa. I had a chance to teach for the summer in a defense course given to high school graduates, but turned that down in order to become a student myself. I am working in electrical engineering and electronics. Whether or not I am given a defense job involving electronics later on, the training will be helpful in connection with electronic computing devices.

I haven't had any chance to work on weather problems recently. I did hear Rossby talk at Iowa City—concerning the training of students for meteorology, etc. Let's hope your own work is getting along well.

Sincerely yours,
JOHN W. MAUCHLY

John V. Atanasoff Testimony, vol. 15, pp. 2176–80.

"Notes on Electrical Calculation Devices"

As identified by John W. Mauchly as his paper written in early August 1941, after his visit to Iowa State College and his reading of Atanasoff's 35-page paper on the construction of the Atanasoff Berry Computer, and his conversations with Atanasoff and Clifford E. Berry. The Mauchly paper was read into the record by Honeywell Attorney Henry Halladay:

–1– Analog versus impulse types – "Computing machines may be conveniently classified as either 'analog' or 'impulse' types."*

I am now reading the asterisk: "I am indebted to Dr. J. V. Atanasoff of Iowa State College for the classification and terminology here explained."

The analog devices utilize some sort of analogue or analogy, such as Chm's Law or the polar planimeter mechanism, to effect a solution of a given equation. The accuracy of such devices is obviously subject to limitations; at times the attainable is more than sufficient, but there is increasing need for more computational aid not so restricted. Impulse devices comprise all those which "count" or operate upon discrete units corresponding to the integers of some number system. There is no theoretical limit to the accuracy to which such devices will work; practical limitations on the bulk or cost or convenience of operation provide the only restrictions. The usual mechanical computing machine, utilizing gears, pauls, etc. are examples of impulse calculators.

No further attention will be given to the analog type here, for although differential analyzers and other analog machines are now used and will continue to be used for some problems, it is in the field of impulse machines that major improvements in speed and accuracy are to be expected and sought for.

−2−For speedy (and noiseless) operation, vacuum tubes and associated circuits are the obvious answer. There are no essential difficulties in designing V.T. apparatus to do the job of ordinary mechanical calculators − but after taking care of stability, freedom from error, ease of servicing, etc., one might conceivably wind up with a design too costly to build. But economically feasible designs are possible. At present it may not be possible to build a commercial competitor for the desk-type mechanical computer, but larger machines for more involved, more lengthy, or more specialized jobs are practical. In some cases it is possible to materially decrease the number of tubes and circuits required in a large machine by having many similar operations performed by one and the same unit, which is switched around in sequence, rather than by having many duplicate units operating simultaneously. This is possible because the time required for a single elementary operation may be very short compared to the time allowable for completing one "step" in the calculation.

−3−The basic units of any computing device are usually the following: (A) Input registers, for putting in, (storing) the numbers to be operated on, (B) the adding (or add-subtract) mechanism for combining such numbers, and (C) the output register for storing, indicating, or making a permanent record of the results attained by the units A and B. There is usually some difference in the function and form of the various registers comprising A and B. For instance, in the ordinary mechanical computing machine, a keyboard may be used to put in the multiplier (which determines the number of times the multiplicand is added in each of several carriage positions), and the resulting product will be read off from dial registers. These dial registers do not make any permanent record, nor can the number in that register be used immediately (without special tricks) as a multiplicant or multiplier.

In a flexible computing machine, it would be very desirable to have all registers in which numbers may be stored immediately usable as either type A or type C. One might imagine a computing control panel such as the following: [sketches].

Atanasoff Testimony, vol. 15, pp. 2171-72.

Mauchly's letter of 30 September 1941 to Atanasoff asking, "would the way be open for us to build an 'Atanasoff Calculator' at the Moore School of Electrical Engineering?" That letter follows:

Dear J.V.:

This is to let you know that I still have the same living quarters, but a different job. During the summer I looked around a bit while sounding out the Ursinus people as to promotions and assistance; I finally gave up the idea of taking an industrial job (or a navy job) and stayed in the ranks of teaching.

The Moore School of Electrical Engineering (Univ. of Pa.) is what I have joined up with, and they have me teaching circuit theory and measurements and machinery – but only 11 hours a week instead of the 33 that Ursinus had developed into.

As time goes on, I expect to get a first-hand knowledge of the operation of the differential analyzer – I have already spent a bit of time watching the process of setting up and operating the thing – and with more such background I hope I can outdo the analyzer electronically.

A number of different ideas have come to me recently: anent computing circuits – some of which are more or less hybrids, combining your methods with other things, and some of which are nothing like your machine. The question in my mind is this: Is there any objection, from your point of view, to my building some sort of computor which incorporates some of the features of your machine? For the time being, of course, I shall be lucky to find time and material to do more than merely make exploratory tests of some of my different ideas, with the hope of getting something very speedy, not too costly, etc.

Ultimately a second question might come up, of course, and that is, in the event that your present design were to hold the field against all challengers, and I got the Moore School interested in having something of the sort, would the way be open for us to build an *"Atanasoff Calculator"* (a la *Bush* analyzer) here?

I am occupying the office of Travis, the man who designed the analyzer here (duplicated at Alberdeen); I think I told you that he is now in the Navy, so I have no opportunity of benefiting by his rich experience.

I hope your defense efforts have been successful, but not so time-consuming as to stop progress on the computer. When you are East, arrange to see us. Perhaps you would like to look over the diff. analyzer, etc.

Convey my best regards to your family, and Cliff Berry and all the gang.

Sincerely yours,

JOHN W. MAUCHLY

John V. Atanasoff Testimony, vol. 15, pp. 2180–81.

Mr. Henry Halladay: Plaintiff's Exhibit 900 of 7 October 1941 reads:

Dear Mauchly:

I am delighted to hear that you are teaching in the Department of Electrical Engineering at the University of Pennsylvania, and I will be sure to get in touch with you the next time I come east which should be in the very near future. At that time we can discuss our mutual interest in calculators.

Our attorney has emphasized the need of being careful about the dissemination of information about our device until a patent application is filed. This should not require too long, and of course, I have no qualms about having informed you about our device, but it does require that we refrain from making public any details for the time being. It is, as a matter of fact, preventing me from making an invited address to the American Statistical Association.

We greatly enjoyed your visit last spring and hope that it can be repeated in the not too distant future.

Very sincerely yours,

JOHN V. ATANASOFF

APPENDIX B

RESOLUTION
Proposing to Confer upon
JOHN VINCENT ATANASOFF
The Honorary Degree Doctor of Science
At the Spring Commencement, 1987
University of Wisconsin – Madison

John Vincent Atanasoff, working between 1936 and 1942, solved conceptual and technical problems which enabled him to design and build one of the first electronic digital computers. This computer utilized four important ideas which are still present in modern computers: first, the use of electronics for control, logic, and arithmetic operations; second, digital rather than analog computation; third, the use of binary numbers; and fourth, a regenerative memory.

It is clear from the record that Atanasoff did indeed enunciate and implement ideas that are at the heart of modern computing.

This work was carried out while John Atanasoff was an Associate Professor of Mathematics and Physics at Iowa State College. He solved the conceptual problems in 1937. In 1939, at the age of 36, he built a model computer for the special purpose of solving linear systems of equations, with the assistance of Clifford Berry, an Electrical Engineering graduate student. During the next two years they built a working prototype computer, but World War Two interrupted their development of a commercial computer.

John Atanasoff received his B.S. in Electrical Engineering from the University of Florida and his M.S. in Mathematics from Iowa State College. He earned his Ph.D. in Theoretical Physics from the University of Wisconsin in 1930, under the direction of John H. Van Vleck. In his own words, "I couldn't have had a better training."

We honor John Vincent Atanasoff, mathematical physicist, businessman, humanitarian, for his contributions to the design of the modern computer and his many inventions and other contributions to modern technology.

Department of Physics	Passed, Oct. 16, 1986
Department of Electrical	
and Computer Engineering	Passed, Nov. 12, 1986
Department of Computer Sciences	Passed, Nov. 14, 1986
Department of Mathematics	Passed, Nov. 20, 1986
Department of History of Science	Supported, Nov. 26, 1986

B. Durand

THE MOST GERMANE DOCUMENTS IN FILE ON ATANASOFF (JVA)

1. Copies of Physics Department card on JVA for the three semesters he was a graduate student here in 1929–30.
2. Copy of JVA's thesis, which is a 1930 Physical Review article, bound and shelved in Memorial Library.
3. JVA's 1940 manuscript, finally published in 1973 in *The Origins of Digital Computers, Selected Papers,* Brian Randell, editor, Springer-Verlag, New York 1973. The article is on pp 305–325, "Computing Machine for the Solution of large systems of Linear Algebraic Equations", August 1940. It contains all essential information, including circuit diagrams and photographs, to build his computer and was successfully used to obtain funding.
4. Excerpts from Judge Larson's 1973 decision in Sperry vs. Honeywell, a concise chronology concluding that (Sec. 3.1.2) "Eckert and Mauchly did not themselves first invent the automatic electronic digital computer, but instead derived that subject matter from one Dr. John Vincent Atanasoff".
5. The first 40 pages of a 90 page article in the *Annals of the History of Computing,* Vol. 3 No. 4, October, 1981, pp 310–399. This is authored by Arthur W. Burks and Alice R. Burks. Arthur Burks was a principal in the development during World War II of the ENIAC. The article's title is "The ENIAC: First General-Purpose Electronic Computer". Pages 310–350 contain the role of JVA. On page 328 the Burkses state, "Thus John Vincent Atanasoff was the inventor of the first electronic computer".
6. An abbreviated first-person account by JVA, written in 1983 for Iowa State University, compressed from the 1984 published article of the same title in the *Annals of the History of Computing,* July 1984. The title is "Advent of Electronic Digital Computing". This 17-page account is fascinating to read.
7. Numerous other documents falling into two categories:
   (a) 1981 *ad hoc* Physics committee's collection of articles and letters
   (b) 1983 Iowa State University collection, some obtained by Rollefson in 1983 and some by me in 1986. Iowa State made a 15–20 minute film in 1983 when it awarded JVA its highest honor, the Distinguished Achievement Citation. (ISU does not offer honorary degrees except every hundredth birthday of the institution.)

JOHN VINCENT ATANASOFF

PERSONAL BORN   4 October, 1903, Hamilton, New York
          FATHER   John Atanasoff, born 1876, Bulgaria, emigrated to USA 1889, married 1900; B.Ph. Colgate University 1900; electrical engineer; died 1956

	MOTHER	Iva Lucena Purdy, born 1881; school teacher (mathematics); died 1983.
	SIBLINGS	Nine, of whom seven survive: Ethelyn, Margaret, Theodore, Avis, Raymond, Melva, Irving.
	FAMILY	Married Alice Crosby, 1949; three children: Elsie, Joanne, John Vincent II; ten grandchildren.
	ADDRESS	P.O. Box 503, Frederick, Maryland 21701. Telephone: 301-865-5400

EDUCATION	HIGH SCHOOL	Mulberry, Florida 1920
	BSEE	University of Florida, Gainesville 1925
	MS, Mathematics	Iowa State College, Ames 1926
	PhD, Theoretical Physics	University of Wisconsin, Madison 1930

Thesis title: "The Dielectric Constant of Helium"

Research adviser: Professor John H. Van Vleck

Committee (Van Vleck was in Europe): Professors Wentzel, Weaver, March, Mendenhall, and Ingersoll.

PROFESSIONAL	OCCUPATION	Mathematical Physicist, Inventor, Businessman
	POSITIONS	Phosphate prospector 1920-21

Gainesville H.S., Teacher, Head of Science Dept. 1925-26

Iowa State College, Mathematics, Graduate Assistant and Instructor, 1926-29

University of Wisconsin, Mathematics, Instructor 1929-30

Iowa State College, Mathematics and Physics

Assistant Professor 1930-36

Associate Professor 1936-42

Professor in Absentia 1942-45

US Naval Ordnance Lab., Washington, D.C.

Chief, Acoustics Section 1942-45

Chief, Acoustics Division 1945-48

	US Army Field Forces, Ft. Monroe, VA, Chief Scientist 1949
	Naval Ordnance Lab., Director, Fuse Program 1949–52
	The Ordnance Eng. Corp., Frederick, MD (sold to Aerojet Gen. Corp. 1957) Founder, President, Director 1952–57
	Aerojet General Corp., Frederick, MD Manager, Atlantic Div 1957–59, Vice Pres. 1959–61
	Cybernetics, Inc., Frederick, MD, President 1961–80
CONSULTANT	Stewart-Warner Corp. 1961–63
	Control Data Corp. 1967–71
	Honeywell 1967–71
PATENTS	32
MAJOR INVENTION	Electronic Digital Computer 1936–42
MEMBERSHIPS	Phi Beta Kappa
	Phi Kappa Phi
	Sigma Tau
	Pi Mu Epsilon
	Tau Beta Pi
	Sigma Xi
	Cosmos Club
	American Assoc. for the Advancement of Science
	Foreign Member, Bulgarian Academy of Science
	Honorary member, Computer Medicine Society
HONORS	U.S. Navy Distinguished Service Award (Navy's highest honor awarded to civilians) 1945
	Citation, Seismological Society of America 1947
	Citation, Admiral, Bureau of Ordnance 1947
	Cosmos Club membership 1957
	Order of Cyril and Methodius, First Class, Bulgarian Academy of Sciences (Bulargia's highest honor accorded a scientist) 1970

Iowa Inventors Hall of Fame
Plaque, Iowa State Univ. Physics
Building 1974
Honorary Membership, Society for
Computer Medicine 1974
Doctor of Science, University of
Florida 1974
Doctor of Science, Moravian College
1981
Distinguished Achievement Citation,
Iowa State Univ. Alumni Assoc.
1983
Doctor of Science, Western Maryland
College

CHIEF FIELDS OF RESEARCH INTERESTS:

Crystal dynamics	1936–42
Original inventor of Electronic digital computer (with assistance of Clifford Berry)	1937–42
Ship dynamics	1942–66
Long range detection of seismic and barometric signals	1947
Original design of automatic systems and cybernetics	1960
Communications theory: written languages, binary alphabet	1942–76

COMMENTARY: CONDENSED HISTORY OF THE
ATANASOFF-BERRY COMPUTER

As a graduate student in Madison, John Atanasoff was frustrated by his need to solve many simultaneous equations and the inadequacy of the cumbersome computing machines of 1930. Later as the director of several graduate students at Iowa State, where he was the only theoretical physicist, this frustration grew to the point that in about 1934 he began "tinkering" with available computers, such as an IBM tabulating machine, a Monroe calculator, and Vannevar Bush's differential analyzer. He decided by 1936 that "analog" (a word he coined) computers would not give the accuracy he desired and switched to thinking about the "digital" (or direct logical) method.

Having been trained in electrical engineering as an undergraduate and physics as a graduate student, he was open to the concept of replacing mechanical computer elements by electronic circuits. Early in his thinking, he considered computing in number systems other than base ten, and decided that the simple binary (base two) system was a natural "on-off" or charged-discharged system for an electronic computer. It is interesting that he learned about binary numbers as a child from his mother, who taught and loved mathematics.

He called the data storage in his computer "memory", a word which has stuck. He was looking for a memory with large storage capacity plus a fast "turn-around" time. His problem solving technique throughout his life has been to load his mind with all available facts, then worry hard until an idea comes. During the winter of 1937, one night he had become too worked up and nervous over the unsolved computer memory problem to think efficiently. He got into his car and drove at high speed to the Mississippi River. Across the river in Rock Island, Illinois, he went into a roadhouse, took off his coat, sat down to have a drink, and realized that the intensity of the drive had relaxed him. His mind was working well and he devised the possibility of the "regenerative" memory, then drove home. That evening, he says in an account of the computer, he made four decisions for his project:

"• I would use electricity and electronics as the media for the computer.
• In spite of custom, I would use base-two numbers (binary) for my computer.
• I would use condensers for memory, but "regenerate" to avoid lapse.
• I would compute by direct logical action, not by enumeration."

By 1939, Atanasoff had obtained money from Iowa State to hire an assistant to help build the computer he had designed. He selected an electrical engineering graduate student, Clifford Berry. They built a model in 1939, then a prototype, which Atanasoff later named the ABC (Atanasoff-Berry Computer) in recognition of Berry's contributions to the actual assembly of the computer. The ABC was Berry's Ph.D. dissertation project, and Berry went on after the War to become a leading mass spectrographer.

In 1940, Atanasoff wrote up what he and Berry had already done and proposed to do, partly as a proposal for further funding. That same year he initiated patent investigations. He also attended the 1940 AAAS meeting in Philadelphia and met Dr. John W. Mauchly of the University of Pennsylvania, who was presenting a paper on an analog electrical system for doing Fourier transforms. Each discussed his work with the other, and they promised to write.

Mauchly wrote several times, then visited Iowa State with his son in June, 1941, as the houseguests of the Atanasoffs. He spent five days examining the computer, reading the manuscript, discussing the ideas with Atanasoff and Berry, and taking notes. In September, 1941, Mauchly wrote to Atanasoff asking if he and fellow researchers at Penn might build an "Atanasoff Calculator". Atanasoff replied that the patent attorney had emphasized the need to be cautious in disseminating information, and his manuscript had not even been submitted for publication.

After Pearl Harbor, Berry had to leave almost immediately. The patent proceedings were left in the hands of Iowa State; and in 1942 Atanasoff went to work for the U.S. Naval Ordnance Lab., where he began a 10-year career in acoustics and seismology. During the War, John Mauchly and J. Presper Eckert developed the ENIAC (Electronic Numerical Integrator and Calculator), funded by the U.S. Army Ordnance Corps. At the end of the War, Atanasoff found that Iowa State had dropped the patent application. In 1983, he told U.W. Prof. Emeritus Ragnar Rollefson, an old friend from UW days, that he had been dumbfounded to learn there was no patent and had never understood why Iowa State had not followed through. Later Sperry-Rand purchased the commercial computer patent rights from Mauchly and Eckert.

From 1971 to 1973, there was a legal dispute over the computer patent. Sperry sued Honeywell for royalties, as a test case. Testimony lasted nine months and Judge Earl R. Larson (Minneapolis Federal Court) took another year and seven months to reach and announce his decision, during which time he studied all the accumulated histories very carefully. He concluded that the Sperry patent, as the Mauchly-Eckert patent before it, was invalid in claiming invention of the electronic digital computer. Atanasoff's natural openness in June, 1941, had given Mauchly his start.

Judge Larson's decision that Dr. John Vincent Atanasoff, assisted by Clifford Berry, had in fact invented the computer from which the ENIAC was derived, was published the day before the Watergate "Saturday Night Massacre" hit the newspapers. The computer decision did not receive much press. Thus World War Two and Watergate both had the effect of keeping Atanasoff and Berry from being "household names" in the computer business. Berry died in 1963 and Atanasoff is retired, living on his farm in Maryland, after a long career in teaching, government, and business.

It is interesting to reflect that Iowa State missed having a "WARF" by not following through on the ABC patent. Clearly Atanasoff learned a lesson. He holds 32 patents for subsequent inventions.

COMMENTARY: ABOUT ATANASOFF BEYOND THE ABC

He very much enjoyed teaching, as had his mother, who lived to age 101½. He is a humanitarian, an early crusader for civil rights (influenced by his childhood in rural Florida), for equal rights, against smoking. He became an expert on Midwest allergies and raised goats to provide milk for allergic children.

He is a quick study. When he founded The Ordnance Engineering Corporation, he gave himself three days to learn accounting and three weeks to learn corporate law. Then he drew up the papers himself.

Early in the War, as a diversion, he started what turned into an avocation: inventing an alphabet to cover all English phonemes. This would make spelling and pronunciation easier. He invented a binary alphabet and worked on improving and publicizing this until he was 80.

He developed real estate in Ames, Iowa, and Monrovia, Maryland. He has owned three farms and lives on one in a concrete house he designed. He also used concrete in farm buildings and boats, and is interested in solar and wind power. His farming interests range from building ponds to raising cattle to raising trees to experimenting with fruits and vegetables and their preservation.

Whatever he is doing, he invents improvements. Among the innovations he has designed are a tree planter, calf feeder, silo, hay curer, garden tractor, windmill boat, electric quartz watch, Postal Service diverter systems, Uniterm filing system for rapid retrieval of documents, automated package handler, the first sweep for pressure mines, detectors/recorders for underground seismic or sonic waves. Some of these are the subjects of his more than 30 patents.

Atanasoff decided to be a theoretical physicist when he was a sophomore in high school. His education included electrical engineering, mathematics, and physics. His contributions to computer science were remarkable, especially in the technological context of the late 1930's. One author describes him as resembling a "minor Thomas Jefferson" in his broad interests, curiosity, and inventiveness. Among our science alumni of the University of Wisconsin, Atanasoff is exemplary.

APPENDIX C

Section 3 of Judge Earl R. Larson's opinion in Honeywell Inc. v. Sperry Rand Corp., et al. *October 19, 1973.*

3.1 The subject matter of one or more claims of the ENIAC was derived from Atanasoff, and the invention claimed in the ENIAC was derived from Atanasoff.

3.1.1 SR and ISD are bound by their representation in support of the counterclaim herein that the invention claimed in the ENIAC patent is broadly "the invention of the Automatic Electronic Digital Computer."

3.1.2 Eckert and Mauchly did not themselves first invent the automatic electronic digital computer, but instead derived that subject matter from one Dr. John Vincent Atanasoff.

3.1.3 Although not necessary to the finding of derivation of "the invention" of the ENIAC patent, Honeywell has proved that the claimed subject matter of the ENIAC patent relied on in support of the counterclaim herein is not patentable over the subject matter derived by Mauchly from Atanasoff. As a representative example, Honeywell has shown that the subject matter of detailed claims 88 and 89 of the ENIAC patent corresponds to the work of Atanasoff which was known to Mauchly before any effort pertinent to the ENIAC machine or patent began.

3.1.4 Between 1937 and 1942, Atanasoff, then a professor of physics and mathematics at Iowa State College, Ames, Iowa, developed and built an automatic electronic digital computer for solving large systems of simultaneous linear algebraic equations.

3.1.5   In December, 1939, Atanasoff completed and reduced to practice his basic conception in the form of an operating breadboard model of a computing machine.

3.1.6   This breadboard model machine, constructed with the assistance of a graduate student, Clifford Berry, permitted the various components of the machine to be tested under actual operating conditions.

3.1.7   The breadboard model established the soundness of the basic principles of design, and Atanasoff and Berry began the construction of a prototype or pilot model, capable of solving with a high degree of accuracy a system of as many as 29 simultaneous equations having 29 unknowns.

3.1.8   By August, 1940, in connection with efforts at further funding, Atanasoff prepared a comprehensive manuscript which fully described the principles of his machine, including detail design features.

3.1.9   By the time the manuscript was prepared in August, 1940, construction of the machine, destined to be termed in this litigation the Atanasoff-Berry computer or "ABC," was already far advanced.

3.1.10 The description contained in the manuscript was adequate to enable one of ordinary skill in electronics at that time to make and use an ABC computer.

3.1.11 The manuscript was studied by experts in the art of aids to mathematical computation, who recommended its financial support, and these recommendations resulted in a grant of funds by Research Corporation for the ABC's continued construction.

3.1.12 In December, 1940, Atanasoff first met Mauchly while attending a meeting of the American Association for the Advancement of Science in Philadelphia, and generally informed Mauchly about the computing machine which was under construction at Iowa State College. Because of Mauchly's expression of interest in the machine and its principles, Atanasoff invited Mauchly to come to Ames, Iowa, to learn more about the computer.

3.1.13 After correspondence on the subject with Atanasoff, Mauchly went to Ames, Iowa, as a houseguest of Atanasoff for several days, where he discussed the ABC as well as other ideas of Atanasoff's relating to the computing art.

3.1.14 Mauchly was given an opportunity to read, and did read, but was not permitted to take with him, a copy of the comprehensive manuscript which Atanasoff had prepared in August, 1940.

3.1.15 At the time of Mauchly's visit, although the ABC was not entirely complete, its construction was sufficiently well advanced so that the principles of its operation, including detail design features, was explained and demonstrated to Mauchly.

3.1.16 The discussions Mauchly had with both Atanasoff and Berry while at Ames were free and open and no significant information concerning the machine's theory, design, construction, use or operation was withheld.

3.1.17 Prior to his visit to Ames, Iowa, Mauchly had been broadly interested in electrical analog calculating devices, but had not conceived an automatic electronic digital computer.

3.1.18 As a result of this visit, the discussions of Mauchly with Atanasoff and Berry, the demonstrations, and the review of the manuscript, Mauchly derived from the ABC "the invention of the automatic electronic digital computer" claimed in the ENIAC patent.

3.1.19 The Court has heard the testimony at trial of both Atanasoff and Mauchly, and finds the testimony of Atanasoff with respect to the knowledge and information derived by Mauchly to be credible.

.

SELECTED REFERENCES

Atanasoff, J. V. "Computing Machine for the Solution of Large Systems of Linear Algebraic Equations." In *The Origins of Digital Computers, Selected Papers,* ed. Brian Randell, Chap. 7.2. New York: Springer-Verlag, 1973.

———. "Advent of Electronic Digital Computing." *Annals of the History of Computing* 6, no. 3(1984):229–82.

Broad, William J., "Who Should Get the Glory for Inventing the Computer." *New York Times,* 22 Mar. 1983, C-1, C-2.

Burks, Arthur W., and Alice R. Burks. "The ENIAC: First General-Purpose Electronic Computer." *Annals of the History of Computing* 3, no. 4(1981):310–89. (Commentaries by John V. Atanasoff, John Grist Brainerd, J. Presper Eckert, Kathleen R. Mauchly, Brian Randell, and Konrad Zuse.)

Ceruzzi, P. E. *The Reckoners: The Prehistory of the Digital Computer from Relays to the Stored Program Concept.* Westport, Conn.: Greenwood, 1983.

Control Data Cases. *Sperry Rand Corp. v. Control Data Corp.,* CA-15823 and CA-15824, U.S. District Court for the District of Maryland.

Des Moines Tribune. "Machine Remembers," 15 Jan. 1942, 2-A.

Eckert, John P. Deposition, 3 June 1969, Bala Cynwyd, Pennsylvania, in *Honeywell Inc. v. Sperry Rand Corporation, et al.,* No. 4–67, Civ.138. U.S. District Court, District of Minnesota, Fourth Division.

ENIAC Trial Records. U.S. District Court, District of Minnesota, Fourth Division. *Honeywell, Inc. v. Sperry Rand Corp., et al.,* No. 4–67 Civ. 138, 1 June 1971 to 13 Mar. 1972, and pretrial depositions taken from May 1967 to the trial date of 1 June 1971.

Gardner, W. David. "The Computer: Born in a Tavern." *Washington Post,* Outlook Section, 13 Jan. 1974, B1, B2.

———. "The Independent Inventor: John V. Atanasoff, Creator of the Automatic Digital Computer, Did It His Own Way." *Datamation* 12–22.

Hanson, Henry L. *Managing Creative Assets.* Chiefton Publishing, 1985.

Honeywell, Inc., "Computerized Trial Arguments and Brief," filed 30 Sept. 1972. 509 pp.

Iowa State College Information Service press release. "Biggest, Fastest Calculator Built by ISC Physicist," 7 Apr. 1942.

Knudsen, O. S. Script for 1983 Iowa State University film, "From One John Vincent Atanasoff."

Larson, U.S. District Judge Earl R. 19 Oct. 1973. Findings of Fact, Conclusions of Law and Order of Judgment, U.S. District Court, District of Minnesota, Fourth Division. *Honeywell, Inc. v. Sperry Rand Corp. et al.,* No. 4–67, Civ. 138. Decision printed in *U.S. Patent Quarterly* 180(1974):673–773.

Ledger, Marshall. "The E.N.I.A.C's Muddled History." *Pennsylvania Gazette,* Nov. 1982, 29–33.

Lundegaard, Bob, staff writer. "Developer of H-Bomb Testifies for Honeywell in Computer-Patent Suit." *Minneapolis Tribune,* 31 Aug. 1971.

Mackintosh, Allan R. "The First Electronic Computer." *Physics Today,* Mar. 1987, 25–32.

Mauchly, Kathleen R. "John Mauchly's Early Years." *Annals of the History of Computing* 6, no. 2(1984):116–38.

Metropolis, N., J. Howlett, and G. Rota, eds. *A History of Computing in the Twentieth Century.* New York: Academic Press, 1980.

Mollenhoff, Clark R. "Court: Computer Iowans Idea." *Des Moines Sunday Register,* 27 Jan. 1974, 1, 8.

Mollenhoff, G. G. "John V. Atanasoff, DP Pioneer." *Computerworld* 13 Mar. 1974, 1–13.

Randell, Brian. *The Origin of Digital Computers.* New York: Springer-Verlag, 1973.

Richards, R. K. *Electronic Digital Systems.* New York: Wiley, 1966.

Ritchie, David. *The Computer Pioneers.* New York: Simon and Schuster, 1986.

St. Paul Pioneer Press and Dispatch. "H-Bomb Aided by Computers," Associated Press, 31 Aug. 1971.

Silag, William. "The Invention of the Electronic Digital Computer at Iowa State College, 1930–1942." *Palimpsest* 64, no. 5(1984):150–77.

Sperry Rand Corp. v. Control Data Corp. CA-15823 and CA-15824, U.S. District Court for the District of Maryland.

Stewart, Robert M. "The End of the ABC." *Annals of the History of Computing* 6, no. 3(1984):317.

INDEX

ABC. *See* Atanasoff Berry Computer

Aiken, Howard, 89

Allegretti, D. Dennis, 106, 107, 113, 119, 132, 155, 156, 174, 175, 198–99

Analog computer, 29–30, 157

Anderson, Harold, 38–39

Annals of the History of Computing, October 1981, 222–24

Atanasoff, Alice, 74, 114, 215–16, 218–19

Atanasoff, John Vincent
Bulgarian background, 12, 150–53
childhood and family background, 12–14, 21
Eckert meeting, 169–70
Honeywell-Control Data lawyers meeting, 112–15
Honeywell deposition, 136–38
honors, 152–53, 232–37, 240–42
IBM lawyers contact, 81, 85–88
Iowa State College studies and research, 21–30, 38
Mauchly and Sperry Rand lawyer interview, 123–27
monitoring Helgoland Island detonation, 72–73
Naval Ordnance Laboratory position, 62–69, 74
personal life, 24–25, 74
research proposal for prototype computer, 36–37, 159–60
testimony regarding Mauchly visit to Ames, 164–66

Atanasoff, Lura, 24–25, 55–58, 66, 74, 113–14, 131

Atanasoff Berry Computer
basic ideas for, 34–37, 158–59
booklet with details of machine, 95, 127, 205, 212
description of, 181–82, 224

dismantling, 73–74

Mauchly examination of, 3–4, 52–53, 55–57, 60–61, 169

patent proceedings. *See* Trexler, Richard R.

press release, 96–97

replica of prototype, 131–34, 135, 164

Auerbach, Isaac M., 115–16, 149, 150

Auerbach Associates, 149

Babbage, Charles, 223, 228

Bair, Freeman and Molinar, 106

Base-two number system, 14, 34–35, 160, 166

Beecher, David, 63, 69, 81, 82, 86

Berquist, Gerald, 147, 148

Berry, Clifford E., 65, 73, 82, 83, 86–87, 94, 95, 160–61, 168. *See also* Atanasoff Berry Computer
correspondence with R. K. Richards, 96–102
death under mysterious circumstances, 103–5
description of Mauchly visit to Ames, 130–31, 164–65, 174
education and family background, 39–41, 61, 169
as ham radio buff, 93
investigation of death, 121–22

BINAC (Binary Automatic Computer), 149

Binary numbers. *See* Base-two number system

Binger, James Henry, 108

Black, Edwin, 241

Brainerd, John Gist, 71, 183

Brandner, Fred, 23

Brandt, A. E., 22, 23, 69, 157

Breadboard model, computer, 8–9, 161, 163, 211

About the Author

Clark R. Mollenhoff, a Pulitzer Prize–winning reporter and author of ten previous books, is a graduate of Drake University Law School. He has received more than twenty-five major awards in forty-five years as an investigative reporter, author, and lecturer on fraud and corruption in government and in other American institutions.

He is a native Iowan, and for more than thirty-five years was on the staff of the Des Moines Register and Tribune Company as an investigative reporter and Washington correspondent. It was as Washington Bureau Chief for the *Des Moines Register* in 1973 that Mr. Mollenhoff first became acquainted with, and fascinated by, the story of the invention of the world's first electronic digital computer at Iowa State College by Dr. John V. Atanasoff and Clifford Berry in the later 1930s.

For the past eleven years he has been a professor of journalism at Washington and Lee University in Lexington, Virginia, and he has continued to work as an investigative reporter in Washington, as an author, and as a legal consultant.

In addition to the Pulitzer Prize for National Reporting, Mr. Mollenhoff has been awarded the Raymond Clapper Memorial Award, the Heywood Broun Memorial Award, the William Allen White Award, the John Peter Zenger Award, the Elijah Parish Lovejoy Award, and three national awards of the National Society of Professional Journalists, Sigma Delta Chi. The Washington, D.C., Chapter of SPJ-SDX has named Mr. Mollenhoff to the Hall of Fame of Washington Correspondents, and in 1980 he was named a Sigma Delta Chi Fellow by the National SPJ-SDX organization.

Since his graduation from Drake University Law School, Mr. Mollenhoff has studied at Harvard as a Nieman Fellow, was awarded an Eisenhower Exchange Fellowship for travel and research in more than forty countries, and has spent two semesters at University College, Oxford, England, as a Washington and Lee University Exchange Fellow.

In 1986 the Drake University Law School selected him to receive an Alumnus of the Year Award, and in 1987 the Richmond Chapter of SPJ-SDX named him as the recipient of the George Mason Award for his contribution to Virginia journalism.